ALL THINGS MADE NEW
THE MYSTERIES OF THE WORLD IN CHRIST

Stratford Caldecott

ALL THINGS MADE NEW

The Mysteries of the World in Christ

ANGELICO PRESS
SOPHIA PERENNIS

First published in the USA
by Angelico Press / Sophia Perennis
© Stratford Caldecott 2011

Series editor: James R. Wetmore

For information, address:
Angelico Press / Sophia Perennis, P.O. Box 151011
San Rafael, CA 94915
angelicopress.com
sophiaperennis.com

Library of Congress Cataloging-in-Publication Data

Caldecott, Stratford.
All things made new: the mysteries of the world in Christ /
Stratford Caldecott. — 1st ed.

p. cm.

Includes bibliographical references.
ISBN 978-1-59731-129-8 (pbk: alk. paper)
1. Bible. N.T. Revelation—Criticism, interpretation, etc.
2. Spiritual life—Catholic Church. 3. Spirituality—Catholic Church.
I. Title
BS 2825.52.C35   2011
228'.06—dc22   2011018285

Front Cover: *Crucifixion*, ink drawing by Daniel Mitsui
www.danielmitsui.com

CONTENTS

To Léonie, who knows the mysteries better.

INITIATION

This book continues and complements the exploration of the Christian mysteries I began in *The Seven Sacraments*, but you do not need that earlier book in order to read this one. That book was about the sacraments and the other patterns of seven mysteries that we find in the tradition, going back to the days of creation in Genesis. (You will find a summary in Appendix 5.) The present book is also concerned with Scripture, but opens with the last book in the canon, one of the most mysterious books of the Bible, the 'Book of Revelation' also known as the Apocalypse of Saint John.

The Apocalypse provides a way in to the heart of the Christian revelation; it gives us our key to understanding both Bible and Tradition. It is about the 'end' of the world, in the sense of the 'meaning' or 'purpose' of the world. For at the end of his life Saint John arrives at an End who is also a Beginning, the Alpha as well as the Omega. His vision of Jesus, the Son of Man, takes place on the Lord's own Day, the Day of the Sabbath when God is at 'rest'. It takes us back to Genesis and re-interprets everything. It is an unveiling of the mystery of the world in Christ himself.

John's is a visionary book. In it we confront the Christian imagination firing on all cylinders. It takes us into the heart of theology, but this is theology in the original sense—that is, theology as it used to be understood in the Church before it became a purely academic subject, divorced from spirituality and prayer. John's Apocalypse is a work of inspired visionary poetry, a kaleidoscope of images full of meaning, sparks thrown out by the impact of Christ. Its approach is the very opposite of 'rationalistic' and 'moralistic'. It does not start with commandments or a logical philosophy. It is more like a gushing stream or rising fountain of living water, from which we drink, perhaps at our peril.

An Outline of Mystagogy

The need for ongoing formation in the mysteries of Christ and of the Church, a catechesis traditionally known as *mystagogia* ('initiation into the mysteries'), has been noted in Catholic circles for years.[1] Mystagogy is a technical term for the stage of exploratory catechesis that comes after apologetics, after evangelization, and after the reception of the so-called 'sacraments of initiation' (Baptism, Eucharist, and Confirmation). While Baptism and Confirmation may be given only once, Christian initiation is a continuing adventure, since the new life of prayer must continue to grow, if it is not to wither and die. The Book of Revelation, I believe, encapsulates the *mystagogia* of the early Church.

The main focus of Catholic mystagogy today is on seven particular mysteries, called 'sacraments'. The word is based on the Latin *sacramentum*, referring to consecration, which in turn was a translation of the Greek *mysterion* or 'mystery'. The sacraments are therefore the Christian mysteries *par excellence*. The whole Christian mystery is, as it were, coiled up inside them. They are a kind of extension of Christ's presence in the world. Their forms and even their number evolved over the centuries, but each leads us back to specific actions of Christ on earth, when he forgave, baptized, and blessed the men and women around him, and gave himself to them in the shape of food.

Each sacrament is a set of rituals and symbols that expresses an aspect of Christ's life, and which is used by him to reach into our lives and transform us, provided we permit him to do so. In other words, they are symbols, but more than symbols: they are conduits of grace. In Baptism we are claimed for Christ, in Confirmation strengthened, in Confession reconciled, in Marriage joined to each other, in Ordination joined to Christ, in Anointing healed, and

1. The modern revival of the ancient Rite of Christian Initiation for Adults (RCIA) by the Catholic Church in the 1960s was an attempt to recapture a sense of the initiatory power of the sacraments as it had been experienced by the early Christians. There is a period of formal mystagogy at the end of the RCIA, which continues from Easter Sunday through Pentecost and then monthly for the remainder of the year. But this does not go nearly far enough. It certainly does not suffice to introduce the catechumen to the full richness of mystical theology.

from the Eucharist, which is Christ, all these other sacraments receive their power.

The Church gave the sacraments a sevenfold form because each could then represent one of the seven days of creation, which were also the seven dimensions of the Old Covenant, and these can be seen to correspond with the seven primary needs of the human heart defined by Christ himself in the Lord's Prayer. In this way the sacraments constitute a re-forging of the Covenant and the re-making of the world itself. The multiple sevens that readers can see in the Book of Revelation also reflect this underlying covenantal structure and emphasize its importance. Although in John's time Christians may not have thought in terms of 'the seven sacraments', the reality they describe was already present.

Numbers were important for the early Christians for many reasons. They are, in a way, inherently mysterious—even today philosophers cannot quite agree what they are, and why they seem to play such a vital role in the order of nature. Are they the thoughts of God? The ancient writers loved the patterns they made, and the simpler the better. Seven is made up of four and three. These numbers when multiplied give us twelve. Each of these numbers—4, 3, 7—is fundamental to Christian mystagogy and has multiple applications throughout the tradition.

Another important theme is introduced by one of the greatest Christian masters of mystagogy, who wrote under a pseudonym around five hundred years after the birth of Christ. Denys the Areopagite, sometimes called Saint Denys (he is also the patron saint of France, where he was thought to have been buried), is called in academic circles the 'Pseudo-Dionysius' or 'Pseudo-Areopagite' because he identified himself with the convert of Saint Paul mentioned in Acts 17:34. Denys divided the Christian Way into three phases called *purification, illumination,* and *union,* and linked these to three hierarchies of angels, who assist in each of these three phases—to put it another way, the active, inner, and contemplative life, reflecting a Trinitarian structure. His division can easily be integrated with other familiar Christian triads, such as the three Theological Virtues of faith, hope, and love, and the Evangelical Counsels which are familiar to many people as the three Vows taken by a monk or nun upon entering the consecrated religious life. The vow of *poverty* corresponds to purification, the vow of *chastity* to hope, and that of *obedience* (the integration of our will with God's) to union.

Consistently with this tradition, the modern *Catechism of the Catholic Church* (paras 2699–2719) divides Christian prayer into three types: vocal prayer, meditation, and contemplation. These, too, can be seen as corresponding to Denys's three phases. *Vocal prayer* brings the body into line with the spirit by expressing the spiritual Word in voice and gesture. We can think of it as a kind of discipline that points us towards God. *Meditation* involves the imagination, the 'eyes of the heart', by which we penetrate gradually to the inner meaning of the words and images of faith. Finally, *Contemplation* is the prayer of silent union with God, a beginning or foretaste of the life of eternity.

One of the most beautiful passages on Denys's three stages of Christian life was written by Blessed John Paul II in the final chapter of his last book, *Memory and Identity*. The Purgative Way, John Paul explains, is based on observance of the Commandments (see Matt. 19:16–17). It enables us to discover and live our fundamental values. But these values, he goes on, are 'lights' which illuminate our existence and so lead us into the Illuminative Way. For example, by observing the Commandment *You shall not kill* we learn a profound respect for life. By not committing adultery we acquire the virtue of purity. This is not something negative, but bound up with a growing awareness of the beauty of the human body, both male and female. This beauty, he says, 'becomes a light for our actions', so that we are able to *live in the truth.*

By following the light that comes from Christ our Teacher, Pope John Paul says, we are progressively freed from the struggle against sin that preoccupies us in the stage of Purification. We become able to enjoy the divine light which permeates creation. This perception of 'illumination' is based on a conscious awareness of the world's nature as gift: 'Interior light illumines our actions and shows us all the good in the created world as coming from the hand of God.' The Illuminative Way therefore leads into the Unitive Way, realized in the contemplation of God and the experience of love. Union with God can be achieved to some degree even before death. And when we find God in everything, created things 'cease to be a danger to us', regaining their true light and leading us to God as he wishes to reveal himself to us, as 'Father, Redeemer, and Spouse'.

Tensions in the Church

Though the Christian religion does not depend on spiritual techniques, it does offer guidance and assistance in developing a life of prayer, and also in putting that prayer into action as a life of love. It offers the lives and examples of the saints, the writings of the mystics, and above all the Scriptures themselves as a treasury on which every Christian may draw. But there is an important difference to note between Christianity and many other religious traditions, where the seeker of wisdom will expect to find a human teacher, a *guru*, to lead him in this quest.

Christians do not need a *guru*. They may have priests, and indeed there are some wise priests and spiritual directors in the Church (thank goodness), but the priest's role is essentially different from that of the Asian 'master'. It is primarily to make the sacramental presence of Christ available to the faithful. The Catholic goes directly to Christ in the Blessed Sacrament and the sacrament of Confession. It is the priest who makes this presence possible. This is particularly important in the present historical period, with so much confusion caused by the mixing of religious traditions. Some of that confusion is reflected in the Church. Thanks to the changes in Catholicism after the Second Vatican Council in the 1960s, some argued that the Church had broken with tradition altogether, and many Catholics felt obliged to reject what they called the 'New Church' of Vatican II and the post-conciliar popes in favour of the 'Church of all times'—which for some appeared to mean no Church at all, just a tradition.

The changes in liturgical practice, the loss of focus in religious education, and the erosion of the sense of tradition and authority within the mainstream Church during those decades have been much discussed. The temptation to set the authority of tradition against that of Rome was felt by many of the most devout, precisely because they felt they understood the tradition so well. Yet the two authorities cannot be so divided. The mistake is partly due to a foreshortened view of tradition, since looking back through history we are apt to tidy up and gloss over the imperfection and instability that are all too apparent when one is living through those times, and in this way we idealize a past state of the Church.

The seven sacraments have survived the liturgical reforms. They always remain valid as long as they are celebrated within the body of the Church, whose true intentions are expressed in the official Latin texts and known to the Holy Spirit who is the soul of the Church. The priesthood and the apostolic succession remain valid. Many individual priests and bishops may be unworthy of their ordination, and that has always been the case, but they are part of something greater than themselves. The continuing health of the post-conciliar Church is demonstrated by the fact that great saints, such as Padre Pio and Teresa of Calcutta, humbly submitting themselves to the authority of Christ and the successor of Peter, have continued to arise and flourish (and work miracles).

Through our participation in the Church, no matter how broken and corrupt it may appear to be at any one time, we are incorporated within the death and humiliation of Christ, comforted by him, taught by him in what happens to us moment by moment, and ultimately resurrected by him in a state beyond corruption and death, in that day when 'all shall be well and all manner of thing shall be well'.[2]

The Way of Prayer

All of this will emerge with greater clarity as we journey through the Book of Revelation. That will occupy the first half of the present book, bringing us to a chapter on the Creed or Profession of Faith. Having been received and initiated into the Church, the Christian is at the end of one journey but only at the beginning of another. For Jesus is the Way, the Way to God, and to be with him and in him is to be on a journey. After we have explored the Apocalypse and what it is trying to teach us, the second half of this book is therefore concerned with the life of prayer—particularly private or individual

---

2. The famous words of Julian of Norwich, from Chapter 32 of her 13th revelation (*The Revelations of Divine Love* exist in many translations).

prayer, although we must bear in mind that no prayer is really 'private' because we pray in the company of the whole Church, including the angels. We will have moved, in other words, from a focus on the inner meaning of the sacraments and the liturgy of the Church (which is John's primary concern) to a focus on the Triple Way of Purgation, Illumination, and Contemplation in the life and practice of the Christian as a member of the Body of Christ.

The organizing theme of this second half of the book is the Rosary of the Blessed Virgin Mary, and its associated devotions. The Rosary is one of the most popular aids to prayer and meditation within the Catholic tradition. Though it is criticized by some Protestants for taking attention away from Jesus and giving it to his Mother, the intention behind it is quite different—indeed, the exact opposite. Correctly understood, the point of the Rosary is to *meditate on the Son* through the eyes of the Mother. Thus the Rosary meditations include the whole span of Jesus' life, from the moment he was conceived in Mary's womb until the moment he welcomes her into heaven and crowns her with glory. So the Rosary is a way of experiencing more fully the Incarnation and Passion of God. In it is reflected the whole of salvation history, and the struggles and destiny of the individual soul on her way to God in the fellowship of the Church. The Virgin Mary represents all of us.

We will also spend some time on the Way of the Cross. This can be considered an expanded version of the Sorrowful Mysteries of the Rosary, describing the way of Purgation. There are fourteen Stations on the Way, representing the final stages of Jesus's earthly life. The life of a disciple is a life of carrying the cross—our own 'cross', meaning our fate or burden, whatever that may be—in the knowledge that Jesus will help us to bear it, and make it light (Matt. 11:30). The Stations of the Cross give us a way to learn the pattern of perfect submission and self-giving that Jesus showed us in his last days on earth, a lesson we can apply not only when we too come eventually to die, but during every moment of our lives.

The final chapter looks at the last of the Glorious Mysteries of the Rosary, the outcome of the Way of Jesus, the fruition of his death on the Cross and of his ascension into heaven. Here the Sorrowful or Purgative mysteries, and the mysteries of Light or Illumination, give way to the mysteries of Union and Contemplation which are already foreshadowed in the Joyful mysteries of Christ's childhood.

After the publication of this book I hope to continue my exploration of Christian spirituality at http://thechristianmysteries.blog spot.com.

Acknowledgements

I am grateful to several friends for their encouragement and advice, not least Phil Zaleski and Ian Boxall, and of course the Publisher, James Wetmore. The book has been several years in development, and part of the material included here formed the basis for two booklets published by CTS: *Companion to the Book of Revelation* in 2008, and *Fruits of the Spirit* in 2010.

As anyone knows who has been bold enough to write on spiritual matters, it is easy to write as if one were wise, and much harder to live that way. I only dared to write this book as a reminder to myself of things that most of the time I forget, or things I fail to live up to. I have drawn on the wisdom of great spiritual writers and the guidance of the Church, and I ask the reader to forgive and overlook whatever comes only from myself.

1

THE BOOK OF UNVEILING

The revelation of Jesus Christ, which God gave him to show to his servants what must soon take place; and he made it known by sending his angel to his servant John, who bore witness to the word of God and to the testimony of Jesus Christ, even to all that he saw.   Rev. 1:1–2

The word translated 'revelation' in the opening verse of the last book of the Bible is *apokalupsis* in Greek, meaning the 'lifting of a veil', but exactly what is being unveiled is unclear from the construction of the sentence. Is it a revelation *of* Jesus Christ meaning 'about' him, or *of* Jesus Christ in the sense of 'belonging' to him—a revelation he has been given by his Father, and which he now transmits through an angel to his Apostle? Since the word is ambiguous, we should probably assume it means both. It is a revelation from the Father to the Son; for, after all, did not Jesus say, 'But of that day and hour no one knows, not even the angels of heaven, nor the Son, but the Father only' (Matt. 24:36)? And it is a revelation not only of 'things that must occur' but in some sense of Jesus himself; that is, of things that Jesus can only learn *about himself* if the Father reveals them.

We tend to scan through the Apocalypse too quickly, catching only the main images—a Woman clothed with the sun, a Dragon, the Four Horsemen, Babylon, the Heavenly City—never stopping to absorb the rest, or ponder their spiritual meaning. 'He who has an ear, let him hear what the Spirit says to the churches', says John in the second chapter (Rev. 2:17), while in the introduction to the book he also writes: 'Blessed is he who reads aloud the words of the prophecy, and blessed are those who hear, and who keep what is written therein; for the time is near' (Rev. 1:3). The Apocalypse was therefore meant to be *read aloud*, to be *heard* (by those who have ears for it), and to be *kept*, or lived. Normally we do none of these three things that John offers us a blessing for doing. Recall that silent reading to oneself (without even moving one's lips!) is a modern invention, virtually unknown to the ancients and medievals. John is implying the presence of a formal lector, reading the text in a liturgical setting, and a congregation who is listening intently to him. We tend to forget this liturgical context when we read the book today in our study bibles.

The Apocalypse was designed to have a certain effect on its hearers when read aloud, and it was to be read *ecclesially*, in the communion of faith. It should not be treated as a mere book-end, nor is it to be dismissed as the eccentric indulgence of an overheated imagination. It has to be received into the soul; it should make a difference to the hearer; it should be taken seriously.

The chapters that follow are written to explore how John's extraordinary cascade of images helps to 'unveil' the whole Christian tradition for us. I want to demonstrate how—with the eyes of faith—the Apocalypse can be seen as a compendium of the Christian mysteries. Of course, that does not mean that it is exclusively of interest to believing Christians. Revelation is a synthesis of all the cosmic and religious ideas of the Middle East, demonstrating a profound harmony between the Christian experience of the first disciples, the visionary mysticism of the Jewish Temple, and the best elements of the Egyptian-Pythagorean wisdom of the surrounding culture. John consciously drew on a wide range of sources to express the 'making new' of all things in Christ. He saw Jesus Christ as the fulfillment of all prophecies and of all myths, the key to unlock secrets hidden from previous ages (1 Cor. 2:6–16). The whole of previous history, the whole of mythology, could now be re-read with Jesus in mind.

The Author of Revelation

But who was John? The traditional view going back perhaps to Saint Irenaeus around AD 180, and now commonly regarded as mistaken, identified him with the 'disciple whom Jesus loved', mentioned in the fourth Gospel and thought to refer the author of that Gospel. If true, that would make him the son of Zebedee, one of the two so-called 'sons of thunder' (Mark 3:17), an Evangelist and member of the Twelve, who had known Jesus personally on earth. *That* John is said to have lived to be a very old man (John 21:20–24), looking after the Virgin Mary, the Lord's own mother, until her assumption into heaven (John's long-term care for her is implied in John 19:27). It was thought that he had written his 'Apocalypse' on the island of Patmos near Ephesus some time before his death towards the end of the first century, say around AD 95. A reference to it in Justin's *Dialog with Trypho* in the middle of the second century seems to support this. Some traditions attributed the three Johannine Letters in the New Testament also to the same 'John', though in the fourth century the Council of Rome identified the second and third of these letters as written by someone else.

Modern critics, basing themselves on the rather rough and ungrammatical Greek style of the Book of Revelation compared to the fourth Gospel, argue for a completely different authorship of the two documents. Not only do they doubt that Revelation was written by the same person as the Gospel of John, but they have questioned the idea that the fourth Gospel was written by an Apostle at all, since the theological texture of the book is so different from that of Matthew, Mark, and Luke—it seems to show a level of erudition inappropriate if not impossible for an unlettered fisherman.

All this is a side-issue. We simply do not know the history of these documents, and more recent criticism has drawn attention to the fact that even the most distinguished scholars make dubious assumptions (such as the impossibility of miracles, or the inability of fishermen to acquire a theological education in the first century) that help to determine their conclusions. John Sweet argues that John's style is deliberately violent, partly to have a certain effect on the reader, partly to preserve elements of Hebrew grammar into the Greek (his control of tenses is, after all, excellent).[1] A striking suggestion was made by J. A. T. Robinson and others that far from being

---

1. J. Sweet, *Revelation*, 16.

a late addition to the New Testament, prompted by the destruction of the Jewish Temple by the Romans in AD 70,[2] the Book of Revelation was probably among the very *first* of the New Testament documents, perhaps written in the year 68 or even earlier. Its composition might have involved translating into Greek various pieces of mystical writing composed previously in Hebrew and commented upon in Aramaic. The fourth Gospel would then have been written down somewhat later than that, i.e. after the fall of the Temple. (It would, of course, make quite a difference to how we read the Gospels, and the fourth Gospel in particular, if we knew that the author assumed that some of his readers were already familiar with the Book of Revelation.) Austin Farrer's view in *The Rebirth of Images* is that all the Johannine material was written by the same person, the different styles being required by the genres in which the work was being done—also that the Gospel was written last, perhaps around AD 90 (the Apocalypse being, in a sense, a necessary preparation for writing it).

In any case, reading the text in the way which interests us here would be substantially unaffected if any or all these documents were attributed not to John the Evangelist but to a Christian leader or even a Johannine community living in the early second century.[3] Whoever he was, and regardless of whether he was a seer in his own right, we know that he was writing in a visionary tradition that went back a long way—probably to the First Temple built by King Solomon, which stood for four centuries until its destruction by the Babylonians in 587 BC. The prophet Ezekiel describes himself as a priest of this Temple in exile. Ezekiel's visions of the divine chariot (*merkavah*) and heavenly temple (see Ez. 1, 10, and 40–47), the visions of Daniel (Dan. 7–12), and the extra-canonical Book of

2. Although the destruction of Jerusalem by fire, famine and pestilence—even the seemingly miraculous survival of the Christian community and of the 'upper room' in Jerusalem—all fit this hypothesis (Scott Hahn, *The Lamb's Supper*, 90–103).

3. Most biblical scholars at least seem to accept the Apocalypse as the work of a single author, given the uniqueness of its style and the careful construction of the whole, though whether it recorded a single vision or a series of visionary experiences over several years is another question.

Enoch, combined with long Jewish meditation on the seven days of creation, the stages of ascent to the heavenly palaces (*hekhalot*), and the Song of Songs, all played a part in inspiring a commentary tradition that by the twelfth century produced in Spain and Provence the flowering of Jewish mysticism known as Kabbalah. But they also lay, much earlier, behind the Book of Revelation, which integrates these ancient themes within a Christian visionary experience.

The Paradox of Revelation

The Apocalypse closes the canon of Christian Scripture, just as the Book of Genesis opens it. Genesis is concerned with the creation of the world; Revelation with its re-creation. John's vision takes place 'on the Lord's day' (Rev. 1:10); that is, on the day that celebrates the Resurrection and also the Sabbath repose of God. The Seer finds himself lifted above his own times, to a vantage-point where he can see more deeply into the spiritual world that lies within and around our own. In the fourth volume of his theological masterpiece *Theo-Drama*, Hans Urs von Balthasar describes John as standing between heaven and earth, exposed to a *mundus imaginalis*, a world of images, that are neither the archetypes of reality nor historical events but something of both, a bridge between the visible and invisible worlds.[4]

Revelation is unique throuhout apocalyptic literature for the profusion of its visual imagery and the paucity of self-interpretation, thus immersing the reader or listener in a symbolic world of extraordinary intensity. 'As an integrated sequence of visionary material, architectonically planned, creating one world of images kaleidoscopically presented, the Apocalypse of John is unique.'[5]

---

4. Here as elsewhere in *Theo-Drama* Balthasar is developing insights of Adrienne von Speyr, who, allegedly without having read the book of Revelation, experienced the same 'world of images' as John in a series of intense visions. She interpreted these in her own two-volume *Commentary on the Apocalypse* which is not yet available in English. See H.U. von Balthasar, *First Glance at Adrienne von Speyr*, 90–94. I have borrowed the phrase *mundus imaginalis*, however, from orientalist Henri Corbin.

5. R. Bauckham, *The Climax of Prophecy*, 177. See also his *The Theology of the Book of Revelation*, 9–10.

John encodes in these images a distillation of history and of prophecy, and herein lies one of the essential paradoxes of Christian existence. Christians in every age must live both history and prophecy, the Cross and the Resurrection, tragedy and comedy, at the same time. They must live simultaneously on two levels, both knowing and not-knowing the end of the story in which they are playing a part. 'The Lord appears to the seer in majesty, with all the emblems of triumph—and yet a struggle is going on (and actually intensifying) in which everything is at stake', says Balthasar.[6]

But Balthasar takes this same paradox to another level. He continues: 'On the secular stage, the prior announcement of victory would be regarded as destroying all dramatic tension; on the apocalyptic stage, however, it is this very victory that causes the real dramatic action to spark into flame.'[7] So it is not simply that we know in advance that the battle has been won; it is that the *awareness of the victory* (of Jesus on the Cross) is what provoked the battle in the first place. This is a weird kind of inverse causality: the outcome of the battle is its cause. It is the real drama that lies behind John's Revelation, encapsulated in this saying from the fourth Gospel: 'If I had not come and spoken to them, they would not have sin; but now they have no excuse for their sin' (John 15:22). The presence of Christ in the world and on the Cross is what brings sin to a head.

Looking back from two thousand years in his future, we can read John's book as a concentrated expression of a tradition and a history that is still unfolding, still intensely relevant to us in our day-to-day lives. It can serve as the starting point for an exploration not just of a certain type of imaginative literature, or of the social milieu of the early Christians, but of Christianity itself, and of the 'Christian experience' shared by all believers.

John consciously models himself on the visionary Old Testament prophets, his task being to point to the One who fulfils all prophecies (a bit like his namesake, John the Baptizer—and similar names in the Bible are rarely coincidental). Whether or not he saw Jesus in the flesh, he writes from within that absolute fulfilment, from

6. Hans Urs von Balthasar, *Theo-Drama*, Vol. IV, 19.
7. *Theo-Drama*, Vol. IV, 21.

within the lived experience of the Incarnation. All the later theological developments in the history of Christianity—from the doctrine of the Trinity and the moral teachings of Saint Thomas in the Middle Ages to Pope John Paul II's 'theology of the body' in the late twentieth century, together with many other developments yet to be unfolded—are germinating within his text. In that sense, the Apocalypse remains for all time a key to the mysteries that Christ revealed to his closest disciples. These mysteries the Church always needs to rediscover, for she will only truly know them if she knows them as if for the first time.

The Structure of Revelation

Revelation opens with John on the island of Patmos being commissioned by God to send a letter to the seven churches in Asia (the introductory verses 4-8 form a kind of executive summary of the whole book). After this prolog, the book unfolds in six or seven main sections, followed by an epilog to balance the prolog. However, the complexity of the text that we find sandwiched between prolog and epilog cannot be overestimated. Whichever way we choose to divide it, there will be repetitions, overlaps, reversals of order, and multiple perspectives on the same events described in different metaphors.

The text appears at first chaotic, a bit like a dream. It is no doubt constructed deliberately to give that impression:

> The dream-like character of Revelation is constructed by focusing: first an object is noticed, comes to the foreground; then action begins to swell out from around it. In the first phase, we see a picture: we notice an object and start wondering what it is for. The longer this goes on, the stranger and more compelling the object becomes. The second phase is cinematic: the object's powers are set in motion by one of the characters. It is like a dream; but it is also like witnessing a religious ceremony in a strange temple, and not knowing what any of the cultic *things* is going to *do*.[8]

---

8. Francesca Murphy, *The Comedy of Revelation*, 215.

It helps to notice that the Apocalypse falls naturally into a simple structure of two parts or halves, with the second beginning at chapter 12 (the famous vision of the woman clothed with the sun and crowned with twelve stars). The first part unfolds as follows.

(1) In the first three chapters, John has a vision of Jesus Christ, who gives him messages for the churches of Asia.

(2) In the next two chapters, John has a vision of heaven, of the heavenly Throne, and of a book in God's hand sealed with seven seals that only the Lamb (Jesus) is worthy to open. The Lamb proceeds to open the first six seals.

(3) The opening of the seventh seal leads to the blowing of seven trumpets. The events associated with the first six trumpets take up the next two chapters.

(4) In the final two chapters of this part, John is given a 'little scroll' to eat, he is instructed to measure the temple, he is told of the two witnesses, and at last the *seventh trumpet* is blown, signifying the final integration of heaven and earth: 'The kingdom of the world has become the kingdom of our Lord and of his Christ' (11:15).

Seven messages, seven seals, and seven trumpets, and we are still only half way through Revelation! The progression in the first part is clear. Jesus has led John through a series of frames. First he steps through a door into heaven. Once there he sees a book. Entering into the book is the second stage in the journey. In fact the opening of the seven seals can be seen as his *journey into the book*, the revelation of the inner meaning of the Hebrew Scriptures. The seventh seal marks a transition to the third stage, signified by seven trumpets, culminating in the 'marriage of heaven and earth' that brings Part One to an end.

The second part of Revelation begins with the opening of chapter 12 and looks forward to Christ's second coming. So:

(1) The woman clothed with the sun is the Church founded by Christ, the Dragon and the two Beasts (the evil echo of the two heavenly witnesses we have seen earlier) are the power of Rome and worldly authority in general.

(2) In chapter 14 we see the Lamb standing on Mount Zion with the 144,000—note, not in heaven but in a place midway between heaven and earth, with the 'sound of many waters' suggesting baptism, therefore again the presence of the Church—and we see in this 'midheaven' three angels (priests?) proclaiming the Gospel.

(3) In the last part of chapter 14 we meet four angels (making a total of seven in this chapter), two of whom carry sickles with which they harvest and reap the earth at the command of the other two.

(4) Chapters 15 and 16 are occupied with another series of seven angels bringing the seven final plagues.

(5) In chapters 17 and 18 we witness the fall of Babylon in detail.

(6) Chapters 19 and 20 concern the vision of heaven and the riding out from there of the Logos himself for the final battle.

(7) Chapters 21 and 22 contain the vision of what happens *after* history: the descent of the New Jerusalem.

(A more detailed outline will be found in Appendix 1 at the end of the book.)

The Theology of Revelation

And what is revealed about God in the Book of Revelation? Primarily, of course, that God is supreme over the cosmos and over man, and that his kingdom will come 'on earth as it is in heaven'. The Apocalypse was written to console and encourage Christians oppressed by the Roman Imperium, seemingly an implacable and all-powerful enemy (the conversion of Constantine lay centuries in the future). More than that, it was intended to reconfigure the imagination of its hearers in order to transform their experience of the world around them—to wean them away from 'Babylon' and summon them to the holy City of God that was and is descending from heaven.

Secondly, the author of Revelation clearly believed in the divinity of Christ and the Trinity of God. Though the doctrine of the Trinity would not be worked out in detail for several centuries, John was already a Trinitarian thinker, recognizing the distinct presence of the Son and the Spirit within the sphere of the divine. This is brought out strongly in Richard Bauckham's books, *The Climax of Prophecy* and *The Theology of the Book of Revelation*. Bauckham points out how, while the Lamb or Jesus is always presented as distinct from the One seated on the throne, he is given the same titles as the God of the Old Testament (for example, compare Isaiah 44:6 with Rev. 1:17). Nevertheless John also carefully avoids using a plural verb or pronoun to refer to God and the Lamb together. Thus the Lamb shares in divinity, yet is never portrayed as a separate object of worship. Father and Son are one God.

As for the third divine Person, Bauckham counts a total of fourteen references to the Holy Spirit in the Book of Revelation. Significantly, these are divided into seven occurrences in the phrase 'what the Spirit is saying to the Churches', and seven elsewhere. Sevenfold patterns are associated by John with divinity, or with the expression of divine power in the world. The Lamb in Rev. 5, for example, has 'seven eyes' and 'seven horns' to represent his perfect knowledge and power. The divine Spirit himself is sevenfold for John (as are the 'stars' or angels of the churches in which the Spirit is present). At the end of Revelation, however, the oneness of this sevenfold Spirit is reaffirmed: 'The Spirit and the Bride say, Come!'

The very opening of the Letters to the seven churches (Rev. 1:4–5) signals this Trinitarian understanding, for 'grace and peace' comes to the reader 'from him who is and who was and who is to come' (the Father), from 'the seven spirits who are before his throne' (the Holy Spirit), and from 'Jesus Christ, the faithful witness, the firstborn from the dead, and the ruler of kings on earth.'

There are also exactly four references in the book to the 'seven spirits' (or the sevenfold Spirit), associated specifically with the victory of the Lamb. Again, this number is significant. In John's symbolic language fourfoldness represents the full extent of the world in its traditional 'four directions', and is often found in combination with seven. So the first four judgments in each series of seven affect the whole world, and the seven phrases by which John designates all the nations of the world are always fourfold (for example, the phrase 'peoples and tribes and languages and nations'). The 7 x 4 occurrences of the title 'Lamb' are probably intended to indicate the worldwide scope of his victory.

In the final, glorious vision of the New Jerusalem we are told (Rev. 21:22) that the City's light is the glory of God, 'and its lamp is the Lamb.' John continues, distinguishing but at the same time stressing the unity of Father and Son:

> There shall no more be anything accursed, but the throne of God and of the Lamb shall be in it, and his servants shall worship him; they shall see his face, and his name shall be on their foreheads. And night shall be no more; they need no light of lamp or sun, for the Lord God will be their light, and they shall reign for ever and ever.[9]

From beginning to end, then, the Apocalypse is implicitly Trinitarian in its theology. Historically it seems to represent a bridge to the more explicitly Trinitarian formulae found in the Gospels (e.g., Matt. 28:19) and the Pauline letters (e.g. 2 Cor. 13:14). But in doing so, it is not unfaithful to the Old Testament tradition either, in which it is so clearly rooted. For the Old Testament, too, can be read as implicitly Trinitarian.[10] The Torah is 'a presentiment of the Logos', and the living relationship expressed in the personal Covenant between God and Israel promises the indwelling Spirit to replace our 'hearts of stone' (Ez. 36:26–7). The Apocalypse, like the Old Testament but more so, is aware of a distinction at the very heart of the absolute, but one that never divides the absolute into several gods in the style of Mesopotamian or Greek polytheism.

With these fundamentals established, we can begin to examine John's theological cosmology in more detail, beginning with the central thrust of the whole book, which relates it directly to the Book of Genesis.

---

9. Rev. 22:3–5; cf. Isaiah 60:19–21. Bauckham's discussion of the titles given to Jesus and to God can be found in *The Theology of the Book of Revelation*, especially on pages 23–30, 54-68.

10. As Giorgio Buccellati has shown in 'Yahweh, the Trinity: The Old Testament Catechumenate (Part 2)', *Communio* XXXIV: 2 (Summer 2007), 292–327.

2

CREATION IN THE
BOOK OF REVELATION

*Then I saw a new heaven and a new earth; for the first heaven
and the first earth had passed away, and the sea was no more.
And I saw the holy city, Jerusalem, coming down out of heaven
from God, prepared as a bride adorned for her husband; and I
heard a great voice from the throne saying, 'Behold, the dwelling
of God is with men. He will dwell with them, and they shall be
his people, and God himself will be with them; he will wipe away
every tear from their eyes, and death shall be no more, neither
shall there be mourning nor crying nor pain any more, for the
former things have passed away.'*

*And he who sat upon the throne said, 'Behold, I make all things
new.' Also he said, 'Write this, for these words are trustworthy
and true.' And he said to me, 'It is done! I am the Alpha and the
Omega, the beginning and the end.'[1]*　　　　　Rev. 21:1–6

In the Norse legends I loved to read as a child there was a prophecy
of the Last Battle at the end of time, Ragnarok, which would destroy
even the gods. But from the destruction, an old wise woman said, a
new and shining world would arise, giving meaning to the Word of
Hope, 'Rebirth', whispered by Odin into the ear of his dead son, Bal-

---

1. The words spoken by God the Father, the One upon the throne, in this passage are practically the only ones spoken directly by God in the Book of Revelation.
They are Trinitarian in structure. God utters *three* sentences in quick succession,
and the second sentence corresponds to the Word, the Logos who in Rev. 19:11 is
described in these same Greek words as being 'trustworthy and true'.

dur the Beautiful, killed by the trickster Loki. This hope of cosmic rebirth reminds me of the opening of the twenty-first chapter of Revelation.

The Apocalypse weaves together mythology, astrology, and numerology to make a garment for the Logos incarnate. I do not, of course, mean that it accepts uncritically the cosmic and mythological determinism of preceding cultures. Christianity liberates humanity from all this, as Pope Benedict XVI rightly emphasizes:

> At the very moment when the Magi, guided by the star, adored Christ the new king, astrology came to an end, because the stars were now moving in the orbit determined by Christ. This scene, in fact, overturns the world-view of that time, which in a different way has become fashionable once again today. It is not the elemental spirits of the universe, the laws of matter, which ultimately govern the world and mankind, but a personal God governs the stars, that is, the universe; it is not the laws of matter and of evolution that have the final say, but reason, will, love—a Person. And if we know this Person and he knows us, then truly the inexorable power of material elements no longer has the last word; we are not slaves of the universe and of its laws, we are free.[2]

This is precisely the message John wishes to convey. It is one of cosmic scope and grandeur, concerning the destiny of all worldly realities. We will see in the next chapter how much of his imagery is adapted from other writers, including Ezekiel, Isaiah, and Daniel— perhaps even the Pythagoreans—and from various Middle Eastern mythologies. But in this chapter we will be concerned with the main notion underlying John's entire presentation, namely that of the 'newness' of things after the coming of Christ: the over-turning, the *making and re-making* of the world by God. Only if this fundamental message is grasped will the rest begin to make sense.

The Meaning of Creation

The central message of Revelation is that God is the one who 'makes

---

2. Pope Benedict XVI, *Spe Salvi*, 30 November 2007, section 5.

all things new'. But what does it mean, to 'make new'? Cosmology, metaphysics, and faith come together when we try to grasp the idea of creation. In a certain sense, the theme of creation serves as a leitmotif of the entire Bible, framed as it is by an account of the world's making and unmaking in Genesis and Revelation, with the 'seven days' echoing through both Old and New Testaments, and a new account of the creation in the opening of the Fourth Gospel which prepares us to understand the role of Jesus Christ. It does seem to be the case that the idea of creation only comes into focus with the revelation of the Trinity, as Angelo Scola puts it:

> the reasons why the human person and the world are distinct from God emerge from the consideration of the life that flows limitlessly within the Trinity itself: in the distinguishing of the eternal Son from the Father is also found the ontological foundation for the existence of the creature in its distinction from the Creator.... To affirm that the permanent intratrinitarian event explains all difference, including the full distinction between God and created reality, is to provide in synthesis an explanation of the ultimate root of the newness of the Christian notion of Creation.[3]

Creation *ex nihilo* (creation out of nothing) appears to have been a distinctively Judaeo-Christian insight. Saint Thomas teaches that 'the newness of the world is known only by revelation, and hence it cannot be proved demonstratively', that is, from within the world.[4] The philosophical interpretation of the Hebrew word *bara* (create) in the first sentence of the Bible only matured gradually, but the Hebrew Scriptures contain several indications of the absolute origin

3. 'The Primordial Relationship between God and the Human Person in Catholicism and Islam', Intercultural Forum for Studies in Faith and Culture, 16 January 2007, Pope John Paul II Cultural Centre. Translation courtesy of *Oasis* (www. cisro.org).
4. *ST* 1, Q. 46, Art. 2. The emergence of the doctrine is traced by Gerhard May in *Creatio Ex Nihilo*, however his assertion that a firm, unambiguous doctrine of creation from nothing was absent from ancient Jewry (23) and had to wait for Christian writers to formulate is disputed, for example by Paul Copan in *Trinity Journal* 17.1 (Spring 1996), 77–93.

of all things in God. Among Christians by the end of the second century after Christ's ascension it was widely understood that God was not only *supreme* over the primordial 'chaos' (*toho wabohu*, the formless void), in the sense of having been being strong enough to reduce it to order as the Gnostic mythologies suggest, but had actually made it in the first place, as part of the act whereby the world was established in seven stages.

So when Genesis tells us, 'In the beginning God created the heavens and the earth. The earth was without form and void, and darkness was upon the face of the deep,' it is saying that God created the void—that is, the earth without form—precisely in order to impose form upon it. The chaos was not a pre-existing 'dragon' to be wrestled into submission, but merely the passive substratum of matter. 'The doctrine of *creation ex nihilo* speaks of a God who gives of his bounty, not a God at war with darkness', not a God who struggles to create, but a God of infinite power and 'unconstrained joy'.[5]

Reflection on Genesis eventually reshaped Christian metaphysics. If God had been faced with chaos from eternity, and if God's very nature was Order, it is hard to see how the making of the world would not be the inevitable result, much as a face cannot help casting its image into a mirror. But if *even the mirror itself* is produced from nothing, what can explain the effect, if not some positive act of will on the part of a supreme being? This implied a more radical freedom on the part of God.

Western thinkers refined their metaphysics by struggling with the equivalent of a Zen *koan*, a mental puzzle that defeats ordinary conceptual thinking. The puzzle could be expressed like this: 'What does it mean *to be*?' What is 'to exist'? According to Plato, a thing is an Idea or Form instantiated in Matter. Reality means participation in the Ideas. Aristotle then refines or reinterprets this notion of instantiation, so a substance is made up of passive Matter 'actualized' (energized) by a Form. But for Aristotle the inner Form or Idea does not exist in its own right separately from Matter. And moreover his God, the 'Prime Mover', is only the first in a chain of such substances, distinguished from all the others by the fact that it

5. David Bentley Hart, *The Beauty of the Infinite*, 258.

alone is both perfectly simple and therefore eternal, and that it is unmoved by anything else. This God of Aristotle may be supreme in a certain sense, but it can hardly become the object of a sincere religious devotion. It is not a *person*.

By the thirteenth Christian century, Saint Thomas Aquinas was in a position to go a step further than either Plato or Aristotle could have done. If neither the Form nor Matter of a thing can exist in its own right, their actual existence together in one substance must depend on a higher, third factor. That cause, unknown to Aristotle, is the cause not just of 'what' something is but 'that' it is. As for the identity of that supreme cause, it can be nothing other than the pure act of being (which is not a noun but a verb: 'to be' or *esse*), since it must be capable of communicating existence to things by virtue of its own nature. This extraordinary and difficult insight, first developed by the Persian thinker Avicenna (Ibn Sina), is confirmed for Aquinas by the name that God gave himself from the burning bush in Exodus 3:14. *Say this to the sons of Israel, 'I AM has sent me to you.'* God is 'making it personal'.

The world of Aristotle (and his other Arab commentator Averroes) was one in which everything must happen eternally by necessity, while the eternal substance that is the cause of all things is entirely self-absorbed and unchanging. No special act of creation is needed. The God of Aquinas, by contrast, creates freely, because existence must be given, and the giving of existence to anything can only be a deliberate action.[6] God loves to create. It is not even that he *chooses* to, as though deciding against the alternative (which is not to create at all). For it is only in a limited creature like us that freedom is conditioned by the choices it is able to make.

Nor does God *have* to create anything. The Platonists tended to say that it is in the nature of the Good to diffuse itself, as it is of the sun to shine, so its nature would be frustrated if it did not do so.

---

6. The distinction Aquinas drew between the existence of a thing and its essence or nature was not universally accepted by Christendom—Duns Scotus, Suarez, and the Nominalists rejected it. This meant that they had to find other ways to preserve God's freedom. For the full story, read Etienne Gilson, *Being and Some Philosophers*.

And for Aristotle one thing leads to another. But here the Christian parts company from both Greek and Muslim. God is a Trinity, which means that every need of the Good to diffuse itself is already taken care of by the self-giving that constitutes the three Persons. These *are* the Good 'diffusing itself', if you like, and they do not automatically produce a world.

This is how Aquinas himself put it:

> The fact of saying that God made all things by his Word excludes the error of those who say that God produced things by necessity. When we say that in him there is a procession of love, we show that God produced creatures not because he needed them, nor for any cause outside of himself, but because of the love of his own goodness.[7]

So God creates whatever exists not because it is necessary to him, but because of 'the love of his own goodness'. And elsewhere Thomas says that God creates because it is *fitting* for him to do so. This notion of fittingness (*convenientia*) lies 'between' the necessary and the arbitrary, and is identified with neither. Thomas writes of the human will that 'When it is inclined to something as absolutely necessary to the end, it is moved to it with a certain necessity; but when it tends to something only because of a certain fittingness, it tends to it without necessity. Hence, neither does the divine will tend to its effects in a necessary way' (*SCG* 1, 82, 8).

Fittingness means suitability, proportion, appropriateness, beauty. Thus we can say with the modern Orthodox theologian David Bentley Hart that for Christianity, 'Creation ... is first and foremost a surface, a shining fabric of glory, whose inmost truth is its aesthetic correspondence to the beauty of divine love, as it is expressed by the Trinity: a sacramental order of light.'[8]

7. Thomas Aquinas, *S. Th.* 1, 32, 1 ad 3.

8. David Bentley Hart, *The Beauty of the Infinite*, 252. Christianity took over and deepened Neoplatonist aesthetics. For the Platonic tradition, beauty corresponds to *unity*, and therefore to common measure, simplicity, proportion, and symmetry. But Christianity transformed the idea of unity by identifying the One as (also) Trinity. The unity to which true beauty corresponds is a unity more intense than that of

The Impact of the Incarnation

In order to understand the *making new* of all things, which the Book of Revelation emphasizes, I began this chapter by speaking of the 'old', the first creation. I suggested that the coming of Christ forced a deeper interpretation of the first verse of the Book of Genesis. The early Christian thinkers had to find a way to express something they felt both heretics and pagans had failed completely to understand. They adopted the vocabulary of Plato and Aristotle but poured into it a new meaning, and re-cast the old debates.[9] The distinction between existence and essence was only part of the story. By itself, that would entail some notion of creation as dependent upon the will of God, but the divine will would remain completely inscrutable; for all intents and purposes arbitrary. God would have made the world on a whim. It was the revelation of the Trinity—of relationship subsisting actually within God himself—that led Christians to their new understanding of the creation as motivated by love rather than necessity.

It is true that Islam also regards God as the Creator *ex nihilo*. Surah 3:47 of the Qur'an is often quoted in this connection: 'God creates what he will. When he decrees a thing he does but say to it "Be", and it is.' These words are presented as having been spoken by the angels in response to Mary's question, 'Lord, how shall I have a son, seeing no mortal has touched me?' (Like Christianity, Islam teaches the virginal conception of Jesus.) One of the sayings of Muhammad, a *hadith qudsi*, relates the idea of the original creation to that of knowledge: 'I was a hidden treasure; I wished to be known

---

the monadic One, namely a unity constituted by the free, loving, and reciprocal self-gift of distinct Persons to one another.

9. We have just seen one example, concerning aesthetics. Christian writers also took over Aristotle's notion of the four types of 'cause' or explanation of things: final, formal, material, and efficient. God is *final* cause because he makes with an end in view, *formal* cause because things imitate aspects of his beauty, *material* cause because he creates them *ex nihilo*, and *efficient* (or 'effective') cause because he separates the gift of being from himself (as non-subsistent *esse*) so they can participate in it. More than an initiator of motion, the truly effective cause is now the origin of the very being of things (see Kenneth L. Schmitz, *The Recovery of Wonder*, 45–6).

[or, to know] and I created the world.' This saying becomes the subject of much commentary by the Sufi shaykhs, notably the great Muhyiddin Ibn Arabi. But in contrast to Christianity it seems to imply that God needs to create in order to be known, or to know himself. This then leads to the conclusion that Divine Being must manifest itself according to all possible modes, and that the world is simply God's way of knowing himself.

So the new philosophy of the Christians was shaped by their theology. The distinctive insight of the Church Fathers (Athanasius, the Cappadocians, Maximus) was to identify all being—even stones and stars—in the light of the Trinity as essentially rooted in the *relational* and *personal*. For Aristotle, dialog or relationship or love could only be an accidental circumstance of being, but in Christianity—thanks to the Trinity—it became as primordial as the very idea of substance.[10] The Orthodox theologian John Zizioulas puts it, if anything, even more strongly. He says 'we must *attribute to love* the role attributed to substance in classical ontology.'[11] Since God is love, 'it is the nature of Christian existence to receive and to live life as relatedness and, thus, to enter into that unity which is the ground of all reality and sustains it.'[12]

> If, within God's identity, there is an Other, who at the same time is the image of the Father and thus the archetype of all that can be created; if, within this identity, there is a Spirit, who is

10. Joseph Ratzinger, *Introduction to Christianity*, 182–3. In an address to the Special Assembly on the Middle East on 11 October 2010, Pope Benedict said: 'As we know well, Aristotelian philosophy tells us that between God and man there exists only a non-reciprocal relationship. Man exists in reference to God, but God, the Eternal, is in himself, he does not change: he cannot have this kind of relationship today and another kind tomorrow. He remains in himself, he does not have a relationship *ad extra*, he does not have a relationship with me. It is a very logical reflection, but it is a reflection that makes us despair. With the incarnation, with the coming of the *Theotókos*, this has changed radically, because God has drawn us into himself, and God in himself is relationship and makes us participate in his interior relationship.' (This speech was translated by Matthew Sherry for the web-site http://chiesa.espresso.repubblica.it.)

11. John D. Zizioulas, *Communion and Otherness*, 108, my emphasis. This book is the sequel to his influential *Being as Communion*.

12. Joseph Ratzinger, *Introduction to Christianity*, 188.

the free, superabundant love of the 'One' and of the 'Other',
then both the otherness of creation, which is modeled on the
archetypal otherness within God, and its sheer existence, which
it owes to the intradivine liberality, are brought into a positive
relationship to God.[13]

And how did Christians come to know for the first time that
within God's identity 'there is an Other'? Through the Incarnation,
obviously. It was the fact that Jesus Christ revealed himself to be
divine,[14] yet simultaneously spoke of the Father and the Spirit as
'other' than himself, that revealed the Trinity. This is the heart of
the unique Christian experience, which is the experience of becoming caught up in a relationship of eternal love that is the very nature
of God. That is why the final book of the Bible is not a work of philosophy, but made up of concrete images of particular beings
engaged in tumultuous relationship. Reality is much closer to these
fleshy images than to the pale abstractions of philosophy.

But the 'newness' with which John's Apocalypse is concerned is
not confined to a re-reading of Genesis in the light of the Incarnation, nor even to an appreciation of the wonderful substantiality of
a world that hangs by a thread from the will of God, manifesting the
beauty of his love and his wisdom. For more important than the
making of the world is its *re-making*. The Eternal became Man not
merely to teach us something we did not know about God, or to
lead us to appreciate the gratuity of creation. He did not just interpret the Scriptures; he fulfilled them. God became Man in order to
give the world a new center, and by so doing to save it.

The centrality of Christ, the 'firstborn from the dead' (Rev. 1:5),
is clearly John's concern from the first page of the Apocalypse. In
Adam, the world had chosen to distance itself from God: the process is represented in Genesis by an exile from the Garden that is
guarded by the Cherubim. The center remained where it was, but it

13. H.U. von Balthasar, *Theo-Logic*, Vol. II, 180–181.
14. In a nutshell, by abrogating laws of Moses, forgiving sins, raising the dead,
claiming to have existed in an eternal present before Abraham ('Before Abraham
was, I am'), and ultimately by rising from the dead. See John Redford's study, *Bad,
Mad or God?*

had become inaccessible to us. It was situated on another level from our daily lives, from history. The Incarnation implanted that now inaccessible center, the Tree of Life, amongst us in the fallen world, in a new form (the body of Christ, hanging on the tree of the Cross). But the coming of the center could not but change the world into which it had been inserted.

Something definitely happened to history when Christ came into it. Even non-Christians have noticed this. But what was it that happened, exactly? Saint Irenaeus writes: 'by bringing himself he brought all newness.'[15] Not only did events arrange themselves around him, but the very substance of the world was transmuted. By that I mean that, starting with his body and those who were in touch with him, all matter, all life, and all personality became reconnected with an eternal source of life, flowing out into the world through the Church.

When God says 'Let there be light', he is breathing his Word into the world (Gen. 1:3). Gradually it takes flesh, and is wrapped in the darkness until it seems to be completely overcome (John 1:5). The light is extinguished on Good Friday, with the separation of the soul from the body of Christ in death. But that separation is equivalent to the tearing of the veil of the Temple (Mark 15:38; Luke 23:44). There were two veils in the Jewish Temple, the outer of which was said to have been woven and embroidered with many colors representing the heavens and the earth. If it was this veil that tore at the death of Jesus, it signified the opening of the Temple to all people, since by baptism into his death all are admitted into the new Covenant (Rom. 6:3–4), but it also signified a return to the first day of creation, before the making of the firmament.

With the Resurrection, the victory of light is revealed and the reign of death is ended. A body of light is revealed.

> But some one will ask, 'How are the dead raised? With what kind of body do they come?' You foolish man! What you sow does not come to life unless it dies. And what you sow is not

---

15. Cited by Henri de Lubac in a section devoted to the impact of Christ's action upon the world, *Medieval Exegesis*, Vol. I, 236.

the body which is to be, but a bare kernel, perhaps of wheat or some other grain. But God gives it a body as he has chosen, and to each kind of seed its own body. . . . What is sown is perishable, what is raised is imperishable. It is sown in dishonor, it is raised in glory. It is sown in weakness, it is raised in power. It is sown a physical body, it is raised a spiritual body. (1 Cor. 15:35–44.)

But as with the first appearance of light in Genesis, the second is the beginning of a history. The remaking of the world is done instantaneously, as a seed is planted, but it takes time to unfold. John's Book of Revelation telescopes the end stages of this process—here at last we see the Lord 'sitting at the right hand of Power, and coming with the clouds of heaven' (as promised in Mark 14:62). Thus at the end of Revelation we find the new heaven and the new earth united in the new Jerusalem, the 'squared circle' of sacred geometry (see next chapter). The circle of time is complete, and so is the square of space, and the two have become one.

What we do *not* have at this point is the beginning of a new cycle of time. The 'world in God' that John shows us is not simply the start of another Golden Age that will in turn be replaced again by ages of Silver, Bronze, and Iron. No, since 'death shall be no more, neither shall there be mourning nor crying nor pain any more, for the former things have passed away' (Rev. 21:4).

King of Ages

It would seem that here we find the most radical break with the ancient cosmology. In most religious traditions we find a doctrine of *yugas* and *manvantaras*—like the Platonic 'great year' of the *Timaeus*, which always begins or ends in fire or flood. The world always existed, even if the evidently cyclical nature of time suggests that it has existed in a succession of world-ages rather than continuously the same. According to Saint Thomas, however, it cannot be necessary that the world exists either for a finite time, or always, since the world need not exist at all: as we have seen, 'it is not necessary that God should will anything except himself' (*ST* 1, Q. 46, Art. 1).

It is possible, nevertheless, that Christian 'newness' of which the

Apocalypse speaks did not require the complete elimination of the ancient cyclic conception of time, but merely its revision or deepening. The world-age described by the Bible is necessarily unique—an image, in its own way, of the uniqueness of God himself. But God must be free to create any number of worlds, each of them an expression of his uniqueness.[16] These worlds would not repeat (as Nietzsche would have it in his doctrine of eternal recurrence); each would be different. 'The eternal has a logical and ontological priority over the whole series of created beings, and this priority is so absolute that one could not increase it by affixing arbitrary limitations to the contents of the world.'[17] This doctrine of other worlds is found even in the impeccably orthodox Maximus the Confessor, who nevertheless concludes, after what seems to be a discussion of this point,

> We know that according to Scripture there is something which transcends the age . . . namely the inviolate kingdom of God. For it is not right to say that the kingdom of God had a beginning or that it was preceded by ages or by time. We believe the kingdom to be the inheritance of those who are saved, their abode and their place, as the true Logos has taught us. For it is the final goal of those who long for that which is the desire of all desires. Once they have reached it they are granted rest from all movement whatsoever, as there is no longer any time or age through which they need to pass. For after passing through all things they will come to rest in God, who exists before all ages and whom the nature of ages cannot attain.[18]

Thus other world-ages do not concern us. Christian salvation transcends the ages of ages; it concerns the lives of persons, who are members of this age, not souls reincarnating in one world after

16. According to St Thomas, 'the power of a Divine Person is infinite, nor can it be limited by any created thing. Hence it may not be said that a Divine Person so assumed one human nature as to be unable to assume another' (*ST* 3, Q. 3, Art. 7). Similarly it may not be said that God cannot create any number of other universes.
17. Robert Bolton, *The Order of the Ages*, 148. The book persuasively advances a Christian Platonist theory of time and history.
18. Maximus, 'Second Century on Theology' in *The Philokalia*, Vol. 2, 159.

another. In that sense Christianity, with its doctrine of creation *ex nihilo*, did finally break the endless chain of cycles. From now on,

> Facts are no longer phenomena, but events, acts. Forthwith something new is wrought—birth, real growth; the whole universe grows to maturity. Creation is not merely maintained, but is continuous. The world has a purpose and consequently a meaning, that is to say, both direction and significance.... Just as God rested on the seventh day after he had created the world, so the world, having completed its course, will rest in God. 'Then time shall be no more' [Rev. 10:6]. All things shall be renewed: *caelum novum, nova terra*. The resurrection, which shall indicate the passing of time into eternity, will be a definitive transformation of the universe: 'A new earth will be created to contain the bodies that have been made new; that is to say, the whole nature of our earth will be transformed into a spiritual state, free, thenceforward, from any change' [Isidore of Seville].[19]

But if there is no change in the world to come, does this not imply a horrifying image of frozen perfection? That is not the world promised by the Book of Revelation, although it is an impression that we find strengthened by the final pages of the *Summa* of Saint Thomas, where the motion of the heavenly bodies ceases with time, and animals and plants disappear, since they have not the same possibility of incorruption as the heavenly bodies, the physical elements, and the human soul. Aquinas seems almost to have forgotten the presence of the Tree of Life with its fruits in John's final vision. The *Summa* portrays a world of light, and luminous rocks, and frozen, blazing stars, with human bodies somehow in the midst of things, resting in God. Perhaps the lesson is that logic alone cannot give us a glimpse of the Resurrection, when even poetry must fail.

I think it helps to remember that the world to come, the world re-made, is not made from *nothing*. It is the old world healed, trans-

---

19. H. de Lubac, *Catholicism*, 142–3. The myth of progress is a secularized version of the [Judaeo-]Christian sense of history. Modernity loves to 'immanentize the eschaton.'

figured, and perfected, just as the risen body of Christ contains everything of value in the old but without the tendency to death. Even his wounds are still present, as he invites Thomas to place his finger in the holes the nails made (John 20:27). As Balthasar says,

> the One who sits on the throne says, 'Behold, I make all things new.' Not: Behold, I make a totally new set of things, but: Behold, I refashion and renew all that is. And our faith tells us that this 'new' reality was already present in the 'old', in our drama, though in a hidden form: 'For you have died, and your life is hid with Christ in God. When Christ who is our life appears, then you also will appear with him in glory' (Col. 3:3f).[20]

—as also will the other living creatures, for if our animal nature is to be resurrected it seems that the rest of creation cannot be excluded. Though, as Saint Thomas argues, individual animals do not possess immortal personhood, each of them expresses a part of the quality of their species, and those species cannot be absent from a world where 'the wolf shall dwell with the lamb, and the leopard shall lie down with the kid, and the calf and the lion and the fatling together, and a little child shall lead them' (Isaiah 11:6). We know that the nobility, agility, patience, and strength of the animals are in the very Cherubim, so that the faces of man, lion, ox, and eagle bend over the throne of God together.

> What the Book of Revelation calls the 'marriage of the Lamb' is not the conclusion but the beginning of a *life* that is to characterize the new aeon. This is portrayed only in shadowy images borrowed from the ancient world, but they suffice to evoke the superabundant, ever-flowing, event-quality of this life: myriad nations throng an open city to which all the treasures of the earth are brought; there the rushing waters of life are constantly heard, the trees of life constantly blossom and bear fruit. Now, at last, things that were formerly only incipient will really begin. . . .[21]

---

20. H.U. von Balthasar, *Theo-Drama*, Vol. IV, 200.
21. Ibid.

Being in God

Hans Urs von Balthasar also asks towards the end of *Theo-Drama*, 'What it is that God gains from the world?' It is a good question. What is the point of the whole thing? This is the question that confronts us when we try to contemplate the 'newness' of creation that Christianity insists upon. What can the world add to God, if all being, all goodness, all beauty, is already his from eternity? If it can add nothing, why did God bother with it at all?

The answer Balthasar gives is an attempt to 'get beyond the apparent contradiction that God is all Being and the world cannot therefore add anything to him (which leads of necessity to a form of *maya* doctrine) or that the world has a genuine being, in which case God cannot be the fullness of Being (which leads logically to the view that the world is necessary to God).' It is that 'the infinite possibilities of divine freedom' (including the completely gratuitous creation of the world) 'all lie *within* the Trinitarian distinctions and are thus free possibilities within the eternal life of love in God *that has always been realized.*'[22]

This enables us to understand the 'newness' of the world in an even deeper way. The place of the creation is not outside God but *within the Trinitarian distinctions*, in other words within God himself; and Balthasar can say this because he believes in the mutual receptivity of the Persons to one another. It seems to me that Leo Schaya echoes this thought in his interpretation of the way God makes 'room' in a part of himself for the creation (by withdrawal or *tsimtsum*) according to the Kabbalah:

> In reality, God, the absolute One, has no 'parts', but an infinity of possibilities, of which only the creatural possibilities have the illusory appearance of separate forms; in themselves, these forms are integrated, as eternal archetypes, in the all-possibility of the One. As for that 'part from which the light has been

---

22. H.U. von Balthasar, *Theo-Drama*, V, 508. One might also say that the second and third Persons of the Trinity 'add' nothing to the Father, since each is identified with the same unique, divine nature. The fact that creation can add nothing to the divine Infinite does not mean that it is not something in its own right, just that the two are not commensurable.

withdrawn' to make room for the 'place' of the cosmos, it is nothing other than the receptivity of God that actualizes itself in the midst of his unlimited fullness; this receptivity has a transcendent aspect, and an immanent aspect. . . .[23]

The doctrine of the Trinity—three Persons freely and joyously giving and receiving the divine nature in its undivided totality—grounds this notion of intradivine receptivity as nothing else could do. And when Schaya goes on to explain that *tsimtsum* is the hanging of a 'curtain' before God, in order to establish a region of immanent receptivity, we recall again the 'rending of the veil' at the moment of Christ's death, which was necessary if the creation was to be made anew.

If God were simply One, all that is other than him could be nothing more than a reflection, or a series of lesser essences arranged in a hierarchy like Russian dolls, just as the number 1 is made up of all the possible fractions we can fit inside it. The world would 'exist' because each form participates in the great Form in its own distinct way, but it would exist only as a shadow that passes, compared to the One that contains the whole plenitude of Being. But if God is Three as well as One, all this changes. The reason it must change is that a God who is a Monad can only *know*, whereas a God who is Three can *love*. Or rather, the Persons can love. As Adrienne von Speyr puts it so succinctly, 'God is not a lover; God is love, and this love has a threefold form.'[24]

As we saw, such a God is free. He can will, and he can give.[25] The things which are in the world are ideas in God; that is (according to the

---

23. L. Schaya, *The Universal Meaning of the Kabbalah*, 64.

24. *The Word Becomes Flesh*, 27.

25. D.C. Schindler, in *Hans Urs von Balthasar and the Dramatic Structure of Truth* (74–93), develops the implications of this insight. 'A conventional reading of Platonism sees the divine ideas only as universal *thought-contents*, or forms. Balthasar, by contrast, sees the divine ideas not only as God's thought of the creature but also his will for the creature' (88). From this follows an understanding of person as 'mission', realized in freedom, which is a creative participation in God's 'moving idea'. This is compatible with the view of Saint Thomas that God knows created things and wills them in the self-same Act, knowing them indeed 'as willed.' Schindler points out that Neoplatonism, by contrast with 'conventional' Platonism, in its own way also saw the Ideas as acts of will.

account given by Aquinas) they are the various ways in which his Essence can be imitated. But God as Person does not only *know* these ideas, as it were implicitly, and does not simply 'preside' over them, as the One presides over the Many; he can actually *give* himself (allow participation in his *esse*) to them, causing them to exist *in relation to himself as Person* (which in fact implies a fuller sense of 'knowing' as well).

For there are three modes of participation, corresponding to the three divine Persons. Saint Thomas argues that every creature bears a trace of the Trinity (1) in being created as an individual, (2) in having a form, and (3) in being related to other things (*ST* 1, Q. 45, Art. 7). So there is, first, participation of the thing through its *esse* (act of existence) in the Being of God, which participation is the actual creation *ex nihilo* of the thing. Second is the participation of a thing through its essence or idea in the Logos (this is the only one of the three participations of which classical Platonism was aware). The third participation of the thing in God corresponds to the Spirit, and is brought about by the Incarnation and Passion of the Son, enabling creation to give itself wholly (and as a whole) back to the Father. That is to say, having received its existence from God, the creation is perfected in its likeness to the Creator by becoming not just a Receiver but a Giver, through our co-operation with the sacrifice of Christ—by becoming 'hypostasized'.

That is to say, God can love things, and so make them real in a new way—that is the truth at the heart of *The Velveteen Rabbit* and *Pinocchio*. He cannot make them real as he alone is Real, but he makes them real by (actively) participating in his Being; real, that is, not just by (passively) embodying ideas, but as persons; or, in the case of the non-human creation, as belonging to an organic relationship with persons.[26]

Creation in its entirety is ordered towards the Incarnation. Its order and intelligibility are due not to its being a pale imitation of the 'contents' of the One, but to the presence within it of the God-Man. This presence is brought about by an *action*, by God's willing to give himself both in eternity and in time—and the latter intention necessitates the creation. The universe is grounded in the freedom of love.

26. John D. Zizioulas, *Being as Communion*, 49n.

3

THE COSMIC ORDER

*And he who talked to me had a measuring rod of gold to measure
the city and its gates and walls. The city lies foursquare, its length
the same as its breadth; and he measured the city with his rod,
twelve thousand stadia; its length and breadth and height are
equal.* Revelation 21:15–16

Christ's advent transformed the very structure and substance of
space and time—its structure, by giving it a center around which to
turn; its substance, by giving eternal life to the shadowy reality of
transient flesh. To the author of Revelation, Christ was not one
more religious leader or prophet, of the kind one finds in every religion; he was the very Logos of God. He was like a comet that strikes
the earth, an event of such overwhelming force that the whole history and substance of the world was changed forever. His advent,
long prepared for, implanted Eternity within Time, giving history a
center and an end. Like a magnet dropped into a field of iron filings,
he oriented all things to himself, for he was their maker and master.

How was such a radical transformation to be expressed in words,
except by adapting and transforming the ancient cosmic symbols?
Yet John's fluent use of symbolism is precisely what makes Revelation hard for a modern reader to understand. It is easier for us to
pass over the symbolic dimension of Scripture, jumping straight to
a moral or theological message. Having long since abandoned the
field of mathematics and cosmology to the scientists, we tend to dis-
miss the numerological concerns of the ancients as primitive, child-
ish or at best incidental. But the result is to reduce the complex
tapestry of the Apocalypse to a single thread: for example, the message that Jesus is the lord of history. When the entire Bible is treated

this way, the multi-leveled teaching of Jesus is reduced to the commandment to be really, really nice to one another.

Even the writers of the *ressourcement* in the twentieth century, concerned to retrieve and revive a fresh, Patristic vision of Christianity, while drawing attention to the cosmological element in traditional exegesis, tended to underplay its significance in order to emphasize the radical break between Christianity and the other religions. For example, in his book *Catholicism*, Henri de Lubac writes that while 'the Fathers' imagination found a great satisfaction in playing with combinations of numbers, whereby they exercised their ingenuity with subdivisions, additions and multiplications' in devising a symbolic arithmetic coherent with Holy Scripture, 'authentic Christianity' no longer attaches any real importance to these, except as pointers to the new order of history.[1] Hans Urs von Balthasar, similarly, is dismissive of the attempts of modern writers like René Guénon and Simone Weil to 'explain' the Cross symbolically or ontologically. 'The point where all the dimensions of the world intersect is also the point of indifference between all contraries, and so the point of redemption—and so forth. In all of that Christian theology is uninterested', he writes rather snootily.[2] It is uninterested because in such writings 'the crucified Christ has become a symbol, denser perhaps than the rest of reality put together, but a symbol all the same. And he is thereby subordinated to the universal.'[3] The danger in dwelling on the symbolism of the Cross is that the historical reality of Jesus Christ and his suffering may be toned down and smoothed over.

The danger exists; nevertheless, provided we are aware of it, the time may be ripe to recover some of these lost dimensions of the Biblical text. It is impossible, in any case, to ignore them completely. Indications abound that there is more to Biblical numbers than meets the eye. One example can be found in the fourth Gospel,

1. H. de Lubac, *Catholicism*, 73, 72.
2. H.U. von Balthasar, *Mysterium Paschale*, 60.
3. H.U. von Balthasar, *Mysterium Paschale*, 65. As Balthasar points out, the 'frontier line is often difficult to make out', being dependent on a choice made in the depths of the soul. Will we allow ourselves to be silenced by this love, or are we just making conversation about it?

where the Lord appears to his disciples by the Sea of Tiberias, after his crucifixion. As the day was breaking, and the weary disciples had caught no fish, a man on the shore tells them to cast the net again, this time on the right side of the boat. They do so, and catch an amazing haul. This trademark miracle causes Peter to recognize the Lord in the morning light, and he runs to him through the water. Later, 'Simon Peter went aboard and hauled the net ashore, full of large fish, a hundred and fifty-three of them; and although there were so many, the net was not torn' (John 21:11).

This number is hardly likely to have been recorded if it was not thought to have symbolic properties. (The number is not even a particularly staggering quantity, as one might have expected from the build-up John gives it.) One hundred and fifty-three happens to be a 'triangular' number with many interesting mathematical properties.[4] The ratio 265/153 is also the closest fraction to $\sqrt{3}$ and was termed by the Pythagoreans 'the measure of the fish', being the ratio of the length to the width of the *vesica piscis*, the symbol of the Dyad, one of the most important geometrical figures in all of sacred art. From Saint Augustine onwards, numerous attempts have been made to explain the presence of this particular number at such a significant point in a Christian Scripture, the most ingenious being that of John Michell,[5] using a combination of geometry and gematria (see the Appendix on this subject), while Balthasar's friend, the seer Adrienne von Speyr, has produced a unique exegesis of her

---

4. For example, 153 is the sum of the cubes of its own digits. Many 'curious properties' of the number are collected by Shyam Sunder Gupta: www.shyamsundergupta.com/c153.htm. The number 153 is also the numerical equivalent of the name of the Archangel Michael in Greek gematria. It is the 17th triangular number, 17 being the sum of 10 and 7, where 10 is the sacred *Tetraktys* of the Pythagoreans and 7 the number of disciples involved in this fishing expedition. In *A Rebirth of Images* (254) Austin Farrer points out that 17 is a well-known whole-number approximation to the diagonal of a square whose sides are 12, making it (in *stadia*) the length of the River of Life that cuts from corner to corner of the City of Revelation, whose four sides each measure 12,000 *stadia*. With these and other arguments he establishes an even stronger connection between the Book of Revelation and the Gospel of John.

5. John Michell, *How the World is Made*, 97–101.

own.[6] At the very least the presence of this number strongly suggests that the author of the Gospel was familiar with the Pythagorean tradition—a fact that must surely be of importance to anyone who wants to interpret Scripture with an eye to the intentions of its human authors.

The Book of Revelation is built around a redoubled threefold repetition of a series of seven climactic events (see Appendix 1), culminating in the vision of a heavenly city in which the number twelve predominates. Seven, three, four, and twelve are the most important numbers in John's vision, and they will dominate the account that follows.

Key to the main symbolic numbers employed in Revelation

1   The primary number, First and Last, unity of God.

½   Limited time, time divided or fragmented.

2   Division, reproduction, symmetry, balance, witnesses;
    the two natures of Christ (divine and human).

3   The divine Trinity, return to unity, primordial relationship;
    the three worlds.

3½ Imperfection ($7 \div 2$), time of trial.

4   The world, universe, seasons, dimensions of material
    cosmos.

6   Sum and product of 1, 2, 3; active days of creation;
    the water not yet turned to wine.

7   Earth joined to God (4 + 3), perfection, God's 'rest', the
    planets.

---

6. In her book *The Fisher's Net* (published posthumously in German in 1969), she lists all the combinations of numbers that add up to 153, interpreting each as the numerical expression of a mission of one of the great saints. The particular symbolic combinations of digits 1–9 comprised in each number express the nature of the mission, and the greatest missions are represented by the prime numbers (Peter is 151). See the summary in English by H.U. von Balthasar, *First Glance at Adrienne von Speyr*, 82–5.

10 Authority (the 10 Commandments), 7 + 3, or else simply a limited number (by contrast with 1000).

12 Tribes, Patriarchs, Apostles; the celestial order of the zodiac; the Church (4 x 3: the world multiplied by the Trinity).

666 In gematria, the number of the Sun, 'Beast' and 'Nero Caesar.'

1000 10^3, simply a very large number, or unlimited time.

1260 Days equivalent to 3½ years (42 months of 30 days).

144,000 12^2 x 1000 (unlimited extension of the celestial order).

The Sevenfold Covenant

The number seven has been held sacred ever since the ancient astronomers counted the wandering stars, or planets, against the stable backdrop of the twelve zodiacal constellations (the interplay of seven and twelve is extremely noticeable throughout Revelation). Throughout the ancient world and right up to the Renaissance these seven visibly moving lights in the sky—the Sun, Moon, Mars, Mercury, Jupiter, Venus, and Saturn—are identified with gods or angels, and with the division of time into the days of the week.[7]

But in the Judaeo-Christian tradition seven acquired a new importance by being associated with the overarching theme of *covenant*. The primordial exemplar is the covenant of creation by which the world is ordered and chaos suppressed in seven days.[8] The Hebrew word for swearing an oath (*shava*), and therefore making a covenant, is the verb form of the word for seven (*sheva*). The seventh day of creation therefore represents God's great oath of binding, an oath that seals the covenant of creation with a 'nuptial' day of rest.[9]

The primordial covenant of the Judaic tradition has three dimensions: the beauty of cosmic order, God's covenant with Adam and

---

7. Even the modern Christian writer C.S. Lewis was able to write that 'the characters of the planets, as conceived by medieval astrology, seem to me to have a permanent value as spiritual symbols – to provide a *Phänomenologie des Geistes* which is specially worth while in our own generation' (cited in Michael Ward, *Planet Narnia*, 30).

Eve, and the sacrament of marriage that unites the first couple. From then on the theme of covenant permeates Scripture. Man breaks faith with God, and the subsequent unbinding of cosmic forces leads to the Flood, after which God makes a new covenant with all creatures (the sign of which is the sevenfold rainbow). His covenant with mankind is renewed through Abraham, Moses, and David. The bond of marriage, loosened by divorce and polygamy, is renewed by Jesus the 'new Adam'. The seven sacraments are the basis of the New Covenant of Christ extended through him not just to 'a couple, a household, a tribe, a nation, or a kingdom—but [to] all humanity.' [10] (The Latin word for a sacrament, *sacramentum*, was also originally the word for a sacred oath.)

In the elaborate number symbolism of the Middle Ages, seven symbolized perfect completeness because it was composed of three, signifying the spiritual world, added to four, signifying the temporal. Three was associated with the spiritual not only because of the Trinity, but from before the Christian era because it represented the return to unity after a primordial division. Four—the redoubling of the primordial division of all things into two during the act of creation—signified the worldly realm. Similarly life in the temporal dimension was represented by the four cardinal virtues, while the

8. See the first chapter of Robert Murray S.J., *The Cosmic Covenant*, and also Joseph Ratzinger, *'In the Beginning...'* (his commentary on the opening chapters of Genesis). Ordering in terms of seven 'days' is not intended to be chronological in the modern sense, any more than the account of John's visions of Revelation is intended to be understood in strict temporal sequence. See my account in *The Seven Sacraments*, and also Harry Lee Poe, 'The Problem of Time in Biblical Perspective.' The number seven is deeply embedded in the structure of Genesis: the first verse contains seven words and four times seven letters, while God's meditation on the creation of man is sevenfold (Gen. 1:26), as are the first recorded words of God to man (1:28). (See also the appendix below on Gematria.)

9. Scott Hahn, *Letter and Spirit*, 60–61. Leo Scheffczyk makes the point that the Genesis account of creation assumed its present form and importance after belief in the saving covenant was established, in order to give that belief 'its supreme justification by anchoring it in the origin of all history, at the same time showing that the God of the fathers, the God of the Sinaitic Covenant, is none other than the Creator of the world' (*Creation and Providence*, 5).

10. Scott Hahn, *Letter and Spirit*, 70. The same author's *A Father Who Keeps His Promises* develops this theme in greater detail.

spiritual life was concerned with the three theological virtues.

Just as the seven virtues were divided into three theological and four moral, the seven sacraments were divided into three sacraments of initiation (Baptism, Confirmation, Eucharist) and four of healing and community (Reconciliation, Ordination, Marriage, Anointing). Together these signified the completeness of Christian existence, based on the union of divine and human natures in Jesus Christ.

It makes perfect sense, therefore, for John's book, which (as Appendix 1 shows in more detail) is a mystical commentary on the Church's liturgy as well as a guidebook to the meaning of both cosmos and history, to be structured in septenaries, with threefold repetition and redoubling as a method of emphasis but also of deepening. The numbers of times a given phrase or word occurs can also be significant to John: Richard Bauckham notes that the title 'The Lord God the Almighty', and the self-designations of God as 'First and Last', 'Alpha and Omega', or 'Beginning and End', each occur precisely seven times, scattered throughout the text— indicating once again, not only the importance of the number seven for John, but the immense craftsmanship that went into his literary construction. The word 'Lamb' occurs precisely 28 (7 x 4) times; furthermore, seven of these occurrences are in phrases that couple God and the Lamb together.[11] Even the puzzling 'time and times and half a time' that John often uses to define the period of the reign of evil (referring back to Daniel 9:27) is on closer examination a divided seven (i.e., one plus two and a half, which is half of seven).

The Fourfold Center

Like the Holy of Holies in the first Jewish Temple, and like the Kaaba, the center of the Muslim world, John's City is in the form of

---

11. R. Bauckham, *The Theology of the Book of Revelation*, 66. As we see in the immediately next section, fourfoldness representing the full extent of the world is also present in many ways throughout the book, often in combination with seven. The first four judgments in each series of seven affect the whole world, and the seven phrases by which John designates all the nations of the world are always fourfold ('e.g., 'peoples and tribes and languages and nations'). The 7 x 4 occurrences of the title 'Lamb' may therefore indicate the worldwide scope of his victory.

a cube. Interestingly, in the world's oldest known story, the Sumerian *Epic of Gilgamesh* dating from around 3000 BC, there is an account of the Flood in which an Ark containing the 'seed of all living creatures' is built in the form of a cube measuring the equivalent of 120 cubits on each side. Furthermore the Hebrew word for 'Ark' (as in the Ark of Noah, the 'basket' in which baby Moses was placed, and of course the Ark of the Covenant) means not a ship but a box or chest, and the related Egyptian word refers to a 'cycle of time'.[12] Such ancient legends and derivations seem to cry out for a metaphysical interpretation.

The cube is one of the regular geometrical forms known as 'Platonic solids', each of which is associated with one of the fundamental elements out of which the world was made: Earth, Water, Air, and Fire—equivalent to the four fundamental states of matter in modern physics: solid, liquid, gas, and plasma. The cube was associated with the element Earth because of its stability.[13] It also represents the universe as a whole, because it faces all six directions of three-dimensional space. Implicit within it, therefore, is a six-armed cross at its center, defining these twice-three directions—up and down, left and right, front and back. The faces of the cube are the filling-out of the possibilities signified by each arm of the cross, hence the frequent use of the cube to represent the completion of a

12. See Robert Temple, *He Who Saw Everything*, 119–21, 132–3. The demonic parody of the golden heavenly city is sometimes found in fiction. The best example is perhaps the grey Borg cube in *Star Trek: The Next Generation* and *Star Trek: Voyager*.

13. In the *Timaeus*, Plato hypothesizes that the elements are made of particles built up from triangles into the forms of the five regular solids. Since the pyramid is the figure with the fewest faces, it must be the most mobile, the sharpest, most penetrating, and lightest. He therefore identifies it as the basic constituent of Fire. Air is composed of octahedrons, Water of icosahedrons. The fifth Platonic solid, the dodecahedron, being the closest in form to the sphere, was associated with the fifth element Aether, the Hindu *Akasha*, or Space. Though the existence of a too crudely imagined 'Ether' as the bearer of electromagnetic waves seemed to have been disproved by Michelson and Morley in 1887, the ancient concept reappeared as Einstein's notion of a unified space-time continuum. The Platonic elements are basic to our experience of the world. The same can hardly be said of two further 'states of matter' recently created in the laboratory by super-refrigeration close to absolute zero, namely Bose-Einstein and fermionic condensates. Symbolically, therefore, the ancient scheme remains intact.

temporal cycle in many religious traditions—such as the Hindu *manvantara*.

It is worth noting that the normal floor-plan of a medieval cathedral, which resembles a cross, can also be read as an exploded cube, whose six faces, when unfolded, create exactly this pattern.

It has been said that all Christian symbolism comes back in the end to the Sun and the Cosmic Tree (with the Moon, reflecting the Sun, as the symbol of the Church). The Cross connects both, being both organic and mathematical: as the former it is a tree made of wood, and as the latter a symbol of the radiation of divine light throughout the world. That radiation of the Cross may be captured in geometrical projection either by a cube or a sphere, a square or a circle. All of these are basic elements of sacred architecture, but it tends to be the sphere or circle that is used to refer to the beginning of things, or the heavens, and the cube or square to the end, or the earth. The temple represents the 'squaring of the circle' or the bringing of heaven down to earth.

Adrian Snodgrass reminds us of the sheer *density* of the traditional symbolic language on which John was able to draw. In the case of the number four, he writes:

> The four arms of the cross correlate with the four columns of the Throne of God, the Four Evangelists, the four cardinal directions, the four winds, the four pillars of the universe, the four phases of the moon, the four seasons, the four walls of the Celestial Jerusalem, the four letters of the name of God (YHVH) and to the four letters of the name of the first man (ADAM). They are 'the four winds from the four quarters of heaven', 'the four quarters of the earth' and 'the four angels standing on the four corners of the earth, holding the four winds of the earth' [from the Book of Revelation]. They also correspond to the four horsemen of the Apocalypse, whose

horses are colored to correspond to the four directions and to
the four parts of the day, thus encompassing space and time:
the white horse is that of the east and the dawn; the red horse
is that of the south and midday; the pale horse is that of the
west and sunset; and the black horse corresponds to the north
and midnight. The four arms of the cross also equate [sic] the
four rivers of Paradise, flowing from Eden in the four directions. In the Christian interpretation of this symbolism the
four rivers are taken to be the cosmos emanating from Christ,
'the artisan of the universe.'[14]

In this way both Adam and the new Adam, Christ, are microcos-
mic in nature—integrating within themselves the totality of the cosmos. We find a similar vision in the Letter to the Colossians: 'He is
before all things, and in him all things hold together' (Col. 1:17).

As to the four Living Creatures or Tetramorph, sometimes called
Cherubim, guarding the way from the fallen world back to the Garden of Eden (Gen. 3), encountered by the prophet Ezekiel in a
vision,[15] and familiar to us from their depiction on ceremonial
books of the Gospel for reasons I will consider below, these also
have an astrological significance, for the constellations Lion, Bull,
Man (Aquarius), and Eagle (the Hebrew equivalent of Scorpio)
form a square around the zodiacal cross formed by the solstices and
equinoxes, dividing the circle of the ecliptic into four sections of 90
degrees. These four figures were also present in Babylonian mythology as the four corners of the universe—their subservience to Christ
in Revelation signifying his supremacy over all cosmic forces.[16]
Thus 'John's vision images a dynamic cosmos, rotating about the
unmoving center of Eternity [Throne]. In his vision the extension
of space in the four directions and the quaternary of the nodal

14. A. Snodgrass, *Architecture, Time and Eternity*, Vol. 1, 291–2. On these matters
of theological and cosmological symbolism see also Jean Hani, *The Symbolism of
the Christian Temple*.

15. Where all four faces appear on the each of the four creatures called cherubim.

16. Margaret Barker suggests that these were the very 'beasts' (*hayyot*) that were
with Jesus in the wilderness when the 'angels ministered to him' (Mark 1:13). See
The Hidden Tradition of the Kingdom of God, 94.

points of the year, the solstices and equinoxes, are coincident. It is a vision of the world in its two coordinates of space and time emanating from the Throne of the Pantocrator.'[17]

Referring also to extra-biblical sources such as the Book of Enoch and the Temple Scroll of Qumran, Margaret Barker concludes that the twelve jewels on which the gates are founded can be associated with the twelve angelic guardians of the ancient calendar. The gates are for the 'stars' to come in and out:

> These stars were the angels who had charge of the calendar (1 En. 75), the four great angels of the quarter days ensuring that the twelve months of thirty days each were divided by the angels of the quarters giving a solar year of 364 days (1 En. 82). The Temple Scroll shows that the plan of the ideal temple was, in fact, calendrical, the alignment of the gates in middle and outer walls on the eastern side coinciding with sunrise at the summer and winter solstices, and the central gate marking the equinoxes.[18]

Certainly a calendrical nature for the Temple would fit with what we know or suspect of the most ancient temple-complexes and sacred buildings all around the world, from the Pyramids to Stonehenge. As for the four Creatures (or the four aspects of one Creature), the most common associations are with the zodiac and the four seasons of the year, the points of the compass, the elements, and the letters of the divine Name YHVH.

To these ancient themes, the Christians added another layer of symbolism. The identification of the four Creatures with the four Evangelists (Matthew, Mark, Luke, and John) is a slightly uncertain process, since the early Christian writers themselves disagreed on which was which, although they all agreed with Saint Irenaeus when he wrote in the second century that it was appropriate for there to be exactly four of them:

> It is not possible that the Gospels can be either more or fewer in number than they are. For, since there are four zones of the

---

17. A. Snodgrass, *Architecture, Time and Eternity*, vol. 1, 298.
18. M. Barker, *The Revelation of Jesus Christ*, 324.

world in which we live, and four principal winds, while the Church is scattered throughout all the world, and the 'pillar and ground' of the Church is the Gospel and the spirit of life; it is fitting that she should have four pillars, breathing out immortality on every side, and vivifying men afresh. From which fact, it is evident that the Word, the Artificer of all, He that sitteth upon the cherubim, and contains all things, He who was manifested to men, has given us the Gospel under four aspects, but bound together by one Spirit. As also David says, when entreating His manifestation, 'Thou that sittest between the cherubim, shine forth.' For the cherubim, too, were four-faced, and their faces were images of the dispensation of the Son of God.[19]

Cherubim are described as having the face of a Man when you look at them from the front, an Eagle from behind, and a Lion and a Bull or Ox if you approach from the left or right side (Ezekiel 1:5–14). These four creatures were taken to represent the four sources of inspiration for the Gospel writers, or the four different ways into the heart of the Gospel; they were, in other words, four faces of a single living organism, the *evangelium* of Jesus Christ. The fourfold book was itself a messenger ('angel') from God.[20]

Irenaeus linked the Lion to John and the Eagle to Mark. So did Saint Ambrose, but Saint Augustine argued instead for John to be identified with the Eagle, the Lion with Matthew and the Man with Mark. Finally Augustine's contemporary in the fourth century, Saint Jerome (the translator of the Bible into Latin), completed the process by accepting John as the Eagle but following the earlier identification of Mark as the Lion and Matthew as the Man/Angel. This was almost universally accepted and became the main iconographic tradition after the fourth century.[21]

The iconography may have been generally accepted because it seemed intuitively appropriate to the style and content of the four

19. *Adversus Haereses* 3.11.8.

20. As fourfold, of course, the Gospels were also the literary form of the four-sided City or Holy of Holies.

Gospels. Matthew (symbol: Man) begins with a human genealogy of Jesus through Joseph that goes back through David to Abraham. He emphasizes the three titles 'Son of Man', 'Son of David', 'Son of Abraham.' This is God with a human face, Jesus as rightful king of the Jews. Mark (Lion) begins with the voice of John roaring in the wilderness. He presents Jesus as a teacher with great power, emphasizing his miracles (of which he records more than any other evangelist) rather than his parables. His syntax is abrupt, the pace of his narrative almost breathless. Alone among the Gospels, Mark describes Jesus as being 'with the wild beasts' after his baptism by John. Luke (Ox/Bull) presents Jesus as the one who suffers for his people, and his genealogy going back to Adam who was made of the dust of the earth. Whereas the Lion is traditionally the noblest of wild creatures on land, the Ox is the noblest of the domestic animals, the fatted calf a symbol of sacrifice, and the Bull represents the powers of the earthly body. John (Eagle) presents Jesus as the one who descends and ascends to heaven. The Eagle is the noblest of birds, the most powerful to fly among the mountaintops, and the most far-sighted creature of all. The four Gospel-creatures were also associated with the four great mysteries or stages in the life of Christ, so that Jesus is a Man in his birth, an Ox in his death, a Lion in his resurrection, and Eagle in his ascension.

Finally, in the Kabbalah the four archetypal principles contained in the divine Name were said to have manifested in the sixth heaven as the Archangels Michael (holiness), Gabriel (strength), Raphael (charity), and Uriel/Fanuel (knowledge, or conversion).[22]

---

21. Until at least AD 150 the Gospel scrolls were read individually; only after that was a codex created containing the four books bound together—and the order was slightly different in the Eastern and Western Mediterranean. See Richard A. Burridge, *Four Gospels, One Jesus?* 25–8.

22. See L. Schaya, *The Universal Meaning of the Kabbalah*, 87–9. Michael is the only Archangel named in the Book of Revelation. The leader of heaven's armies, he defends God's honour against those who claim to be 'like God.' Uriel, who appears to Ezra in an apocryphal O.T. text, is identified by tradition with the wielder of the 'fiery sword' who guards the way back to Eden (Gen. 3:24), and also with the stranger who wrestles with Jacob at Peniel (Gen. 32:21).

1	Y (Yod)	Man	Matthew	Incarnation	Michael	*Who is like God*
2	H (He)	Lion	Mark	Resurrection	Raphael	*Healing of God*
3	V (Vau)	Bull	Luke	Passion	Gabriel	*Strength of God*
4	H (Heh)	Eagle	John	Ascension	Uriel	*Light of God*

Correspondences like these—regarded as reflecting an archetypal idea in God's mind impressed on every level of the created universe—were employed in the construction of Christian churches throughout the middle ages, with the astrological alignment of the building and the choice of images and forms throughout the church reflecting a schema of elements, directions, and natural processes. A typical schema might look something like this:

Elements	Qualities	Seasons	Colors	Processes
Fire	Dry/Hot	Summer	White	Combustion
Air	Hot/Moist	Spring	Red	Rarefaction
Water	Cold/Moist	Winter	Yellow	Liquefaction
Earth	Cold/Dry	Autumn	Black	Solidification

The details might vary, but the underlying geometric structure remained consistent. Churches, of course, were always cruciform in shape, expressing the body of Christ outstretched, head to the east, face upwards gazing towards the Father. The church building itself could therefore be identified with the body or womb of the Virgin Mary in which the Son of Man was conceived, and from which he goes out to the world. The body, soul, and spirit of man were then imaged in the three main sections of the church plan: nave, chancel, and sanctuary.

The Twelve Gates

The City of John's final vision has four sides, but there are three gates on each side, making twelve in all. Twelve, like seven, had a cosmological significance. The fact that our calendar year is still organized in weeks of 7 days grouped into 12 months of approximately 4 weeks each is a vestige of this ancient way of thinking, which sought to conform daily life to the forms and rhythms connecting earth with heaven, time with space.

The circuit of the heavens was divided first into four by the solstices and equinoxes, then into the twelve symbolic signs of the zodiac, while the circuit of the sun is also measured by four seasons and twelve lunar months. The twelve months of the year were echoed in the twelve hours of the day and the twelve of the night. Mathematically, applying the number twelve to the circuit of the heavens permitted the simplest combination of both odd and even symmetry through the interplay of three and four. Thus the twelve tribes of Israel gathered around the presence of God in the Temple, and the twelve apostles gathered around the Lamb,[23] represented the totality of the temporal world measured by the stars of the Fourth Day, with the great Mediator or supernal Sun at the center of all.

Twelve, like seven, is made out of three and four, but by way of multiplication rather than addition. Ancient and medieval writers believed that multiplication diffuses a property into a given number of directions or objects.[24] They thought twelve therefore especially appropriate to describe the mystery of the Church, through which the spiritual life is diffused throughout the four directions of space and time, or the four dimensions of the corporeal world. Furthermore, if for Christians the number seven signifies the creation and recreation of the world in the sacraments, then twelve can also signify the fruition and end of this creation: in other words *the transcendence of the sacraments*. Henri de Lubac writes:

> 'When the consummation comes, the sacraments will be employed no more.' That axiom must be given all the breadth of meaning that Tradition permits. Human mediation, now indispensable and of primary importance, will have no *raison d'être* in the Heavenly Jerusalem; there, everyone will hear

---

23. The two twelves together make up the twenty-four Elders we find seated around the Throne, for example at Rev. 4:4. This is one of the ways the Book of Revelation represents the unity of the Old and New Covenants.

24. Hopper, *Medieval Number Symbolism*, 82.

God's voice directly and everyone will respond to it spontaneously, just as everyone will see God face to face. And more than this; in this 'regime of perfect inwardness' the perfect and glorious knowledge of God will fill the elect 'as the covering waters of the sea.' The Source of Life will spring up in each one of them: 'The whole city shall be one with the temple', and the only temple will be God himself, and its only lamp the Lamb. The altar will be an altar of incense and not of holocausts, and the whole Church will be one single sacrifice of praise in Christ. At the Day of the Lord when the *catholica societas* will be realized in its perfection, everything will be at once unified, interiorized and made eternal in God, because 'God [will be] all in all.'[25]

John sees the New Jerusalem 'prepared as a bride adorned for her husband' (Rev. 21:2). But we are a long way here from the erotic symbolism of the Song of Songs. The Beloved is described with a mathematical objectivity that seems cold by comparison with the allegory of the Canticle ('Your two breasts are like two fawns, twins of a gazelle, that feed among the lilies'). The Liturgical City of John's vision is laid out within a great wall in the shape of a square, each side having three gates, each gate corresponding to one of the tribes of Israel and having inscribed on its foundation the name of one of the twelve apostles. The wall is 12,000 *stadia* long, and the city is in the form of a cube, for 'its length and breadth and height are equal' (Rev. 21:16).[26] Each wall is said to be 144 (that is, 12 times 12) cubits thick, and faces one of the four directions, east, west, north, and south. Each gate, moreover, is a single pearl; each foundation (apostle) is adorned with a particular kind of jewel.

Despite the importance of numbers to the author of Revelation, the measurements of the City supplied by the angel are much less precise and complex than the detailed Temple description to be

25. Henri de Lubac, *The Splendor of the Church*, 49–50.

26. One *stadium* or *stadion* was equivalent to 185 meters, so the city wall is a square roughly 1,367 miles on each side. The number 12,000 is obviously intended to be symbolic rather than physical, being the multiplication of 12 by the 'unlimited' number 1000.

found in chapters 40 to 48 of the Book of Ezekiel, or for that matter the instructions to Moses of how to construct the ark and tabernacle of the Covenant in Exodus (25:8–27:21), which some have thought was for the ritual enactment of the cosmic vision of the Seven Days vouchsafed to Moses on Sinai.[27] Of course, in the case of Revelation there was no intention of suggesting that the City or Temple should be actually constructed. John's vision, after all, is of a City that we are *part of*, one that is being built up by God out of the lives of the saints. The symbols (whether these are numbers, colors, or stones) are merely clues to its nature and purpose. Nevertheless, the measurements John does choose to give us are there for a reason. As Hans Urs von Balthasar puts it, 'all the religious concepts of measure contained in the Old Testament are taken up and superseded. . . . In the New Testament, these numbers become the expression of the living missions of the saints, and the measurements of the heavenly Jerusalem are the measurements of the living eschatological bride of the Lamb.'[28]

We recall here that the twelve gates of the City are not crystals but pearls; they are white, and reflect light, like the moon in relation to the sun. These represent the tribes of Israel because it is through the tribes—now scattered to the four directions but eventually to be reunited—that all the peoples of the earth are to be brought into God's kingdom. The tribes represent the Church. But if the gates are pearls, Revelation also tells us that the *foundations of the gates* are precious stones, which being crystals shine by *transmitted* light. These are the apostles of the Lamb, who (though born later in time), are to be kings and judges over the tribes, according to Jesus's words in Luke 22:30.[29]

---

27. See John H. Sailhammer, *The Pentateuch as Narrative*, 298–9; also M. Barker, *The Revelation of Jesus Christ*, 17-20.

28. H.U. von Balthasar, *The Glory of the Lord*, Vol. VII, 314–15. 'This whole possibility of combining the measureless profusion of grace on the one hand and allocation and measure on the other hand is the decisively Christian element in a theological aesthetics, because its essential basis is the inner Trinity of God and the coming-forth of this Trinity in the Incarnation' (ibid., 314). The Triad is no doubt sacred in many if not all traditions. The question of the relation of Triad to Trinity has been touched upon in an earlier chapter.

Was John a Pythagorean?

The Liturgical City stands at the center of the world. Its gates are open, but guarded. Israel's mission was to be precisely such a center among the nations, and it has never been as isolated as some would have liked it to be. Even its darkest periods of exile—in Egypt (a sojourn begun in friendship, as described in the tale of Joseph and his brothers, although by the time of Moses it had degenerated into slavery) and in Babylon (after the conquest of Jerusalem in 599 BC and the subsequent destruction of the Temple)—have been important times of cultural give and take.

Many early Christian and Jewish writers believed that the Greek philosopher Plato was influenced by Moses. Perhaps the influence began even earlier, with Pythagoras. Margaret Barker has revived this tradition by claiming that the similarities between Israel's mystical First Temple tradition and the Pythagorean-Platonic tradition of mathematics and philosophy are more than coincidental. Pythagoras, the father in many ways of Western civilization, was a direct influence upon Plato, whose cosmological dialogue *Timaeus* was well known and appreciated by the early Christians. Barker writes:

> My reconstruction suggests that the priests of the first temple knew an invisible, heavenly world on which the tabernacle or temple had been modelled; that they spoke of forms: the *form* of man and the *form* of a throne; that they described the heavens as an embroidered curtain; that they knew the distinction between time, outside the veil, and eternity within it. They knew that time was the moving image of eternity. They knew of angels, the sons of God begotten on Day One, as Job suggests. They concerned themselves with the mathematics of the creation, the weights and measures. They believed that the creation was bonded together by a great oath or covenant. They believed that the stars were divine beings, angels, and they

29. For much more on 12 as a cosmological number and the geometric structures that express this function see Michael Schneider, *Constructing the Cosmological Circle*. See also 'Entering the City', below.

described a creator whose work was completed not by motion but by Sabbath rest. What I have reconstructed as the secret tradition of the world beyond the temple veil would, *in any other context be identified as Plato's Timaeus*, written in the middle of the fourth century BCE.[30]

The *Timaeus*, Barker thinks, contains a muddled version of Jewish cosmology, with the fourfold Living Creature upon which the world is modelled being equivalent to the Jewish Logos, or Wisdom, and the tetramorph. Her chapter 'Temple and Timaeus' argues in detail for the formative influence upon Pythagoras of the First Temple tradition: the Pythagorean veneration of a fiery cube at the center of the universe recalls the gold-covered Holy of Holies, while their account of creation seems to transpose the mythological and visionary description of Day One into a philosophical key.

Here I should interject that the question of what exactly the 'Pythagoreans' believed may never be known. Recent studies suggest that a great deal may have been projected onto the figure of Pythagoras by Plato's Academy.[31] Pythagoras seems to have travelled widely, and is may have derived the key idea associated with his name—that divinity is defined by number—from the religious cult associated with Orpheus. But the origins of Orphism are obscure. Some believe it may have come to Greece from Babylon, while others suggest a provenance in Egypt between 1500 and 1200 BC (perhaps the very period when the Tribes of Israel were there, before the Exodus). At least one scholar (Ernest McClain) has argued for a common source in the musical culture of ancient Sumeria around 3000 BC.[32]

Despite this obscurity, the idea of there being a common heritage or shared legacy of understanding between the Jewish and Christian

30. Barker, *The Great High Priest*, 201.

31. By 'recent' I mean since Walter Burkert's influential study, *Lore and Science in Ancient Pythagoreanism*, which appeared in English in 1972. For what is currently known and surmised about Pythagoras see Charles H. Kahn, *Pythagoras and the Pythagoreans*.

32. For an introduction to Ernest G. McClain's work see www.ernestmcclain.net and his book, *The Myth of Invariance*.

Scriptures and the Pythagorean/ Platonic movement remains very appealing. There is a strong emphasis on number symbolism, on divine order, and measurement of the cosmos in the Scriptures, and many Jewish and Christian mystics from Philo to Pico have recognized this affinity.

Numbers in the Pythagorean tradition are archetypes: less measures of quantity, as we tend to think of them today, than qualities or states of being—perhaps even, in a sense, 'gods', subordinate to the One from which they derive. The sacred *Tetraktys*, or Decad, is a pattern created by arranging the first four natural numbers 1, 2, 3, 4 (referred to in the Oath of the Pythagoreans as the four 'letters' of the divine Name) on four levels in the shape of an equilateral triangle, the elements adding up to Ten:

$$1$$
$$1 + 1$$
$$1 + 1 + 1$$
$$1 + 1 + 1 + 1$$

The Greeks, of course, did not use Hindu/Arabic numerals but rather assigned numerical values to the letters of the alphabet. They used a quasi-decimal system of counting, but without a sign for zero. Pythagorean mathematics was more qualitative than quantitative. Each number reveals an aspect of oneness, together forming a whole that reflects the structure of the universe. Though I have represented the Decad for convenience as a series of units, the numerical series from 1 to 4 or 10 should not be seen as the simple repetition of 1, but as a process by which the contents of the One are unpacked, as it were, and then returned to unity through the form of the triangle or Triad.[33] For this reason the Decad can also be represented as a square (the enfolding One) divided 'noughts and crosses' style into three rows of three smaller squares.

33. As the principles of oddness and evenness, the Monad and the Dyad were sometimes not even regarded as numbers; the first real number was then the Triad because it joins the Two with the One. The Greek word for number is *arithmos*, which has the connotation of 'joining.'

The *Tetraktys* represented not only the four elements of the cosmos (in the order of density: Fire, Air, Water, Earth), the three dimensions of space unfolding from the point (two points determine a line, three a triangle, four a pyramid), and the fundamental harmonies of music ($1:2$ the octave, $2:3$ the fifth, and $3:4$ the fourth), but also the principles of form in general. It has been seen as the origin of the much later Kabbalistic 'Tree of Life', with its ten Sefiroth divided between four levels or worlds of being: Aziluth (Power), Beriah (Creation), Yetzirah (Formation), and Assiah (Action).

It is within this tradition that Plato's school is situated (or situated itself), for without knowledge of symbolic mathematics no one was admitted to the Academy. And yet Plato was not an out-and-out Pythagorean—or at least, he seems perfectly capable of satirizing the Pythagoreans (see *Republic* 546 b–c), and John Michell has argued that his whole symbolic narrative of Atlantis was constructed as a critique of the Pythagorean veneration of 10.[34] If Plato supplanted 10 by 12, that certainly brings him closer in spirit to the author of John's Apocalypse. Yet he remains within the broader tradition for which the 'music' of mathematical harmony, ratio, and proportion, based on numerical ratios, reflects the beauty of God himself—making the practice of mathematics a type of worship. For Christians, Platonists and Pythagoreans alike, the earthly liturgy, our service of the Infinite, in order to transcend the limitations of individuality, must be integrated with the service rendered by the angels who govern and represent this musical order of the cosmos (as Dionysius the Areopagite makes clear in his *Celestial Hierarchy* and *Ecclesiastical Hierarchy*).

An appreciation of symbolic cosmology did not die out after the Age of Cathedrals, but continued to flourish in Neoplatonist and Hermetic circles both in and after the Renaissance, whether underground in the secret societies or in broad daylight, in the case of a number of eccentric visionaries that include the German cobbler Jacob Boehme and the English engraver and poet, William Blake. The latter's prophetic poem *Jerusalem*, around 1800, is a powerful reminder that the symbolic properties of nature and number have a

---

34. John Michell, *How the World is Made*, 251–261.

long history, and perhaps may always be visible to a certain sort of consciousness:

> The Four Living Creatures, Chariots of Humanity Divine Incomprehensible,
> In beautiful Paradises expand; These are the Four Rivers of Paradise
> And the Four Faces of Humanity, fronting the Four Cardinal Points
> Of Heaven, going Forward, forward irresistible from Eternity to Eternity.[35]

But what should today's Christians—especially those more concerned than Blake was to appear orthodox—make of this kind of cosmological symbolism? The theologian Yves Congar remarks that it is certainly a characteristic feature of Johannine writings: 'At the root of all this is obviously the theology of the prologue to St John's Gospel.' But he adds: 'A genuine cosmic value is implied and parallel teaching can be quoted from the study of the history of religions, but, in the Apocalypse, this value is *incorporated into the positive facts of the history of salvation*, itself dependent on a free act of God's will, by which moreover the word has been created as an ordered and measured whole.'[36]

Congar's little comment (tucked away in a footnote) gives us an important clue. The Christian story is both mythological *and* historical. That is because it concerns the historical incarnation of the One whom *all myths represent*. Thoth, Hermes, Apollo, and a hundred other gods are images of the Logos or Mediator whom Christians believe was born as a human child, died on a Cross, and rose from the dead two thousand years ago. 'By this you know the Spirit of God: every spirit which confesses that Jesus Christ has come in the flesh is of God, and every spirit which does not confess Jesus is not of God' (1 John 4:2–3). Nor does a 'literalist' belief in historical incarnation render imagination and the use of symbolism redundant—if anything it legitimizes them.

---

35. Cited in Laura DeWitt James, *William Blake and the Tree of Life*, 29.
36. Y. Congar, *The Mystery of the Temple*, 219 (my italics).

And this goes even for the symbolism of number. Pope Benedict XVI makes the essential point:

> The mathematics of the universe does not exist by itself, nor ... can it be explained by stellar deities. It has a deeper foundation: the mind of the Creator. It comes from the Logos, in whom, so to speak, the archetypes of the world's order are contained. The Logos, through the Spirit, fashions the material world according to these archetypes.[37]

---

37. Joseph Ratzinger, *The Spirit of the Liturgy*, 154. On the subject matter of this chapter, see also my *Beauty for Truth's Sake.*

4

A BOOK OF
SPIRITUAL EXERCISES

Truly, truly, I say to you, you will see heaven opened, and the
angels of God ascending and descending upon the Son of man.

John 1:51

Having examined at the metaphysics and cosmology implicit in the
text, we perhaps need to look more closely at the detailed structure
of the narrative. In the first appendix I explore the order of the
images and messages as John presents them—marveling at the patterns in the kaleidoscope. (The main pattern, as I have already suggested, is *liturgical*—a reflection of the liturgy of heaven.) In the
present chapter I move through the whole text, picking out particular groups of images, to try to bring out their spiritual meaning for
us today: the Letters to the Churches, and a series of visions of
heaven that describe successive stages of Christian consciousness.

How can we explain the tremendous complexity of this book?
How can we get a handle on it? Hans Urs von Balthasar quotes the
spiritual writer Valentin Tomberg as saying, 'Nowhere can we find a
key to St John's Apocalypse, for we cannot interpret it in such a way
as to make a philosophico-metaphysical or a historical system out
of it. The key to the Apocalypse is to practice it, that is, to use it as
a book of spiritual exercises calling forth deeper and deeper layers
of consciousness.'[1] Though Balthasar adds we must take Tomberg

---

1. *Theo-Drama*, Vol. IV, 51. Balthasar is quoting from the German edition of
Tomberg's anonymously published masterpiece, *Meditations on the Tarot*.

'with a grain of salt', he nevertheless agrees with this verdict.[2] In the end, making sense of the Apocalypse will only be possible if we live it, transforming our consciousness by participating, here and now, in the *eschaton*. This is what happens if we enter into the mysteries of the Church through the liturgy, and allow the liturgy to shape our daily lives.

Letters to the Churches

Messages to the representative churches of Asia Minor serve as a sevenfold introduction to the Book of Revelation, tailoring it to the specific needs of the congregations to which it is sent from Patmos (and from heaven). Since the messages reflect the Book of Revelation as a whole, reading them with care will also prepare us to understand the deeper meaning of the book as it applies to ourselves. We find, when we do so, that they form a natural progression. What we see in these seven messages is God confronting the sins of the Christian community and offering to heal them with his mercy. (Other interpretations—for example, the identification of each letter with one of seven ages of the Church—are not excluded.)

Rev. 2:1–7:
Message to Ephesus—Return to Paradise

The second chapter of Revelation opens with the introductory message to the church in Ephesus—the closest to Patmos, reputedly the last home of the Virgin Mary, and a congregation that had probably been governed at one time by John himself. More precisely, it is addressed to the 'messenger' or 'angel' of the church, which may mean its bishop, or may have a more purely spiritual meaning. The fourfold structure of this first message will be replicated in all those

2. Tomberg, who died in 1973, was a convert to Catholicism from Anthroposophy, the movement founded by Rudolf Steiner. The 'pinch of salt' is a reference to the fact that Tomberg's thinking never became entirely orthodox in Catholic terms, though Balthasar felt that it was full of valuable insights. Unlike Theosophy, from which it broke away, Anthroposophy gives a central role in world history to Jesus Christ, laying great emphasis on the development of human consciousness, and has a high regard for Saint Thomas Aquinas, combining this with a theory of reincarnation that is incompatible with orthodox Christian anthropology.

that follow. It begins (1) with a characterization of the one from whom the message comes, in this case, *The words of him who holds the seven stars in his right hand, who walks among the seven golden lampstands.* Immediately after this comes (2) a description of the spiritual state of the church in question, and this is followed (3) by a promise. The closing remarks (4), as in each message, include the formula, *He who has an ear, let him hear what the Spirit says to the churches.*

Ephesus is described as a church that has toiled and endured but *abandoned the love you had at first.* The Ephesians are told, therefore, to remember *that from which you have fallen, repent and do the works you did at first.* (There is also an approving mention of the church's hatred of *the works of the Nikolaitans* or early Gnostics.)[3] Finally, the promise: *To him who conquers I will grant to eat of the tree of life, which is in the Paradise of God.* There is an echo here of the introduction of the message, since the 'golden lampstands' are themselves 'trees of life.' The theme of the whole message is renewal, a fresh start, a return to Paradise where the tree of life still grows—a fitting theme with which to begin the sequence of messages, and one that looks forward to John's final vision of the new Jerusalem.

In order to turn these messages into a spiritual exercise, it helps to read them as an examination of conscience, as if in preparation for the sacrament of Confession. The message to Ephesus cues us to do so, with its call to repentance. We need to compare how we are now with the way we were when we first felt the impact of divine grace, when with Adam we walked with God among the trees in the garden.

3. The Nikolaitans are followers of Nikolaus, a name which means 'conquer [*nikao*] the people', in an allusion to the theme of spiritual warfare that runs all through Revelation, and will be discussed further in the next chapter. Jean Daniélou saw echoes of the early Christian contest with the dualistic sect of the Syrian Nikolaitans in several references to 'star' throughout Revelation as well as to the name of Balaam in the Letter to Pergamum—Balaam having prophesied that 'a star shall come forth out of Jacob' in Numbers 24:17—and links this to the visit of the Magi at Matthew 2:2, which signified the overcoming of magic and the submission of the astrologers to Christ (see his *Primitive Christian Symbols*, 102–123).

Rev. 2:8–11:
Message to Smyrna—Strengthening for the Test to come

The Lord addresses himself to the second church as *the first and the last, who died and came to life.* In other words, he announces himself as the one who has power over life and death. He characterizes the church as follows: *I know your tribulation and your poverty (but you are rich) and the slander of those who say that they are Jews and are not, but are a synagogue of Satan.* (This, by the way, implies that to be a Jew is a good thing, because the people who are claiming to be Jews are nothing of the sort. The exact nature of the dispute being referred to here is not known.) Then he warns them of what is to come: *Do not fear what you are about to suffer. Behold, the Devil is about to throw some of you into prison, that you may be tested, and for ten days you will have tribulation.* This message is therefore addressed to Christians about to experience persecution. The promise follows: *Be faithful unto death, and I will give you the crown of life*—the crown that he has won by conquering death.

Reading this message, again, as a spiritual call not to some ancient congregation long dead, but to ourselves here and now, we see that in the suffering of our lives (suffering often caused by the malice of others) the only real consolation is in Jesus, the Alpha and Omega—the one who is *before* and *after* all that we must suffer, who has been through and transcends it all. Even death is now only a doorway that he has opened for us.

Rev. 2:12–17:
Pergamum—Bread from Heaven

Jesus addresses himself to this church as the possessor of *the sharp two-edged sword.* He tells them, approvingly: *I know where you dwell, where Satan's throne is; you hold fast my name and you did not deny my faith.* The sharp sword is the blade of discernment, the one that cuts between good and evil, the surgeon's knife of the spirit. The church and therefore the soul he is addressing has already made that discernment—living in the very place of Satan's throne, in the fallen world where he rules, the name of Jesus has nevertheless been upheld and remembered, and for this he gives due praise. But at the same time he calls us to repentance, for *you have some there who hold the teaching of Balaam, who taught Balak to put a stumbling block before the sons of Israel, that they might eat food sacrificed to idols and practice immorality.* Part of us is still drawn to idolatry, and will be for as long as we are not completely one with God.

It is this fragmentation of our person, this subtle corruption of our integrity, that the message calls us to confront. The promise that Jesus makes is that through the Eucharist and in the resurrection we will receive our true identity, the rock on which our eternal life can stand: *To him who conquers I will give some of the hidden manna, and I will give him a white stone, with a new name written on the stone which no one knows except him who receives it.*

Rev. 2:18–29:
Thyatira—Loving Faithfulness

Christ addresses this church simply as *the Son of God, who has eyes like a flame of fire, and whose feet are like burnished bronze.* He continues: *I know your works, your love and faith and service and patient endurance, and that your latter works exceed the first.* Whereas the church of Ephesus was told to *repent and do the works you did at first,* those of Thyatira are congratulated for doing greater works. Yet with greater spiritual gifts, greater achievements, there is also a greater temptation, a greater possibility of sin. The stakes have been raised. So Jesus goes on: *But I have this against you, that you tolerate the woman Jezebel, who calls herself a prophetess and is teaching and beguiling my servants to practise immorality and to eat food sacrificed to idols.*

This is one step beyond anything Pergamum was accused of, and the results will be serious indeed. *Behold, I will throw her on a sickbed, and those who commit adultery with her I will throw into a great tribulation, unless they repent of her doings; and I will strike her children dead.* The Jewish Scriptures had long seen in adultery a metaphor for the breaking of God's Covenant. John is talking of something more than a temptation to heresy; he has in mind the active seeking out of the Devil's secrets, *what some call the deep things of Satan.* And yet all is not lost, for part of us remains anchored in God through faith. To them he says: *I do not lay upon you any other burden; only hold fast what you have, until I come.*

Finally comes the promise: *He who conquers and who keeps my words until the end, I will give him authority over the nations, and he shall rule them with a rod of iron, as when earthen pots are broken in pieces, even as I myself have received power from my Father; and I will give him the morning star.* For the Son of God alone (as he describes himself in the opening of the message) has the right to rule over men, a right given by his Father, whose kingdom must now come to be *on earth as it is in heaven.* Revelation is a profoundly subversive text, subversive of Roman power and of all earthly authority.[4]

Rev. 3:1–6:
Sardis—Strengthening at the Point of Death

The words of him who has the seven spirits of God and the seven stars. I know your works; you have the name of being alive, and you are dead. The accusation here is even worse, it seems, than the one levelled against Pergamum. The corruption has gone further: the children of Jezebel have been struck dead. *Awake, and strengthen what remains and is on the point of death, for I have not found your works perfect in the sight of my God.* The urgency intensifies: *If you will not awake, I will come like a thief, and you will not know at what hour I will come upon you.* Yet as long as we remain part of the church there is hope for we can let ourselves be led by those in the community who possess the virtues we lack: *you still have a few names in Sardis, people who have not soiled their garments; and they shall walk with me in white, for they are worthy.* We ourselves can become worthy of eternal life even at the point of death, when all seems lost. *He who conquers shall be clothed like them in white garments, and I will not blot his name out of the book of life; I will confess his name before my Father and before his angels.*

Rev. 3:7–13:
Philadelphia—Power of the Keys

The words of the Holy One, the true one, who has the key of David, who opens and no one shall shut, who shuts and no one opens. Jesus presents himself as the ultimate priest, the priest who is also a king,

4. On this point see R. Bauckham, *The Theology of the Book of Revelation*, 35–9.

the one who gave the Apostles the power of the keys, the power to forgive sins, when he appeared to them after his resurrection (John 20:23). His words now are of divine mercy, even after all the sins of which he has accused the churches and the individual soul, for *I know that you have but little power, and yet you have kept my word and have not denied my name.* He is addressing himself to the faithful, to that part of us that has not slept with Jezebel, or has repented of doing so in response to his call. *Behold, I have set before you an open door, which no one is able to shut.* The way to heaven lies open before us. If we only *hold fast*, then he will keep us from (that is, keep us safe through) the *hour of trial that is coming on the whole world*, the hour that is described in such graphic detail in the rest of the book. And as we approach the end of the series of churches, the promise that he makes now refers to the final stages of the vision of fulfilment. *He who conquers, I will make him a pillar in the temple of my God; never shall he go out of it, and I will write on him the name of my God, and the name of the city of my God, the new Jerusalem which comes down from my God out of heaven, and my own new name.*

The four successive mentions of 'my God' refer to the four levels of being we encountered in the chapter on cosmology, the worlds in which God manifests himself, beginning with the lowest and ending with the highest.

Of the 'pillar', Romano Guardini writes:

> He who is made pillar in the temple of God, the Christ, is one destined to participate in the eternal construction of divine love; he can never be broken out of his sacred place. The name of God engraved in the pillar is God himself; it is what gives the chosen one his true essence.[5]

The 'new name' of Christ is 'the name which is above every name' (Phil. 2:9), but it also echoes the 'new name' promised to each faithful believer in Pergamum, for here in the *eschaton* the name entrusted to each Christian is that of Christ himself, in order that 'they may be one, even as we [Jesus and his Father] are one' (John 7:11). What this 'oneness' implies will be seen in the message that follows.

5. R. Guardini, *The Lord*, 524.

Rev. 3:14–22:
Laodicea—Doing Penance

Having assured the Christians of Philadelphia of his love, the speaker saves his final warnings for the Laodiceans, for this is the community of those who take that love for granted. Jesus speaks as *the Amen, the faithful and true witness, the beginning of God's creation*; that is, as the end and the middle and the beginning of all things. The word translated as 'beginning' here also means self-grounded 'principle' or 'head', as in the opening of John's Gospel ('In the beginning was the Word'), implying Christ's absolute divinity.

I know your works: you are neither cold not hot. Would that you were cold or hot! So, because you are lukewarm, and neither cold nor hot, I will spew you out of my mouth. There may be a kind of 'in joke' here, because Laodicea was situated between the cold water springs of Colossae and the hot ones of Hierapolis. The waters of the Laodicean church, therefore, have neither refreshing nor healing properties. They have ceased to resemble the 'waters of life' that flow in God's kingdom and from the Temple.

For you say, I am rich, and I need nothing; not knowing that you are wretched, pitiable, poor, blind, and naked. These five adjectives add up to a fair description of the human condition, and indeed this final message seems to be addressed not just to single congregation but to all of us at the deepest level of our common humanity— fallen, redeemed, and still in desperate need of grace. *Therefore I counsel you to buy from me gold refined by fire, that you may be rich, and white garments to clothe you and to keep the shame of your nakedness from being seen.* The 'white garment' is the mantle of grace, with which human beings were clothed in the Garden and which they lost through sin, restored now through the sacrifice of Christ ('washed in the blood of the Lamb'). We are told also to buy *salve to anoint your eyes, that you may see.* As Ian Boxall points out, 'the whole purpose of John's Apocalypse is that you may really see: a particular depth of apocalyptic insight which enables the privileged to draw back the curtain and view reality from a new perspective.'[6] But *Those whom I love, I reprove and chasten; so be zealous and*

6. I. Boxall, *The Revelation of St John*, 77.

repent. After all the harsh words, we are reassured that it is love that treats us so.

Then, the promise: *Behold, I stand at the door and knock; if any one hears my voice and opens the door, I will come in to him and eat with him, and he with me. He who conquers, I will grant him to sit with me on my throne, as I myself conquered and sat down with my Father on his throne.* The series of promises is very carefully constructed to reach its culmination with this promise of the throne (equivalent to divinization by grace). This in turn prepares the ground for the vision John now receives, only three verses later; namely a revelation of the heavenly throne itself (4:2), the very center of heavenly worship. The Christian approaches this throne with amazement and awe, and with the staggering promise that he will one day sit upon it himself, in the most intimate friendship with the One who reigns there resplendent 'like jasper and carnelian' at the heart of a gigantic rainbow.

The Eight Visions of Heaven

The grand vision of heaven that immediately follows the seven messages to the churches of Asia is one of a series of such visions that punctuate the Book of Revelation. It is these I now want to examine in more detail. These 'stations' in John's journey offer us another way into the heart of his message. Each reveals another aspect of the Communion of Saints. In the sequence below I will concentrate on these stations, marking the stages of John's inner journey, but skipping over the passages that separate them.

The First Vision of Heaven (1:12–20): *Christ*

John hears a voice like a trumpet, and 'turns to see the voice' (Rev. 1:12). The 'voice' that he sees is the resurrected Christ, who resembles a 'Son of man' (Dan. 7:13).[7] He is standing in the midst of seven golden lampstands: a *menorah* with seven branches for the days of creation. Each branch of the *menorah* also represents one of the churches.

John's first and immediate vision, therefore, is not of the divine Throne, but of Christ, who becomes his point of entry into the mysteries. It is by being with and in Christ, as every baptized Christian is with and in Christ (though perhaps, in John's case, also as one who had known Jesus in the flesh before, during, and after his death on the Cross), that the author of Revelation hears and sees all that is to follow. And the first things that are given to him are the seven messages we have just examined in some detail.

The Second Vision of Heaven (4:1 to 5:14): Trinity

In chapter 4, after receiving the messages, John sees an open door in heaven, and the same Voice that he heard at the beginning calls him through it in the Spirit to see 'what must take place.' But he is not shown the future, as one might expect; he is given a glimpse of Eternity. He sees a throne on a crystal sea, crackling all around with lightning, surrounded by Four Creatures full of eyes and continually singing. Each possesses three pairs of wings, indicating their ability to move freely throughout the three worlds. The One seated on the Throne (not Christ but the Father) shines like the precious stones jasper and carnelian, white and red, and is surrounded by a rainbow described as being 'like an emerald.'

Corresponding to the seven stars which John saw in the hand of the Son in the first vision, which were there called the 'angels of the churches', he now sees seven torches burning before the Throne,

---

7. The term calls for a comment. It is frequently used by Jesus himself, especially in Mark's Gospel, but this seems to be the only place in the new Testament where it is used of Jesus by someone else apart from Stephen the first martyr: 'Behold, I see the heavens opened, and the Son of man standing at the right hand of God' (Acts 7:56). Stephen's dying vision looks back to Jesus's promise at Mark 14:62, and forward to the whole Book of Revelation. Pope Benedict XVI explores the meaning of the phrase in *Jesus of Nazareth*, 321–35. In one sense it means simply 'man', but it has connotations like that of the 'Perfect Man' in Sufi tradition, and by using it Jesus will have been identifying himself with the 'one like a son of man' who appears to the Prophet Daniel in the clouds of heaven before the Ancient of Days, to whom is given an everlasting 'dominion and glory and kingdom' (Dan. 7:13–14), the kingdom—says the Pope—'in which the world attains its goal.' He goes on: 'The enigmatic term 'Son of Man' presents us in concentrated form with all that is most original and distinctive about the figure of Jesus, his mission, and his being. He comes from God and he is God. But that is precisely what makes him—having assumed human nature—the bringer of true humanity.'

described as the 'seven spirits of God.' We can think of them as the spirits of the seven days of creation, the makers and re-makers of the world, the archetypal forms of the branched candlesticks which he glimpsed in his vision of Christ.

The twenty-four Elders seated around the One represent the assembled patriarchs of Old and New Testament, but also the powers of heaven, the governors of the cosmos. The word for Elders, *presbyteroi*, also means 'priests.' In response to the song of the Four, these 'royal priests' are continually throwing themselves down and casting their crowns before the Father. This signifies that the power of God is not imposed by force upon creation, but is given to him willingly; he rules by love not fear.

The whole image, startlingly intense, resembles an oriental *mandala*. The One seated on the Throne is portrayed in two shining colors, surrounded by a third color (green) at the center of the rainbow, with seven torches, encircled in turn by the Four Creatures (covered in eyes and wings), and the twenty-four Elders (dressed in white and gold). But the image is no mere static tableau, for it is full of overwhelming sounds and dynamic movement, of song and voices and thunder.

The vision of the Father is now followed by a vision of the Son. The Father holds a sealed scroll that no one else is worthy to open. John weeps at this, feeling so intensely on behalf of the whole creation the need for the scroll to be opened. The Lion-who-is-the-Lamb is in the 'midst' of the Throne, with seven rays of light and the seven spirits upon him. The Lamb takes the scroll, whereupon the Creatures and the Elders sing 'a new song', the song of the Redeemer. Whereas the first song, to the Father (Rev. 4:11), began, 'Worthy are you . . . for you created all things', the new song, accompanied now by the harps and incense of a heavenly liturgy representing the prayers of the saints, begins, 'Worthy are you to take the scroll and open its seals, for you were slain and by your blood you ransomed men for God. . . . ;' and every creature in heaven and earth and under the earth and in the sea, together with the millions of angels, joins in the praise, for the world that was created by the Father has been redeemed, united with God in the Spirit through the Lamb's eternal sacrifice.

The Third Vision of Heaven (7:9 to 8:5):
The Church

The first vision had been a vision of Christ in his earthly though transfigured form. Through him John was given a second vision, a vision of the Father, and of the Trinity and cosmos in spiritual unison. This vision now continues and is extended into the third, for the opening of the seals now takes place in heaven, though we also see its impact on the earth. We are standing with John in heaven, looking at the world from the perspective of the *Merkavah*. He is standing, in other words, on the plane of consciousness represented by the glassy sea, that of the 'upper waters' (Gen. 1:7). What he sees now, after the opening of the first six seals, is a vision of the Church, of the 144,000 descended from Israel and an unnumbered multitude from every other nation who have come out of the 'great tribulation.'

Whether or not this 'tribulation' refers to an historical persecution, such as the one that may have taken place in John's lifetime under the Emperor Nero, symbolically it may be taken to represent the trials of life in the fallen world, and at the hands of evil men, from which the Lamb has rescued us. Those who have washed their clothes 'white in the blood of the Lamb' (Rev. 7:14) have received a baptism of blood, for indeed 'all of us who have been baptized into Christ Jesus were baptized into his death' (Rom. 6:3). And the Elder who is speaking to John (perhaps the spiritual counterpart of John himself) describes their situation (Rev. 7:16–17) in what amounts to a summary of the Sermon on the Mount that simultaneously looks forward to the vision of the New Jerusalem at the end of the whole book:

'They shall hunger no more, neither thirst any more;
the sun shall not strike them, nor any scorching heat.
For the Lamb in the midst of the throne will be their shepherd,
and he will guide them to springs of living water;
and God will wipe away every tear from their eyes.'

In keeping with the fact that this is a vision of the Church, the opening of the seventh seal is followed by an offering of the prayers of the saints by angels standing at a golden altar before the Throne, after which the seven trumpets are sounded.

The Fourth Vision of Heaven (11:15–19):
The Woman

During the sounding of the trumpets and the plagues that ensue, John's vantage-point shifts back to the earth. It is from there that he sees the mighty angel with 'legs like pillars of fire' (Rev. 10:1) holding the little scroll that is given him to eat. But after he has measured the temple and the altar on earth, and seen the two witnesses called up to heaven in a cloud, and when the seventh trumpet is sounded, John is given his fourth glimpse of heaven. The first vision was of Christ, the second of the Trinity, the third of the Church; the fourth in this logical series is of the Woman, *Ecclesia*, who is revealed by the Judgment of God. For the Elders chorus (Rev. 11:17–18):

'We give thanks to you, Lord God Almighty,
who are and who were,
that you have taken your great power and begun to reign.
The nations raged, but your wrath came,
and the time for the dead to be judged,
for rewarding your servants, the prophets and saints,
and those who fear your name, both small and great,
and for destroying the destroyers of the earth.'

With this vision, something new is revealed in heaven: 'God's temple in heaven was opened, and the ark of his covenant was seen within his temple.' John has just been measuring the earthly temple (which, by the way, may suggest that this text was written before the Romans destroyed it in AD 70); now he is shown the heart of the temple that is its archetype. But the vision of the Ark of the Covenant at once gives way to another vision of what is essentially the same thing under a different aspect: the Woman whose flesh carries within it the New Covenant of Jesus Christ. For now 'a great sign appeared in heaven, a woman clothed with the sun, with the moon under her feet, and on her head a crown of twelve stars; she was with child and she cried out in her pangs of birth, in anguish for delivery' (Rev. 12:1–2).

The adventure of the Woman, the Dragon, and the two Beasts that unfolds in the succeeding chapters is the story of the Covenant and the Anti-Trinity. But it is also the story of the creation, and of the fallen angels, and of their long battle with God. The Woman is the personification of the whole created order 'full of grace' (clothed with the sun), and the child with whom she is pregnant is the light that darkness cannot overcome (John 1:5). The second sign that appears in heaven in this vision is the spirit of evil: a red Dragon with seven heads (opposed to the sevenfold Spirit of God). Having failed to devour the child in heaven (because he is immediately taken up to God's throne), the Dragon is thrown down to the earth by Michael. There, with the Child now out of reach, he seeks to sweep the woman away in a flood of water. But 'the earth came to the help of the woman', by swallowing the flood, so his third ploy is to make war on the Church: 'the rest of her offspring, on those who keep the commandments of God and bear testimony to Jesus' (Rev. 12:17)—meaning the good Jews and Christians. This he does by means of the Beasts from the sea and the earth.

The Fifth Vision of Heaven (14:1–13): The Priests and the Harvest

At the beginning of chapter 14, the tale of the two Beasts is interrupted by the fifth vision of heaven, which is like a reprise of the third, the vision of the Church, for it concerns once more the 144,000 who are singing the 'new song' of the Redeemer. But in each successive vision, there are important variations, or some new element is added, and this time the Lamb and the 144,000 are standing on Mount Zion, and we are told that the seal on their foreheads includes the name of the Lamb and of the Father. In other words, these are the formally baptized, seen in this state of spiritual consciousness. But where is Mount Zion? Meister Eckhart comments here: 'Now John says he saw a lamb standing on the mountain. I say John was himself the mountain on which he saw the lamb. And whoever wants to see the lamb of God must himself be the mountain, and ascend into his highest and purest part.'[8]

There are also three angels proclaiming the Gospel, and the voice of the Holy Spirit is heard directly: a voice from heaven tells John to

8. Sermon 24, in *Meister Eckhart: Sermons and Treatises*, Vol. I, 193.

write the Beatitude, 'Blessed are the dead who from now on die in
the Lord', and the Spirit responds, 'Blessed indeed, that they may
rest from their labours, for their deeds follow them' (Rev. 14:13).
The voice of the Spirit is 'like the sound of many waters and like the
sound of thunder', it is 'like the sound of harpists playing on their
harps, and they sing a new song before the throne' (Rev. 14:2-3)—
musical, then, but on a scale and with an intensity that human
words cannot adequately describe. Francesca Murphy comments on
the significance of the fact that the voice sounds like waters (as also
when it is the voice of Christ in 1:15):

> Water and Spirit come together in the actions of creation and
> baptism: this is the aspect of God which brings about *relation*.
> Water is a sign of a communication which is not just a transfer
> of information from one ego to another, but a flowing
> exchange of self. Coming out of the water is the moment of
> liberation, the birth of the person. When John's attention is
> drawn to the Lamb who holds the book and feels all around
> him voices like the booming of the sea, he is immersed in
> something wild and primeval, but also in a medium of com-
> munication, which transforms his understanding.[9]

Christ has led John into the heart of the Trinity and shown him
the Church in her heavenly and universal form, the 'Church Trium-
phant.' Now he is to see the Church on her way to that final state
through the suffering that measures our distance from heaven,
transformed into an offering by the actions of her priests: 'the earth
was reaped' (Rev. 14:16), and 'the wine press was trodden outside
the city, and blood flowed from the wine press, as high as a horse's
bridle, for 1600 *stadia*' (Rev. 14:20). The very specific figure of 1600
mentioned here is the square of 40—a number associated with
Noah's flood, representing also the tenfold multiplication of the
four directions of space. The world is submerged not in water this
time but in blood (albeit only 'as high as a horse's bridle'); that is, in
human life poured out before the throne of God, blood becoming
wine.

---

9. F. Murphy, *The Comedy of Revelation*, 216.

The Sixth Vision of Heaven (Rev. 15):
Purification, the Seven Angels

In the sixth vision John sees the sea of glass again, but now it is mingled with fire (Rev. 15:2). The 'temple of the tent of witness in heaven' is opened, and the seven last plagues are sent forth in the hands of the seven angels clothed in white with golden sashes: the bowls or vials of wrath. These evoke the ten plagues that Moses unleashed on the Egyptians—and indeed the Song of Moses (celebrating the crossing of the Red Sea and the escape from the Egyptians) is invoked at the beginning of this chapter. They are the last plagues, the final purification of the earth before the new can be revealed. In human life they are also the seven 'anti-sacraments', the seven results of denying and rejecting the love of God present in the sacramental mysteries of the Church.

After this John is shown in great detail 'the judgment of the great harlot', the City of Babylon, and how she is mourned by the merchants of the world. For Babylon has to be completely destroyed if the new City, the City of God, is to descend from heaven. It must be rooted out from every soul, and we must be made to feel the anguish of that separation: 'Alas, alas, for the great city that was clothed in fine linen, in purple and scarlet, adorned with gold, with jewels, and with pearls!' (See next chapter.)

The Seventh Vision of Heaven (19:1–10):
The Victorious Army

In heaven John hears and sees the celebration that ensues when the harlot city is cast down, in three great hymns, a triple Hallelujah, the third of which introduces a new theme: 'Let us rejoice and exult and give him the glory, for the marriage of the Lamb has come, and his Bride has made herself ready' (Rev. 19:7). The angel tells John, 'Blessed are those who are invited to the marriage supper of the Lamb.'

By this point it is admittedly hard to distinguish one vision of heaven from another, for the visions succeed one another so quickly, and the actions of the angels are interwoven with the drama being enacted on earth. (In fact Ian Boxall distinguishes seven separate visions of the Church just between 19:11 and 22:11.) The Word of

God rides forth on his white horse, with his armies (Rev. 19:11–16), for the last battle, and the 'supper of God' which sounded so charming in the previous verses is revealed to be the antithesis of the marriage supper of the Lamb, a meal made of the 'flesh of kings ... the flesh of all men, both free and slave, both small and great' (Rev. 19:18). In this war the Dragon is finally defeated, and with his two Beasts is thrown into the lake of fire and brimstone, to be tormented for ever.[10]

Now John sees 'a great white throne and him who sat upon it; from his presence earth and sky fled away, and no place was found for them' (Rev. 20:11). The book of life is opened, the dead are judged, and Death and Hades themselves are thrown into the lake of fire.

The Eighth Vision of Heaven (21:1 *to* 22:5): *The Bride*

The final two chapters of Revelation are of a radically different tone and mood than the others. It is impossible not to note the transformation in mood and atmosphere. All the turmoil and conflict of the Judgment and Purification of the earth has been resolved and overcome: the storm in the night is over, and a new day is dawning, the eighth day of creation.

These verses reveal the ultimate effect John's visions were aiming at, and the change in consciousness they were designed to bring about. With each successive heavenly vision in this series, the integration of heaven and earth comes closer, and now it has been achieved.

The Consciousness of the Christian

Entry to the City is by way of twelve whole pearls that form the gates of the Tribes. A pearl is a living jewel formed around some

---

10. The chronology here is hard to interpret, no doubt because it was not intended to be taken literally. It is said in chapter 20 that Satan will be bound for a thousand years while the martyrs reign with Christ in the 'first resurrection', i.e. *before* the final judgment. This is probably most safely interpreted with Augustine as referring to the period of the Church on earth, in which the saints reign with Christ from the altar and in the liturgical calendar. But as Balthasar points out, we are ignorant of 'heavenly super-time' and its relation to world-time, which makes these problems insoluble for us (*Theo-Drama*, Vol. V, 358–9).

impurity that has entered under the oyster's shell, or (symbolically) some suffering endured and transformed. One meaning of this is surely that it is through the suffering of the children of Israel that mankind will enter the City. But the image applies individually, as well as collectively. Each of us must transform our own impurity into its opposite, for nothing unclean can enter the City (21:27), and only the pure in heart will see God (Matt. 5:8).

The jewels upon the city walls and its foundations incorporate the beauty of the stars into the adornment of the City, and the pearly gates the beauty of the moon. Within the walls, 'the street of the city was pure gold, transparent as glass' (21:21). The sea of glass (4:6) mingled with fire (15:2) has become the golden crystal of the city street, as the warmth and glory of love has entered into and transmuted the substance on which it stands, and the earth is now united with the sun. Thus the City is the final form of the Woman clothed with the sun, standing on the moon, crowned with stars.

There shall no more be anything accursed, but the throne of God and of the Lamb shall be in it, and his servants shall worship him; they shall see his face, and his name shall be on their foreheads. And night shall be no more; they need no light of lamp or sun, for the Lord God will be their light, and they shall reign for ever and ever.[11]

This is a depiction of the final state of the world, but also of the mind of the Christian united with God. The state being described here—in which we see by the 'light' that is God—is called the Beatific Vision. According to Saint Thomas, in this life we can only know things by the mediation of an idea in our mind (as it were by 'reflected' light), but in the next we will know God directly, since the place of the idea in our mind is taken by the actual essence of God.[12] An inward light from God will make us shine without the need of lamp or sun, because only like can see like. So it is that 'when he appears we shall be like him, for we shall see him as he is' (1 John 3:2). In that glorified state, to know is to be known, as bridegroom and bride: 'Now I know in part; then I shall understand fully, even as I have been fully understood' (1 Cor. 13:12).

---

11. Rev. 22:3–5.
12. See St Thomas Aquinas, *Summa Contra Gentiles*, bk 3, chap. 51.

This is a staggering notion, and it should be contrasted with all other religious notions of 'enlightenment' and *gnosis*. It is true that, as with the Asian religions, the final state of perfection in Christianity is one of knowledge, since that is the paradigm of spiritual union. But for Christianity the vision of God, in which all happiness is comprised, is not our natural state, to be regained by some method of meditation or insight that will dissipate the clouds of ignorance we have wrapped around ourselves. It is something new, something of which we only become capable by being transformed. That transformation makes us 'sons in the Son', *logoi* in the Logos.

We could only hope to come to know God in this way because God knows himself in an even higher way—because he has a Son, because he is a Trinity. It is the Son who reveals the Father: 'No one knows the Son except the Father, and no one knows the Father except the Son and any one to whom the Son chooses to reveal him' (Matt. 11:27). It is only through union with him, who first gave himself to us, that we can hope to see the Father without being simply extinguished in him.

The Christian lives in the anticipation of the blissful Vision of God, but because he is a temporal creature the goal is not yet achieved. We do not yet experience the influx of the *lumen gloriae*; we are not yet incandescent. The infused virtue of faith must serve in the place of this light, for the time being. We know God but not by sight, rather by touch, like children in the dark holding their mother's hand. This is the characteristic of a Christian consciousness: a constant awareness of God as a presence behind the world, by the power of a faith that we know is flowing into us from beyond ourselves, which we might lose at any moment but for that very reason assures us that God is there. The authentic Christian consciousness is therefore marked by *joy* and *gratitude*, which are the twin fruits of the experience of being loved. Even when these are not consciously felt or adverted to, they remain as a kind of subconscious substance in our souls for as long as faith continues to be alive in us.

The joy, ecstasy, and serenity that we sense at the end of Revelation, in the final vision of the City, is precisely this, the fruit of a faith so intense that it has dissolved all but the last veil between ourselves and the throne of God.

5

THE LOGOS RIDES TO WAR

*Nation will rise against nation, and kingdom against kingdom;
there will be great earthquakes, and in various places famines
and pestilences. . . . And there will be signs in sun and moon and
stars, and upon the earth distress of nations in perplexity at the
roaring of the sea and the waves, men fainting with fear and with
foreboding of what is coming on the world; for the powers of the
heavens will be shaken. And then they will see the Son of man
coming in a cloud with power and great glory.*

Luke 21:10–11, 25–8

We have already seen that the second half of the Book of Revelation
is particularly concerned with the Second Coming, the coming in
glory of the God-Man. That 'glory' is ultimately the serene splendor
of the Holy City itself, the descent of which is itself an image of the
Second Coming. But before this final resolution is achieved, the
descent of the Logos provokes a war throughout the cosmos. It is as
though all evil, in order to be eliminated, must first be flushed out
from hiding, and confronted. The details of this process concern us
intimately, and therefore it is important to give them some attention in this chapter—along with the whole problematic of evil, and
of God's relationship to a suffering world.

The horrors described in Revelation are not at all at odds with
the Gospels, as we can see from the passages in Luke, just quoted,
and Jesus's extended prophecies concerning the fall of Jerusalem
and the 'close of the age' as recorded in Matthew 24 and 25.

When time is unmasked by the eternal, nothing is safe. The prophetic eye measures the distance between earth and heaven, and the

79

violence of these apocalyptic scenes reflects the greatness of this distance, the intensity of the contrast, when the one is brought kicking and screaming into the light of the other. In order to understand what is meant by the Second Coming, we must let the images speak. *All that you know is at an end.*

Monsters from the Pit

Even the computers of the modern film industry would find it hard to generate some of the images John evokes:

> In appearance the locusts were like horses arrayed for battle; on their heads were what looked like crowns of gold; their faces were like human faces, their hair like women's hair, and their teeth like lions' teeth; they had scales like iron breastplates, and the noise of their wings was like the noise of many chariots with horses rushing into battle. They have tails like scorpions, and stings, and their power of hurting men for five months lies in their tails (Rev. 9:7–10).

These particular monsters are associated with the 'first woe', that of the fifth trumpet, which afflicts those who do not wear the seal of God upon their forehead. Though in the form of locusts, they are given the command not to hurt 'the grass of the earth or any green growth or any tree' (9:4). The next to be released (by the sixth trumpet) are four angels that had been bound at the Euphrates,[1] with a cavalry of 'two myriads of myriads' (200,000,000): 'the riders wore breastplates the color of fire and of sapphire and of sulphur, and the heads of the horses were like lions' heads, and fire and smoke and sulphur issued from their mouths' (9:17), although their power to kill lies also in their tails, which are like serpents.

Two armies of monsters, then, one from the Pit and one from the Euphrates, with the power to sting and wound and kill, but they can

---

1. This is the fourth of the rivers that are named in Genesis (2:14), and is mentioned again at Rev. 16:12 as being dried up by the sixth Vial 'to prepare the way for the kings from the east'—about whom no more is said. The Euphrates marks the boundary between this world and the East, which may represent the higher world of our origin and the domain of wisdom, or more mundanely the region from which conquerors often come.

only affect those who have rejected God—and the time for repentance seems to be past, for none of those who survive these trials, it seems, will give up their idol worship or murdering or sorceries or thievery (9:20–21).[2] Their afflictions are simply the natural consequence of attachment to sin, a refusal to be rescued from a fallen and collapsing world full of false and transient delights.

God's overlordship is clear: it is by divine command that the monsters are released, and they can only act within the limits he sets. Does this make him responsible for the suffering they inflict? He permits it, and does so for a purpose—to bring the whole world ultimately to the transformation glimpsed at the end of the book. When we commit evil we only see the beginning of a process, one that may appear pleasant enough. If we could perceive rightly we would see even in the beginning of the act its natural end, which is the torment it stores up for us, by virtue of its true nature, in the Pit. But even God cannot prevent us seeing this at last, if the process is to run its course. The result is either repentance or a hardening of the heart, and it is the hardened heart that we are concerned with here. This hardening is what permits the separation of the saved from the damned who 'shall be tormented with fire and brimstone in the presence of the holy angels and in the presence of the Lamb' (14:10), while the blessed 'rest from their labours.' Final impenitence makes the divine presence a torment.

The violence that takes place in Revelation simply reveals what has been under the surface of things since the Fall. Like the suffering of Jesus on the Cross, it is intended to open our eyes to reality, the reality of sin. Once that has been done, and done definitively, we can each make our choice between life and death, and the harvest of the earth, now 'fully ripe' (14:15), can be gathered in.

'I saw Satan Fall like Lightning'

Philosophers love to talk about the 'problem of evil', by which is meant the apparent contradiction between an all-powerful and good God on the one hand, and the immense suffering (often inno-

---

2. Cf. Rev. 11:13, where the destruction of a tenth of the city leads to the repentance of the rest.

cent suffering) in the world he has created on the other. Even if it is conceded that all suffering may be due to some wicked deed at the beginning of time (but what about the poor animals?), God's decision to let the evil unfold and take its toll is hard to reconcile with our conception of goodness. It is easier, perhaps, to jettison the idea of God's omnipotence. But John's Revelation does not allow us to take that road.

John describes the suffering of both the innocent and the guilty in graphic detail, yet his God is clearly omnipotent. Indeed, though the One is enthroned at the center of reality and far above the mêlée of history, the divine Lamb stands 'as though slain', in the midst of history and alongside the myriads who bleed and die with and for him. So God is not aloof. Our bloodstained history is the arena in which an omnipotent and infinitely good God chooses to deal with evil. This is what we have to try to understand.

The possibility of evil enters into creation as soon as there is something that is not God. Only God is so intensively One that by definition, as it were, he is both infinitely free and yet incapable of wrongdoing. He is goodness itself. But this does not mean that the possibility of evil grows the further one descends along the great chain of being, moving away from God towards *materia prima*. Evil may be a 'privation of being', but in fact a creature who has less being than another is not therefore more evil: a fly is not worse than an angel. Evil lies in the privation of a good that *ought to have been present*; that is, in the marring of reality, not its degree.

Furthermore the greatest possibility of evil lies closest to God. It is one who stands nearest to divinity, and who resembles it most, that is most tempted to sin, and who becomes the most evil when he yields. Those who 'know not what they are doing' can be forgiven, or at least deserve a degree of mercy; the one who *knows* what he does is guilty of the greater crime. That is why Satan was struck from the heavens like lightning (Luke 10:18). A cosmos is a very fragile thing: it can snap down the middle.

The *mystery* of evil is how a creature can reject God, except in a state of ignorance. We have to assume that Lucifer's decision was made in the full knowledge of the consequences; the long defeat and endless punishment to come. An angel is an intellectual being and can see such things much more clearly than we can. He got exactly what he wanted; he regrets nothing. And what was it he wanted, that was worth such a price? Presumably, his own singular nature, his own glory, which he would have had to give up for others if he had accepted the gift of grace. God's invitation to the Beatific Vision, the interior life of the Trinity, above and beyond the natural capacity of any creature, was the occasion of angelic sin. Grace cannot be forced on anyone, and that means there must be a real possibility of rejecting it, even at the highest spiritual level.

The Beastly Trinity

The consequences of that rejection are played out in history and in the 'world of images' presented to us in the Book of Revelation. In Chapter 12, we are shown two great signs in heaven: the Woman and the Dragon, archetypes recognizable from every culture. Yet this is no serene image of majesty, not yet: the great Queen, though crowned with the stars of heaven (representing the Apostles, or the Tribes), is crying out in the pangs of birth, and the Dragon now stands before her like a horrific midwife, to devour her child. When the child is born, he is wrenched from her by God, and she for her part is cruelly separated from him by being sent into the wilderness. Yet this apparent harshness is really kind: the child, after all, is kept safe from the Dragon, and the woman nourished and protected.

If we identify the Woman with Mary,[3] these six verses sum up the advent of Christ: almost as soon as he is born (for thirty years must have gone by in a flash) he reaches his manhood and dies on the Cross, leaving his mother and the Church behind in the wilderness as he ascends to the Father. Yet the cycle of the Incarnation from conception to Ascension is only a prelude to the battle his coming provokes, which culminates in his eventual return. This battle begins in heaven, not on earth, as all things do. 'Now war arose in heaven, Michael and his angels fighting against the dragon; and the dragon and his angels fought, but they were defeated and there was

---

3. She is also the Church, no doubt, and the Shekinah, since the vision of the Woman follows immediately from the opening of the temple in heaven and the Ark of the Covenant (11:19).

no longer any place for them in heaven. And the great dragon was thrown down. . . .' (12:7–9). Being archetypal, the battle is contemporaneous with any point in time.

The serpent is cast down not into hell, but rather 'to earth and sea' (12:12), to pursue the woman and, failing her, the Church. 'And he stood on the sand of the sea' (12:18), linking earth and sea like the great angel of Rev. 10:1–3, and from the two places where he stands arise the two beasts, the one with ten horns and seven heads, who is the demonic counterpart of God's Son, and the other with two horns like a lamb but speaking like a dragon (13:11), who is the Unholy Spirit, making men worship the first beast (whose number is 666) and bringing fire from heaven. Against the two beastly witnesses are ranged the two 'olive trees', we encountered earlier (in chapter 11).

As for the Antichrist and his reign, a helpful account may be found in the penultimate chapter of Josef Pieper's little book, *The End of Time*. The experience of two world wars, the continuing development of modern weapons, and the growth of universal surveillance in response to the threat of terrorism, are among the factors pointing towards the possibility that a supreme world ruler of the future might emerge to institute the most impregnable of tyrannies. Such a ruler might well be greeted by the world's peoples as their deliverer from a period of chaos and danger, as in the 'Short Story of Antichrist' penned by Vladimir Solovyev in the last years of the nineteenth century. For Pieper, writing in the first half of the twentieth, it is entirely to be expected that 'the place of external wars would be taken by internal "police actions", the character of which would approximate very closely to the extermination of pests.'[4] Who could fail to see the lineaments of such a future in the preparations our societies have been forced to make as part of the 'War on Terror'?

The overthrow of the evil kingdom is accomplished by the 'Vials of Wrath' in chapter 16. No doubt this, too, will find historical expression in the reign of Antichrist, just as the victory of the saints

4. J. Pieper, *The End of Time*, 122. Pieper's book could profitably be read in conjunction with Romano Guardini, *The End of the Modern World*.

will have to be accomplished through persecution. The word for 'wrath', *thymos*, means also 'passion', and God's anger must always be understood as a manifestation of love—the same love that was poured out on the Cross. The seven bowls that are given to the angels by the cherubim (15:7) are tipped like a libation upon the earth. The result is ostensibly a series of terrible plagues, visited on those who worship the beast, and on the throne of the beast itself, and on the elements, turning the waters to blood and scorching men with the heat of the sun. The plagues correspond to the sacraments, outpourings of divine grace, here experienced as so many forms of torment by those who have rejected the love of God, and the last of them cleaves the Unholy City into three parts.

Babylon the Great

Before we reach the new city, we must leave the old. We must detach ourselves from all that binds us to the world that is passing. The extended prophecies concerning Babylon, that form a central narrative in the second half of Revelation, remind me of Plato's myth of Atlantis, but also to those detailed meditations on death and decay (sometimes conducted in a graveyard) that the Buddhist monk is enjoined to practice in order to detach him from the world.

The narrative is presaged at Rev. 14:8, when the second of the three angels who are summarizing the message of Revelation as a whole says, 'Fallen, fallen is Babylon the great, she who made all nations drink the wine of her impure passion.' Then, after the harvesting and reaping, and the seven bowl-plagues, we return to a more detailed account of her fall in chapters 17 and 18.

The introduction to this fall is hard to interpret. The woman/city is seated on the scarlet beast with seven heads and ten horns, which signify (according to the angel who is John's guide at this point) seven hills, seven kings—five of whom have already fallen—and ten kings who are due to rule for an hour. I dare not venture into the thicket of interpretations that have grown up around these verses. The only thing that seems to be fairly certain is that the seven hills are those of Rome—unless Margaret Barker is right and 'Babylon' is meant to refer to the Jerusalem of the Second Temple.

More interesting is the reference to the beast that 'was, and is not, and is to ascend from the bottomless pit and go to perdition' (17:8). This is in deliberate counterpoint, repeated three times, to the three-times repeated title of God, 'the One who is and who was and who is to come' (1:4, 1:8, 4:8).[5] The ontological contrast between God and his opponent is clear: the latter belongs to the past, not the eternal present, and he is 'coming' (from below) only to be judged and expunged.

In chapter 18 an angel with great authority and splendor repeats the earlier phrase, 'Fallen, fallen is Babylon the great...'; perhaps it is the same angel, but God never seems to run out of these radiant beings as far as John is concerned. The extended meditation begins, and it takes the form of a dramatic dialog or musical piece for several voices:

- the first angel (18:2–3);
- a voice from heaven that calls, 'Come out of her, my people, lest you take part in her sins, lest you share in her plagues' (18:4–8);
- the kings of the earth weeping and wailing over the smoke of her burning (18:9–10);
- the merchants of the earth bewailing because 'no one buys their cargo any more' (18:11–17), cargo listed in splendid detail;
- shipmasters and seafaring men (18:17–20);
- the angel who throws a millstone in the sea (18:21–24).

This music of several voices, beginning and ending in the angelic, then gives way to the song of the multitude in heaven, joined by the Elders and Living Creatures before the Throne.

The dialog is important to read line by line, and preferably aloud, as John would have intended. We are meant to feel the charm of the great worldly city in our own hearts, for we are all tempted by her 'fine linen, purple, silk and scarlet, all kinds of scented wood', gold, jewels, and pearls. If we are to 'come out of her', it is this temptation we need to reject. We will be helped by the vision of an alternative:

5. As Richard Bauckham points out, there are also two abbreviated occurrences at 11:17 and 16:5, 'the One who is and who was', the omission of 'who is coming' being due to the fact that at this point in the vision he *has already come*.

the heavenly city of John's final vision.

If we think the images quaint, just because they refer to spices and slaves and harpists and minstrels rather than restaurants and credit cards and computers then we have missed the point. We are all implicated, we are all entangled in a way of life that will eventually come crashing down around us, like a great millstone in the sea. What happens next is up to us.

The Return of the Child

We last saw the child of the woman clothed with the sun, 'one who is to rule all the nations with a rod of iron', being caught up to God and his throne at 12:5. Now he is fully grown.

> Then I saw heaven opened, and behold, a white horse! He who sat upon it is called Faithful and True, and in righteousness he judges and makes war. His eyes are like a flame of fire, and on his head are many diadems; and he has a name inscribed which no one knows but himself. He is clad in a robe dipped in blood, and the name by which he is called is The Word of God. And the armies of heaven, arrayed in fine linen, white and pure, followed him on white horses. From his mouth issues a sharp sword with which to smite the nations, and he will rule them with a rod of iron; he will tread the wine press of the fury of the wrath of God the Almighty (Rev. 19:11–15).

We have been told that each person who conquers will receive a white stone, with a new name that no one else will know (Rev. 2:17). This is a deep mystery, for as we see here it connects us with God himself, whose own name is also secret. Even 'Logos' or 'Word', by which Scripture refers to him, is not that name, but only the one by which others call him. 'God's love for each individual is totally personal and includes this mystery of a uniqueness that cannot be divulged to other human beings.'[6] The interior dimension of the 'I', where each of us is alone in the presence of God, is an essential part of our likeness to the Son, whose interior life is open only to the Father in the Spirit.

6. J. Ratzinger/Benedict XVI, *Jesus of Nazareth*, 128–9.

The coming of the White Rider causes the Beast and the kings of the earth with all their armies to gather in opposition, making war on God. Their final defeat is inevitable: 'and all the birds were gorged with their flesh' (19:21). How many of those will burn in hell? We cannot know, for the number of the saved, though relatively small (144,000) compared to the billions who have lived, is symbolic.[7] Many of the most influential theologians of the twentieth century—Karl Barth, Karl Rahner, Hans Urs von Balthasar— came close to arguing for 'universal salvation', believing as they did that Christians may legitimately hope that in some sense hell would turn out, in the end, to be empty (at least of human beings). Others have warned that this would reduce much of Scripture, and many of the statements of Christ, to the status of threats that a grown-up uses to terrify children into good behavior, and which he has no intention of carrying out. It seems to me that this does not follow. There may be a real possibility that I will walk over a cliff, even if I never do. To put it another way, God does not have to make sure that some people actually do fall over the cliff in order to ensure that his warnings against walking too close to the edge not remain an 'empty threat.' To the extent we remain creatures in time, without having reached our final destination, we remain in peril.

I would go so far as to say that most of us are in much greater danger than we realize, since we do not take the state of our souls as seriously as we should, and our sense of sin has become numb. As a society, too, we are used to hiding our own cruelty under the carpet. We pride ourselves on being civilized, yet our wars are as brutal as any in history, millions of our children are exterminated in the womb, and the 'abomination of desolation' has entered the souls of a whole generation.

Our spiritual peril is depicted graphically in the Book of Revelation. The Lord's return signifies a restoration of order both in the

---

7. Not only is the number made up of twelve twelves, but it is a nice coincidence that 144 is the only 'square' member of the famous Fibonacci sequence, a pattern of ascending numbers that governs much of biological growth (a fact that was presumably unknown to the author of Revelation), and as such a good number to fill the New Jerusalem.

world and in our souls that must come, if the will of God is to be done 'on earth as it is in heaven.' But while the Apocalypse reveals what has become of us, and the perils that face us, it also gives us a choice. We do not have to sink with Babylon. There is another place to go.

In a note on this subject in the final volume of his *Theo-Drama*, Balthasar mentions the 'daring statement' of Saint Ambrose, that if we are to be judged on our lives as a whole, then each of us will be partly saved and partly condemned; thus the Christian must hope to find that 'what is damnable in him has been separated from him and thrown out with the unusable residue that is incinerated outside the gates of the Holy City.'[8] We do know that nothing unclean will enter into the shining City to stain its radiance, and that beyond the horizon presented by an everlasting torment of fire and brimstone (20:10) there is a moment when Death and Hades themselves will be thrown into the lake of fire (20:14). The unclean elements of the old world, with all that pertains exclusively to the old order, including death, will be cast off like slag, and dissolve like dreams as the dawn rises.

8. H.U. von Balthasar, *Theo-Drama*, Vol. V, 321.

6

ENTERING THE CITY

*And it had a wall great and high, having twelve gates, and in the
gates twelve angels, and names written thereon, which are the
names of the twelve tribes of Israel. On the east, three gates: and
on the north, three gates; and on the south, three gates: and on
the west, three gates. And the wall of the city had twelve foundations, and in them, the twelve apostles of the lamb.*

Revelation 21:12–14 (KJB)

The life of a Christian is already the life of the Kingdom, even if we
are not always conscious of it. John's Revelation is the *unveiling* of
this life for us.

The Twelve Tribes

We begin with the walls of the city, through which anyone must
pass if they are to draw life from the waters within. We are told there
are twelve gates, corresponding to angels, tribes, jewels, and apostles. These walls and gates are particularly important because they
represent the interface, the transition, between our world and that,
between time and eternity.

In the next chapter I will write about the twelvefold Apostles'
Creed, which is an 'image in dogma' of the visionary City. And as we
have seen, the twelve tribes represent the guardians of time, the
zodiacal signs. Their transposition from the circle of the heavens to
the square of the City represents the stopping of the circuit, the
ending of time, the squaring of the circle, in order to open the
earthly to what lies above. The moon which the pearly gates resemble can be taken as marking the transition between earthly and
heavenly realms—it represents the sphere of memory, and therefore

Tradition, through which we enter into the new City founded on the Apostles.

To the modern mind, the most boring and pointless parts of Scripture are probably the lists of names. But to the ancients themselves, these lists were both fascinating and important. They were important not so much for the historical information they contained, which may have been limited in any case, but for their symbolic meaning (as in the case of the two genealogies of Christ, in Matthew 1 and Luke 3, where different lines of ancestors have been selected).

The twelve tribes are descended from the patriarch Jacob, son of Isaac, who was renamed 'Israel' after he wrestled with a mysterious figure at the ford of the river Jabbok all through the night (Gen. 32:22–32). The figure tells him, 'Your name shall no more be called Jacob, but Israel,[1] for you have striven with God and with men, and have prevailed.' Jacob himself adds, 'I have seen God face to face, and yet my life is preserved.' Reading this passage as the Church Fathers might have done, we can see in the mysterious figure not just an angel, but a type of Christ, who is both God and man ('you have striven with God and with men').

After the death of King Solomon, the tribes of Judah and Benjamin formed the Southern Kingdom (Judah) around Jerusalem, while the remaining ten formed the Northern Kingdom of Israel. The latter were then scattered (becoming known as the 'lost tribes of Israel') after an invasion by Assyria. Judah survived longer, but its population was eventually deported to Babylon. It was the descendants of Judah and Benjamin, then, who returned to build the Second Temple around 520–515 BC, and who constituted the Jewish people of Jesus' time.

There are at least twenty slightly varying enumerations of the twelve tribes in the canonical scriptures alone.[2] One particularly important example is found in the Book of Numbers (2:2–33).

---

1. The name means both 'He who strives with God' and 'God strives'.
2. For example: Gen. 35:22–5, 49:3–28; Ex. 1:1–5; Num. 1:3–15, 1:16–50, 25:5–62; Deut. 27:12–13, 33:7–26; Judges 5:12–19; 1 Chron. 2:1–2; Ez. 47:13–48:30, 48:31–35; Rev. 7:4–8.

There Moses commands the tribes to pitch their camps under their standards around the Tent of Reunion, which was the mobile Temple, three by three in the four directions starting in the east. Joseph and Levi are replaced with Joseph's sons Ephraim and Manasseh, for Joseph's tribe divided into two, and the tribe of Levi was never assigned a geographical territory but instead supplied priests for the Temple. Thus according to Snodgrass: 'The three tribes to the east (Issachar, Zebulun, and Judah) were gathered under the sign of the Lion; the three tribes to the south (Reuben, Simeon and Gad) had the sign of the Man; those to the west (Ephraim, Manasseh and Benjamin) had the emblem of the Bull; and the three to the north (Dan, Asher and Naphtali) had the sign of the Eagle.'[3]

Ezekiel, on the other hand, gives two lists, both of them including Levi among the Twelve and one including Joseph. The list given in the seventh chapter of Revelation, unlike the others, omits Dan and includes both Joseph and one of his sons (Manasseh).[4] Austin Farrer explains the arrangement by means of a zodiacal square, assigning the order of the tribes on the four sides according to their different mothers.[5]

It is worth emphasizing again that many traditional and tribal societies were ordered according to the calendar or zodiac in the same way. Plato in the *Laws* describes an ideal city centered on an 'acropolis' sacred to Hestia, Zeus, and Athena, the land around divided into twelve portions, just as Solon divided Athens into twelve tribes and clans corresponding to the zodiac around the Acropolis, with each family belonging to one of the tribes having certain religious duties depending on the time of year. We need read no more into the actual ordering of the tribes by Saint John. But we do know this: they stand as a symbol for the celestial cosmos, and

3. Adrian Snodgrass, *Architecture, Time, and Eternity*, Vol. 1, 294. The identification of the four standards under which the tribes were gathered seems to be from a *targum*, one of the Aramaic versions of the Hebrew Bible, not the Biblical text itself.

4. John may have replaced Dan in this way because the Danites fell into idolatry (Judges 18:30) and effectively disappeared from the history of Israel.

5. *The Revelation of St John the Divine*, 106–8. A more complex argument unfolds in Farrer's *A Rebirth of Images*, 216–44, but this was written earlier and he seems to have reconsidered many of the details.

for the whole of mankind insofar as it was to be redeemed and brought back from exile into the Temple/City of God.

The River of Life

Having entered the City, what is the first thing we find? Not houses, apparently (or at least John does not mention them), but a river. The main street of the City runs with the life giving waters that flow down from a great fountain, the eternal spring which is the throne of God.

> Then he showed me the river of the water of life, bright as crystal, flowing from the throne of God and of the Lamb through the middle of the street of the city; also, on either side of the river, the tree of life with its twelve kinds of fruit, yielding its fruit each month; and the leaves of the tree were for the healing of the nations. (Rev. 22:1–2)

The visions described in Revelation have close ties with those of Ezekiel dating back to the Babylonian exile. Ezekiel shows us the restored Temple with water flowing 'from below the threshold of the temple towards the east' from under the right side of the altar, teeming with life and freshening the stagnant pools into which it flows (Ezek. 47:1–11). There are echoes, too, of the Garden of Eden, for we are told at the very beginning of the Bible that a river flows out of Eden to water the Garden, just as a river flows out of the Temple and out of the City. But then it divides and becomes four branches (Gen. 2:10).

The language of natural symbols, such as stars, trees, numbers, mountains, cities, and geometrical shapes, is both precise and universal. The river is one such universal symbol, and something of the meaning it has for John can be ascertained by a glance at this wider context. There is a clear symbolic distinction, for example, between water flowing as a river, and the salt waters of the sea into which all rivers tend, though the two archetypes merge in the mythological Oceanus, the world-encircling ocean only loosely based upon the material Atlantic and Pacific. The sea tends to represent primordial chaos, or potentiality, *prakriti* in the Indian tradition—or alternatively the goal to be reached through the long journey of existence.[6]

Rivers have a number of specific functions, including forgetting and remembering (Lethe and Mnemosyne respectively in Greek mythology), and the washing away of sins (Ganges, Jordan). Or they mark a boundary or threshold in the nature of the world (Styx), in which case they may be closely associated with a bridge or ferry from one side to the other. But the river's function of giving life is, of course, the most common theme, and with good reason. A great river like the Nile or the Euphrates brings life to the wilderness around it, and in the ancient Middle East such rivers were the foundation of civilization. Egyptian cities were built along the Nile where periodic floods and perennial irrigation made the desert bloom.

The transition from one river to four, as for example in the river that flows from the center of the Garden of Eden, also has a precise meaning. It marks the transition between the essential or celestial world, or the *axis mundi* (the vertical ontological axis along which descends the influence of heaven), and the material or terrestrial world, with its four horizontal directions defining spatial and geographical extension.[7] (In the case of the New Jerusalem, we are dealing with a celestial city or city descending from above. Thus *within the city* the River is single; it is only outside the four-square walls that one may imagine the waters dividing into four.)

To the symbolic imagination, the life-giving river is akin to the flowing blood within the human body, or the sap in the tree, representing the life-force flowing through the organism as it does through a landscape. Blood, for most traditional peoples including the Jews, represented life,[8] and the human being was a microcosm reflective of the whole universe. Thus it is no surprise to find that

6. There is an important distinction between the waters above and below the firmament (Gen. 1:7), which are equivalent to the waters of form and the waters of formlessness respectively.

7. This is presumably the reason the way back to the Garden is appropriately guarded by the (four-faced) Cherubim.

8. 'For the life of the flesh is in the blood; and I have given it for you upon the altar to make atonement for your souls; for it is the blood that makes atonement, by reason of the life. Therefore I have said to the sons of Israel, No person among you shall eat blood, neither shall any stranger who sojourns among you eat blood' (Lev. 17:10–12, etc.).

the Gospels make use of this symbolic language. John the Evangelist emphasizes that when the heart of Jesus Christ was pierced upon the Cross, 'there came out blood and water' (John 19:34), and the Church Fathers saw in this double flow a symbol of the sacraments, as well as the union of divine and human natures in Christ. It represents the convergence in the Sacred Heart of the inner, human reality (blood) with the outer, cosmological reality (water)—and thus Christ is confirmed as the true microcosm uniting the inner with the outer world, from which flows the River of Life itself.[9]

The other key occasion when we see the figure of Christ in close relation to a 'river' is, significantly enough, in the scene of his baptism in the Jordan, which has been portrayed as a veritable compendium of archaic symbols by the iconographers. The moment of Christ's death and the moment of his baptism are connected, because as St Paul says, 'Do you not know that all of us who have been baptized into Christ Jesus were baptized into his death? We were buried therefore with him by baptism into death, so that as Christ was raised from the dead by the glory of the Father we, too, might walk in newness of life' (Romans 6:3–4). It is Jesus's death on the Cross that transforms John's baptism of water into a baptism 'with the Holy Spirit and with fire' (Luke 3:16); which is to say, a sacrament.

We may see the River as a symbol, too, of the Scriptures themselves, the words of God that are written down under the inspiration of the Holy Spirit to be 'trustworthy and true' for all time. This connection is made in the words that immediately precede the epigraph to the present chapter: *Also he said, 'Write this, for these words are trustworthy and true.'* The river of Eden flows, according to legend, from a rock at the center of the Garden on which stands the Tree of Life, the rock that is Christ. Here we have a symbolic image of Revelation flowing from Christ, and dividing into four branches as it reaches out into the world—the four Gospels.

---

9. The spear of the centurion Longinus, along which the blood and water flow when the Lord is pierced, thus becomes another symbol of the *axis mundi*, conveying grace from heaven, hence the tradition of Longinus's instantaneous conversion when the drops reach his hand.

Water from the Throne

John tells us that the waters of the River of Life were flowing *through the middle of the street of the city* (Rev. 22:1). One can picture this in a variety of ways. For example, it might be that the River runs down the middle, dividing the traffic on the left from the traffic on the right. I prefer to think that the street is itself the bed of the River: that to walk up the street is to walk submerged in the waters of life, through Baptism, upstream towards the center of light and eternal resurrection.

Reading John's account without reference to Ezekiel chapter 47, some have wondered how a tree of life can be on both sides of the river at the same time. The simple explanation is that the Greek word does not imply a single tree, but probably describes a grove (like a grove of cyprus or pine) covering both banks of the river. This would echo Ezekiel's vision, where 'on the banks, on both sides of the river, there grow all kinds of trees for food. Their leaves will not wither nor their fruit fail, but they will bear fresh fruit every month, because the water for them flows from the sanctuary. Their fruit will be for food, and their leaves for healing' (Ezek. 47:12).

However we decide to read this, the River and the Tree and the Street (the word for which may also refer to any 'public space') are clearly connected, as aspects of the same vision of healing and immortal life. But the image of the rushing water full of light predominates, for it flows straight from the Throne. In the Bible we often find the waters conjoined with the Holy Spirit. In the very beginning, the Spirit of God moved over the formless ocean, and God said 'Let there be light' (Gen. 1:2–3). When Jesus emerges praying from the waters of baptism, the Spirit descends like a dove, and a voice is heard from heaven saying, 'You are my beloved Son; with you I am well pleased' (Luke 3:22).

Thus the ever-flowing river of life, love, and holiness is best interpreted as a symbol of the Holy Spirit, as the Gospel itself makes plain (John 7:37–9; cf. John 4:14).[10] What we have here in the Liturgical City is the Holy Spirit no longer descending upon the water or

10. See the beautiful meditation by Jean Corbon, *The Wellspring of Worship*, and Jean Daniélou's survey of early Christian imagery in *Primitive Christian Symbols*.

hovering above it, but actually within it. 'There are three witnesses, the Spirit, the water, and the blood: and these three agree [are one]' (1 John 5:7).

The three are one, for the light and life of the Spirit is the substance of the water, and the giving of life is the same as the giving of light and immortality, because to see God is to die in this world, or to become eternal like him: 'God is love, and he who abides in love abides in God, and God abides in him' (1 John 4:16). There, when those waters flow through me and all that I have, and am, is flowing directly from the Throne, 'I shall understand fully, even as I have been fully understood' (1 Cor. 13:12).

Faith, love, and hope are single river, without banks and without end, that flows from God and returns to God. They are one and formless, the life and light of grace. Now God himself is threefold, and as such his life has form. He is the God of order even in love, and that is why he gives us the life and light of his word in a definite form. This form is the Church, which contains and dispenses the sacraments, the source of life and light, within a certain order.[11]

The grace of the Holy Spirit is faith, hope, and love, poured into the form of the sacraments (three into seven) in order to make the Church.

These life-giving waters nourish the Tree of Life and make possible the twelvefold fruit. Traditional commentaries identify these fruits with the twelve fruits of the Holy Spirit described by Saint Paul in the Vulgate translation of Galatians 5:22–3. As such they are all aspects of love, or charity, as Saint Francis de Sales explains: 'Now charity is called a fruit inasmuch as it delights us, and inasmuch as we enjoy its delicious sweetness, the sweetness of a true apple of paradise, gathered from the tree of life, which is the Holy Spirit, grafted on our human spirits and dwelling in us by his infinite mercy.'[12]

For those who might be interested, in another book I have tried to show how the Fruits grow from the Cardinal Virtues as these are 'supernaturalized' by the Holy Spirit.[13]

---

11. Adrienne von Speyr, *The Word Becomes Flesh*, 75.
12. Francis de Sales, *Treatise on the Love of God*, bk 11, chap. 19, 522–3.

Cardinal Virtue	Theological Virtue	Fruit of the Holy Spirit
	Faith	Peace
PRUDENCE	Hope	Joy
	Love	Love
	Faith	Faithfulness
JUSTICE	Hope	Gentleness
	Love	Generosity
	Faith	Patience
FORTITUDE	Hope	Kindness
	Love	Goodness
	Faith	Modesty
TEMPERANCE	Hope	Continence
	Love	Chastity

The Bride Descending

The ultimate purpose of Christ's union with humanity is to present his people to the Father, for the Father to love as he loves himself. The Son returns to the Father 'in glory', clothed not only in a human body but in the cosmic vestments of a purified humanity, bringing with him the whole restored and beautified creation. We may therefore conceive of the Bridal City as a personification of the creation redeemed and perfected in Christ, offered to the Father by the Son as an eternal Eucharist: the human nature he has joined to himself through the Holy Spirit.[14] Appearing on earth first in the Virgin Mary (Bride of the Holy Spirit), she is extended to include all humanity through the Holy Church (Bride of the Son), and is finally to be offered up by Christ in the heavenly Liturgy. The final image, the Bride of the Father, is sometimes identified with the figure of Wisdom.

Could we then call the third and highest manifestation of the City the 'Bride of the Father'? Perhaps, and if we were then to identify the Bride with Wisdom, or *Sophia*, we would have arrived at a

13. Stratford Caldecott, *The Fruits of the Spirit*.

14. Bulgakov describes the confluence of Mary, Church, and Sophia in the final vision of Revelation (the Holy City) at the end of his book, *The Bride of the Lamb*.

Trinitarian interpretation of this mysterious Biblical figure. Our theological guides, however, do not go so far, and tend to interpret Sophia as the eschatological Church, or as the Virgin Mary in her heavenly form. Louis Bouyer describes her as 'the glory which was the Son's at the side of the Father before the creation of the world, a glory the Father bestows on him through his crucifixion in histori-cal time, a glory which the glorified Son will then impart to the faithful when he gives them the Spirit.' 'Appearing with Christ, and descending with him from the side of the Father', Bouyer adds, 'will be his eternal Bride, the eschatological Church, the redeemed, saved and glorified cosmos. And eternal Wisdom will be revealed as the goal of all history both for the cosmos and for mankind.'[15]

Sophia is thus an image of the final perfection of creation, of holiness and beauty. For wisdom is the beauty of holiness.[16] It is in human holiness that we glimpse the true and final order of the cos-mos, and thus the beauty and the purpose of creation. What else of greater value can we seek than this? But important moral implica-tions follow from such an interpretation of the meaning of Sophia. We are speaking of the fiery, transcendental Beauty that is the 'unspotted mirror' of God's majesty and goodness, and into which no defiled thing can ever fall without being consumed. This Beauty is the radiance or self-gift of being.

But Beauty in this sense, so closely identifiable with the Wisdom and Glory of God, may be witnessed and known only by those *who are in some way akin to her.* In the words of the Russian Sophiologist Pavel Florensky: 'Purity of heart, virginity, chaste immaculateness is the necessary condition for seeing Sophia-Wisdom, for acquiring sonhood in Heavenly Jerusalem—'the mother of us all' (Gal. 4:26). It is clear why this is so. The heart is the organ for the perception of the heavenly world.'[17] Chastity, or purity, or spiritual virginity, turns out to be the very key to the knowledge of God. In a certain way, it integrates the other seven virtues, as white light includes

15. L. Bouyer, *Cosmos*, 192, 230-31, 264. Cf. Heb. 12:18–24; Rev. 7:12.
16. A phrase borrowed from the poet Robert Bridges. Cf. John Saward, *The Beauty of Holiness and the Holiness of Beauty.*
17. P. Florensky, *The Pillar and Ground of the Truth*, 254–5.

within itself the colors of the rainbow.

The marriage of the Lamb, to which Revelation looks forward, is the moment when the creation, united with the Holy Spirit in the person of Mary and then extended to all creation in the person of the Church, is united with the Son as the fruit of his sacrifice. In that same moment the purpose of creation is achieved, for the Son is united in self-giving with the Father, and the creation (now part of him) is united with the Father also. As such, it has indeed become 'the Father's Bride'. But the descent of the Bride is also the ascent of those who belong to her. As she descends, they ascend to meet her, and *become* her even as she appears on the new earth.

> And the twenty-four elders and the four living creatures fell down and worshipped God who is seated on the throne, saying, 'Amen. Halleluja!' And from the throne came a voice crying, 'Praise our God, all you his servants, you who fear him, small and great.' Then I heard what seemed to be the voice of a great multitude, like the sound of many waters and like the sound of mighty thunderpeals, crying, 'Halleluja! For the Lord our God the Almighty reigns. Let us rejoice and exult and give him the glory, for the marriage of the Lamb has come, and his Bride has made herself ready; it was granted her to be clothed with fine linen, bright and pure'—for the fine linen is the righteous deeds of the saints. And the Angel said to me, 'Write this: Blessed are those who are invited to the marriage supper of the Lamb' (Rev. 19:4–9).

The descent of the Bride and the ascent of the saved both refer to the mystery of *theosis*, or divinization, or deification. 'God became man so that man could become God.' This formulation of Saint Athanasius, much used by the early Church Fathers, may seem dangerously bold, though it is perfectly scriptural. 'Beloved, we are God's children now; it does not yet appear what we shall be, but we know that when he appears we shall *be like him*, for we shall see him as he is' (1 John 3:2).[18] The goal of our earthly existence is to

---

18. See also John 10:34–5 (Ps 82:6); 1 Cor. 15:49; 2 Peter 1:4. I return to this point later.

become in the end, as the Blessed Virgin Mary was from the beginning, 'like him', not by nature but by grace. This deification comes about through the Holy Spirit. As the *Catechism of the Catholic Church* says, God 'gave himself to us through his Spirit. By the participation of the Spirit, we become communicants in the divine nature.... For this reason, those in whom the Spirit dwells are divinized' (n. 1988).

After her Assumption into heaven, Mary is clothed by the whole reality of the Communion of Saints, and her union with the Son in glory is wholly oriented towards the definitive fullness of the Kingdom, when 'God will be all in all'. Mary is, in fact, in her earthly life already the Church (and the embodiment of Wisdom) that the rest of us are summoned to become through repentance and purification. She is *nature perfected* in a single person, and transfigured by the grace to which she offers not the faintest shadow of resistance.

The Spirit and the Bride say, Come!

7

JEWEL OF FAITH: CREDO

In the rest of this book we will be exploring the tradition of Christian prayer, with particular attention to the Rosary of the Blessed Virgin Mary. But before doing so, it seems fitting that at the end of our study of the Book of Revelation we look at the Apostles' Creed, which resembles the Holy City at the end of the Book of Revelation, and is used to introduce every full cycle of Rosary mysteries. In the context of the Rosary, as we shall see, it becomes a prayer. It is a masterpiece of harmony, structured by number, like a jewel that reflects light in all directions. The twelve clauses of the Creed are like the facets of this jewel, or the 'gates' of the City, corresponding to the twelve Tribes and the twelve Apostles.

1. *I believe in God, the Father almighty,*
   Creator of heaven and earth,

2. *and in Jesus Christ, his only Son, our Lord,*

3. *who was conceived by the Holy Spirit,*
   born of the Virgin Mary,

4. *suffered under Pontius Pilate,*
   was crucified, died and was buried;

5. *he descended into hell;*
   the third day he rose again from the dead;

6. *he ascended into heaven, and is*
   seated at the right hand of God the Father almighty;

7. *from there he will come to judge the living and the dead.*

8. *I believe in the Holy Spirit,*

9. *The holy catholic Church,*
   the communion of saints,

10. *the forgiveness of sins,*

11. *the resurrection of the body;*

12. *and life everlasting. Amen.*

There is in fact an ancient legend, described by Henri de Lubac SJ in his book *The Catholic Faith*, that the Apostle's Creed was drawn up by the twelve disciples of Jesus Christ under direct inspiration from God, each of them contributing one of the twelve sections.[1] Whether this is true or not, the first four clauses do at least echo the concerns of the four Evangelists, Matthew, Mark, Luke, and John. For Saint Matthew's Gospel was written for the Jews in Palestine and the text is full of citations from the Old Testament—the Covenant that revealed God as Father (see clause 1 of the Creed). The purpose of Mark's Gospel seems to have been primarily to bring the good news of salvation to the Gentiles, and so he lays great emphasis on the miracles as proving the cosmic significance of the Son (clause 2). Saint Luke also wrote for the Gentiles, but his emphasis is on the loving kindness of Christ and especially on the story of his Annunciation and Nativity (clause 3). In fact, Peter Kreeft writes:

> To my mind, the two most distinctive and attractive features of Luke's Gospel are its emphasis on Mary and on the Holy Spirit. Both are mentioned far more often than in the other Gospels. The Holy Spirit is mentioned twenty-two times in Luke. He

---

1. De Lubac regards this division into precisely twelve parts as rather forced, though less so than the division into two sets of *seven* favoured by both Saint Thomas Aquinas and Saint Bonaventure (the first set of three listing the mysteries of the divine Trinity, the second of four the mysteries of the divine humanity of Christ). In fact, despite the high repute of both these great saints, and despite the importance of the number seven, the Catholic tradition as a whole did not follow them in this. In the case of the Creed, a twelvefold division was felt to be more faithful to the more ancient texts as well as more convenient for memorization.

tells the story of Jesus' birth from Mary's point of view; Matthew tells it from Joseph's.[2]

Finally, Saint John the Evangelist gives us the most detailed, profound, liturgical account of the Passion of Christ, his death on the Cross (clause 4). At the same time, he speaks most directly about the Church, for example by giving us the words of our Lord at the end of the Last Supper, for example: 'And now I am no more in the world, but they are in the world, and I am coming to thee. Holy Father, keep them in thy name, which thou hast given me, that they may be one, even as we are one' (John 17:11).

The Creed, therefore, while it may not have been composed by the Twelve Apostles as group, certainly reflects the very earliest concerns of the Christian community and, in a particularly clear way, the main lineaments of the Apostles' teaching. It also possesses a clear Trinitarian foundation. In his book *Introduction to Christianity*, which is an extended commentary on the Apostles' Creed, Joseph Ratzinger summarizes its history. The risen Christ had told his disciples to baptize 'in the name of the Father and of the Son and of the Holy Spirit' (Matt. 28:19). The candidate for baptism was therefore asked, 'Do you believe in God the Father... in Christ... in the Holy Spirit?'—questions to which he responded with a tripartite affirmation, linked to a triple renunciation of the Devil, his service, and his work.

This threefold assent, in the context of the symbolism of drowning and resurrection, effected an 'about turn' in the person's whole existence. As the Creed evolved from this simple question-and-answer format into a continuous statement of belief by the third century (the legend of its apostolic origin emerging in the fourth), each section was expanded into a fuller account of Christian belief, being eventually imposed throughout his empire in a standard form by Charlemagne. (From this fact, and the precise form that was adopted, arise certain well-known tensions with the Christian East.) Ratzinger adds that 'in spite of its chequered history this Creed does represent at all decisive points an accurate echo of the ancient

2. Peter Kreeft, *You Can Understand the Bible*, 195.

Church's faith, which for its part is, in its kernel, the true echo of the New Testament message' (87).

The Trinitarian structure of the Creed can be made plain if we display it as follows, placing all the sections after the first into two unequal columns:

1. I believe in God, the Father almighty, Creator of heaven and earth

2. and in Jesus Christ, his only Son, our Lord,

3. who was conceived by the Holy Spirit, born of the Virgin Mary	8. I believe in the Holy Spirit
4. suffered under Pontius Pilate, was crucified, died and was buried;	9. the holy catholic Church, the communion of saints,
5. he descended into hell; the third day he rose again from the dead;	10. the forgiveness of sins,
6. he ascended into heaven; and is seated at the right hand of God the Father almighty;	11. the resurrection of the body,
7. from there he will come to judge the living and the dead.	12. and life everlasting.

The point of dividing it into two columns in this way is to emphasize the fact that, after the second clause introducing the Second Person of the Trinity, there are five clauses that expand upon the work of the Son in the world. Only then is the Holy Spirit formally introduced as an object of faith (in clause 8)—but this and the four clauses that follow (which all concern the work of the Holy Spirit) 'shadow' the five clauses referring to the work of the Son's incarnation, as I show below. They seem to unpack the Creed's very first mention of the Spirit, found in clause 3, where it refers to the Son's conception and birth.

The shape of the Creed is therefore extremely elegant. But pairing up the clauses in this way also helps to reveal the Creed's theological structure, for three important facts about the Trinity and our knowledge of the Persons are shown by it.

First, it shows that the work of the Holy Spirit is indissolubly linked to the Incarnation at every stage. The Son reveals the Spirit, and the Spirit the Son. The Holy Spirit makes his first appearance in the Creed as conceiving the Son within the womb of the Virgin Mary. The Spirit is revealed by his role in the Incarnation.

Second, we also learn something important about the Virgin Mary right away, namely her intimate relationship with the Holy Spirit. (Normally she is termed the 'spouse' of the Spirit, but at least one saint—Maximilian Kolbe, one of the saints of Auschwitz—went so far as to call her the Spirit's 'quasi-incarnation.')

Third, if each of the 'Spirit clauses' is to be read against one of the 'Son clauses', the Creed can assist us in understanding the work of the Spirit in relation to specific aspects of the Son's mission on earth, as follows:

1) His suffering, crucifixion, death, and burial are directly connected with the establishment of the Church, the communion of saints (4/9).

2) His descent into hell and rising from death are directly connected with the forgiveness of sins (5/10).

3) His ascension to the right hand of the Father is directly connected with our own resurrection on the last day (6/11).

4) His second coming and final judgment are directly connected with our own everlasting life (7/12).

Together, these four points give us the main threads that run through the mission of the Son on earth, which are the very reasons for his incarnation. Each, however, calls for a more detailed meditation. The following series is intended only to initiate this process, which the reader can continue alone:

Clauses 4 and 9 *refer to the burial of Jesus and establishment of the Church.* The Incarnation bears fruit, but the seed must be buried. Others, beginning with Jesus' immediate family and first disciples, begin to live with the Spirit of Jesus Christ within them, and in this way the Church is born. It is born specifically in and through Baptism, which is a way of dying with Christ, a process of being 'buried' with him in the sacramental waters (according to Romans 6:3–4).

Clauses 5 and 10 *refer to the descent into hell, resurrection, and forgiveness of sins.* The sin of Adam that initiated the Fall, together with all the personal sins that have contributed ever since to our alienation from the Creator, are the *felix culpa* ('happy fault') that occasioned the Incarnation. Forgiveness, and liberation from the state of slavery to sin, is what Jesus came to give us. In order to accomplish it, though, he must first descend into the hell to which sin has brought us. This is a mystery about which Adrienne von Speyr wrote profoundly, the mystery of Holy Saturday, which lies at the heart of the sacrament of Reconciliation. In this sacrament Christians experience the turning from death to life.

Clauses 6 and 11 *refer to the ascension of Jesus and our raising from the dead.* After Jesus rose from the dead he was, for a time, still upon the earth, but at the Ascension forty days later his earthly existence was taken up and reintegrated with the eternal life he possessed with the Father in heaven. Our own resurrection will not be into a second earthly life, but into a new state we cannot now imagine. 'It is sown a physical body, it is raised a spiritual body' and 'as is the man of heaven, so are those who are of heaven' (1 Cor. 15:44, 48).

Clauses 7 and 12 *refer to Jesus' second coming and the granting of everlasting life.* When we are raised, there is one further stage we must go through, and it is the judgment. The Book of Revelation ends with the words, 'Come, Lord Jesus!' This is the consummation, the fulfilment to which the saints look forward. Through judgment comes the final human state, the state that the Church Fathers called *theosis* or divinization, the Beatific Vision, the vision of God 'face to face', which is the real meaning of the phrase 'everlasting life'.

Thus we see in the few lines of the Apostles' Creed a masterpiece of summation, condensing a whole world of theology into a few bold strokes.

Twelve Marian Mysteries

Interestingly, when we meditate upon the mysteries of the Virgin Mary's life as presented in Scripture, we discover a twelvefold structure in these mysteries too. She too has twelve gates or facets. This is what Hans Urs von Balthasar finds when he reflects on Mary in his *Theo-Drama*:

Twelve such mysteries can be enumerated (though they can be subdivided): (1) Annunciation (Luke 1); (2) Pregnancy (Joseph's suspicion in Matt. 1); (3) Visitation of Elizabeth and John the Baptist, the Magnificat; (4) Nativity; (5) Presentation in the Temple; (6) Flight; (7) Finding of the Child in the Temple; (8) Cana; (9) Dismissal of his Mother and brothers; (10) 'Blessed are those who believe'; (11) At the foot of the Cross; (12) At prayer together with the Church (Acts 1). These individual scenes are like stars: they demand to be seen as a constellation, and they become brighter and deeper the closer they are brought together. The effect is often surprising: thus the 'sword' prophecy in Luke clearly points to the scene at the Cross in John; and the 'Spirit' and the 'power of the Most High' that comes upon Mary in Luke 1:35 points to the 'Spirit' and the 'power from on high' that comes upon the Church in Luke 24:49 and Acts 1:8.[3]

Thus when the Church meditates upon her faith, whether in relation to Jesus or in relation to Mary, it is twelve facets that seem to present themselves, twelve gates through which our minds can travel into the City of Faith that lies behind them. And when we juxtapose the twelve phrases of the Apostles' Creed with Balthasar's twelve Marian mysteries (in bold type), an interesting pattern emerges.

1. I believe in God, the Father almighty, Creator of heaven and earth,
   Annunciation

2. and in Jesus Christ, his only Son, our Lord,
   Pregnancy and Joseph's suspicion

3. who was conceived by the Holy Spirit, born of the Virgin Mary,
   Visitation of Elizabeth and John the Baptist
   —the Magnificat

3. Hans Urs von Balthasar, *Theo-Drama*, Vol. III, 299 fn.

4. suffered under Pontius Pilate, was crucified, died and
   was buried;
   Nativity—the mystery of the Incarnation

5. he descended into hell; on the third day he rose again from
   the dead;
   Presentation in the Temple

6. he ascended into heaven, and is seated at the right hand of
   God the Father almighty;
   Flight into Egypt

7. from there he will come to judge the living and the dead.
   Finding of the Child in the Temple

8. I believe in the Holy Spirit,
   Cana—the turning of water into wine

9. the holy catholic Church, the communion of saints,
   Dismissal of his Mother and brothers

10. the forgiveness of sins,
    'Blessed are those who believe'

11. the resurrection of the body,
    At the foot of the Cross

12. and life everlasting.
    At prayer together with the Church—Pentecost

This is how I read the connections between the two sets of mysteries as juxtaposed:

I believe in God, the Father almighty, Creator of heaven and earth,
Annunciation
The annunciation of the angel Gabriel to Mary, that the great promise of God would be fulfilled through her, was accepted by her as an act of faith in 'God the Father almighty', the Father of her people. It was the greatest such act of faith that had ever been made, and the purest.

and in Jesus Christ, his only Son, our Lord,
Pregnancy and Joseph's suspicion
The result of Mary's act of faith was the conception of Jesus himself within her womb. He entered, Saint Augustine tells us, 'through her ear' (in the sense that she conceived not in the way of fallen humanity but by accepting the Word that had been spoken to her). Whether Joseph suspected her of adultery or not is unknown; that he was nonplussed and puzzled is without doubt, since it would not have been clear to him what part he could possibly play in this mystery of God's Son until the Angel told him that he must become the legal father of the boy, in order to graft him into the stock of Israel and of David, and to protect both Mother and Child.

who was conceived by the Holy Spirit, born of the Virgin Mary,
Visitation of Elizabeth and John the Baptist
In the Gospels the pregnancy of Mary's old cousin Elizabeth and Mary's own are intertwined, as are the destinies of their two sons. Mary is informed of Elizabeth's miraculous pregnancy during the Annunciation itself, but she travels to visit her cousin not to confirm the message of the Angel but to help in the birth of John, just as Jesus will travel to John in the wilderness so that John can assist in the 'birth' of his ministry through baptism in the Jordan River.

suffered under Pontius Pilate, was crucified, died and was buried;
Nativity—the mystery of the Incarnation
Here our juxtaposition of mysteries reminds us that Christmas and Easter, birth and death, are two sides of the same coin, and especially so in the case of Jesus, whose birth into the world as a man separate and distinct from all others is for a purpose that is only fulfilled in his death for sin, in which he draws all men to himself and becomes the second Adam.

he descended into hell; on the third day he rose again from the dead;

Presentation in the Temple

What is the connection between the Presentation, the descent into hell and the rising from the dead? Jesus is brought by his parents to the Temple for the normal rites of purification after a birth. They meet the old prophet, Simeon, and the prophetess, Anna, who see in the Child the redemption of Israel, and Mary is told 'a sword shall pierce through your own soul also' (Luke 2:35). That sword is the death of her Son, and his resurrection is the salvation that is promised at the same time.

he ascended into heaven, and is seated at the right hand of God the Father almighty;

Flight into Egypt

Ascension into heaven is not a flight from the earth: that would be too easy. But we can see a strange inversion here. In the Ascension Jesus is welcomed by his heavenly Father and given his eternal throne; on earth, far from offering him a throne, the king tries to kill him and Joseph has to take him into concealment far from home. Yet in the eyes of heaven abasement is the same as glory.

from there he will come to judge the living and the dead.

Finding of the Child in the Temple

Mary and Joseph do not find him hiding in the Temple, but 'sitting among the teachers, listening to them and asking them questions; and all who heard him were amazed at his understanding and his answers' (Luke 2:46–7). Icons show him holding court, as it were—an anticipation of the role he will fulfil at the Last Judgment, when the fate of our souls will be defined by the answer to such questions as these: 'Lord, when did we see thee hungry or thirsty or a stranger or naked or sick or in prison, and did not minister to thee?' (Matthew 25:31–46.)

I believe in the Holy Spirit,

Cana—the turning of water into wine

In the Jewish tradition, wine and blood, blood and spirit, are closely connected, so much so that the consumption of the blood of an animal was forbidden and the touching of blood could render ritually unclean, because it was sacred, the bearer of life. In the first miracle of Jesus recorded by John, done in answer to Mary's instruction, the 'Spirit' of Jesus, which is the Holy Spirit, is revealed. Water becomes wine, enlivening the wedding banquet: what better symbol of the pouring out on all flesh of the Holy Spirit, who is the archetypal source of all marriage?

the holy catholic Church, the communion of saints,
Dismissal of his Mother and brothers
When someone in the crowd tells Jesus that his Mother and cousins are calling him from outside the house, he replies, looking at those sitting with him, 'Here are my mother and my brethren! Whoever does the will of God is my brother, and sister, and mother' (Mark 3:31–5). In other words, he defines the nature of the Catholic Church and the communion of saints. It is made up of all who have become his family through the gift of the Holy Spirit and their acceptance of it. His mother does not need to come in, and he does not need to depart, for she is already there.

the forgiveness of sins,
'Blessed rather are those who hear the word of God and keep it'
(This sentence of Jesus from Luke 11:28 is rendered by Balthasar in the extract reproduced earlier in this section in an alternative translation, 'Blessed are those who believe.') Jesus is replying to a woman in the crowd who cries out, 'Blessed is the womb that bore you, and the breasts that you sucked.' Mary knows, of course, that she is eternally blessed, so this is hardly intended as a rebuke directed at her. She is the *first* of those who heard the word of God and kept it, as the same Gospel tells us. Forgiveness of sins is only possible because of this hearing and keeping, this receiving of the word that is the incarnation of the Father's mercy.

the resurrection of the body,
At the foot of the Cross

John tells us that he receives Mary into his home, as his own spiritual Mother, from the moment that Jesus tells him 'Behold, your mother!' (John 19:27.) With that, Jesus knows that all is completed. Mysteriously, Jesus on the Cross has given birth, like a mother, to the Church, in the form of the communion of John and Mary. He has made Mary the mother of John and of all disciples, so that as his body dies, its rebirth from the tomb is already anticipated by the birth of the Church.

and life everlasting.
At prayer together with the Church—Pentecost
The life everlasting is the life of the indwelling Holy Spirit who descends on us at Pentecost like tongues of fire, when Mary is at prayer with the disciples (Acts 1:14, 2:1–4).

These are the contents of our faith. But Victor White reminds us: 'A dogma is not only an article of faith to be believed; it is also a task to be achieved.' The Creed is not a manifesto, but a challenge. We have to grow into it. This is something that comes across very strongly in the Book of Revelation, which, though it culminates in the vision of the Bride of God, the Heavenly City, in whom the soul finds rest, is concerned to address all Christians, including those who are still wading through blood to get there.

8

THE HOLY WAY

The *Tao Te Ching*, a book of ancient Chinese wisdom, famously says that the Way that can be spoken of is not the Eternal Way, and the name that can be named is not the Eternal Name.

That is true enough. But what if the Way should speak of itself? What if the Name should name itself?

One of my favorite sayings from a great Taoist sage is this:

'You understand how to fly using wings,
but you have not yet seen how to fly without them.
You understand how to act from knowledge,
But you have not yet seen how to act from not knowing'
(Chuang Tzu).[1]

There is a way to act from not-knowing, to fly without wings. It is the way of the Spirit.

The Spirit is like a wind that 'blows where it wills, and you hear the sound of it, but you do not know where it comes from or where it goes' (John 3: 8). The wind of the Spirit blew Philip to the side of a man reading the Prophets in his chariot, a man to whom he explained the meaning of the Scriptures, who then asked to be baptized. Having baptized him, Philip was caught up by the Spirit and disappeared, reappearing in Azotus (Acts 8: 26–40).

---

1. This translation is taken from Gia-Fu Feng and Jane English, *Chuang-Tsu: Inner Chapters*, 68. A wonderful Christian-Taoist synthesis may be found in Hieromonk Damascene, *Christ the Eternal Tao*. The classic work of what might be called a kind of 'Christian Taoism' is *Abandonment to Divine Providence* by the French Jesuit Jean-Pierre de Caussade (d. 1751), rendered in contemporary English as *The Joy of Full Surrender*.

The same Spirit is speaking to us today, and can blow us any-where. It is with us because the Way has entered the world as a man, walking and talking. Jesus does not simply *know* the Way; he him-self, in his own person, *is* the Way of the Spirit. 'I am the way and the truth and the life' (John 14:6). It is this person, Jesus, who lives in the Spirit and sends the Spirit to those who accept him.

The Way of the Spirit is the spiritual path that we walk in faith— through the air, when necessary (there are saints, such as Padre Pio of Pietrelcino and Joseph of Cupertino, who have traveled that way, just as others have followed Christ by walking on water). It is the path of the seeking soul, the way to the Father's 'house of many mansions' (John 14:2), the way through hope to love. But when love is manifested as man, as Jesus, it suffers the natural fate of truth in a fallen world. Though the light will, in the end, triumph over dark-ness, it does so through persecution and hardship. We cannot avoid the Way of the Cross, for 'he who does not take up his cross and fol-low me is not worthy of me' (Matt. 10:38, cf. Luke 9:23 and 14:27). And yet we know that 'he who loses his life for my sake will find it' (Matt. 10:39).

Difficulties in Prayer

The classic Catholic definition of prayer is 'raising the heart and mind to God'. But this is not always an easy task—as Hamlet's father found. 'My words fly up, my thoughts remain below: Words with-out thoughts never to heaven go' (*Hamlet*, Act 3, Scene 3, lines 100-103).

In a sense the *core* of our being does not need to be raised to God because it is already there. What does need to happen is that we need to journey into that core. We are normally living somewhere else, somewhere shallower. This 'shallower' self, a less real or less authentic part of ourselves, has to be transformed.

Prayer is less something we do than something the Spirit does in us. That is a consoling thought. We do not have to force ourselves to pray. St Paul tells us, 'the Spirit helps us in our weakness; for we do not know how to pray as we ought, but the Spirit himself intercedes for us with sighs too deep for words' (Rom. 8:26).

But in order for the Spirit to be able to 'sigh' in us, our own faculties must be at the Spirit's disposal. We must be alert, focused, clear, or 'one-pointed'. Thus many Christians find their verbal prayers becoming briefer and briefer, until it is just one word, 'Lord' or 'Jesus', repeated over and over again like the beating of wings that raise the soul to God. Eventually, the saints tell us, even this may disappear, as the Holy Spirit 'intercedes for us with sighs too deep for words' and we simply glide on the breath of God.

Prayer is attention (Simone Weil). We use words to direct our attention, and the words of a prayer are intended to direct our attention towards God. But God can never be seen or grasped in the mind. It has been rightly said that 'If God were visible we would see nothing else' (John Powell Ward). Words in prayer tend to give us images, metaphors, symbolic ways of relating to God, but all these are merely pointers that show in which direction he lies, not labels that stick to him.

If *prayer is attention*, many of our problems in prayer seem to boil down to various kinds of distraction. (That includes sexual fantasy, money worries, and a whole lot else.) Prayer is a question of focus, and yet we are a bundle of disordered energies pulling in many directions, unable to concentrate for more than a moment on any one thing, let alone the invisible God. Distraction is our normal state. It always has been a problem and a temptation, but in the modern world it has become a way of life. The electronic media that permeate our lives, the advertisers who vie for our attention with images calculated to stimulate and entice, the music that provides a 'soundtrack for our lives'—these distractions exist on a scale never before experienced. To invoke the presence of God through prayer is to open a zone of interior silence, to turn our faces towards him, to cease talking to ourselves or allowing ourselves to be entertained. 'It requires a detachment from the self and the other voices in the heart, a going out from the self, to listen to Someone other than the self' (Sister Ninian OSB).

Prayer requires to be nourished, or it will die. We can do that in several ways. Firstly, we must give it time—that is, we offer up (sacrifice) time that might have been spent on more immediately productive tasks by devoting it to prayer. Secondly, we may read Scripture or some of the vast library of spiritual texts in a reflective way that leads back to contemplation. But the most important way to nourish and enliven our prayer is by trying to live it. For although I have been describing prayer as an 'interior' journey, that is not quite accurate. Prayer involves the whole of us, and that naturally includes our will, our behavior, and all our outward actions. Going out from the self interiorly cannot be separated from going out exteriorly—that is, acting towards others with love. For that reason 'faith without works is vain' (James 2:20).

St Paul writes that 'in my flesh I complete what is lacking in Christ's afflictions for the sake of his body, that is, the Church' (Col. 1:24). The question I have to ask myself is, what is it that Christ has left undone, in order that I may do it?

Pathless Prayer

I have been writing about forms of prayer that involve a journey— from God, to God. The Rosary in particular represents this journey. But there is also a form of Christian spirituality that does not involve travelling at all, even in a circle. If God is with us already, we do not need to go anywhere. This is the realization that opens a way that is not a way, sometimes called 'the sacrament of the present moment.'

Let us imagine I am sitting in an airport. My flight is delayed; I will probably miss an important meeting. There is no other way to get there. My job, my livelihood, and my ability to pay the mortgage on my home, are hanging in the balance. Normally I would be consumed with anxiety in these circumstances. Perhaps, if I am a believer, I remember to pray. Here is an example of the journey of faith, the pilgrim mentality. There is somewhere to get to, and plenty of good reasons for going there.

If I am praying as a Christian prays the Lord's Prayer, and I really want God's will to be done more than my own, then as I pray for particular things I will always insert a little unspoken proviso; that if God decides not to give me what I want, at least the experience should somehow bring me closer to him. The place I want to get to— a job, a house, a comfortable life for those I love—is not what I am ultimately most interested in. Beyond all that, my real goal is higher. I am aiming for perfection, for infinite happiness, for God himself.

But there is a stage beyond even this. Let me try to imagine myself into it. What I still need to see, or to realize fully, is that God is here right *now*. The goal of my life has come to me already. There is nothing left to want. Not even the happiness of my family, because that happiness, too, lies in the hands of the God who is already with me. Meister Eckhart puts it like this: 'If our will is God's will, that is good, but if God's will is our will, that is far better.'

This would change the way I relate to the present. It would no longer be a way-station, a highway; it would become the destination. This does not mean that I will have lapsed into passivity or become inert. (That would be the heresy called 'Quietism'.) The present is a dynamic thing, constantly moving. To remain in the present we must ever be moving along with it. I am *at* the destination, but the destination itself is moving. Each moment is a new gift. To be passive would mean to be stuck in the moment immediately past, rather than living in the present.

Let us pretend that my plane is indeed delayed, and I miss the meeting. I am at peace, because I know that God wants me to experience this disappointment for a reason. In fact I do not even experience it as a disappointment. To be interiorly at rest while continually moving is a state like that of which Lao Tse speaks, or the Buddha— a state of mindfulness, one-pointedness, detachment—but with one important difference. I am conscious of receiving every moment from God's hand. I am living in faith; I am hand-in-hand with God.

The disciple has given up everything in order to follow Jesus: wealth, brothers, sisters, mothers, and fathers. What he receives in return is a hundredfold (Mark 10:30), an intensification of those very things, because they are now experienced in Jesus, along with eternal life, because he has been raised up with Jesus into eternity. The idol of the self is left behind. He no longer knows who he is or where he belongs (*foxes have holes but the Son of Man has nowhere to lay his head*). He belongs only with Jesus and in him, and he makes his home wherever Jesus goes, where Jesus takes him.

To be detached in a Christian way is not to escape time, not to become empty, but to enter time more completely, to be filled with a new life that is flowing into the Christian continually from above and transforming him gradually into a new creation. That this happens to very few of us—that there are hardly any honest-to-goodness saints, any true disciples—is a scandal, perhaps, but it is only to be expected. (The number in whom the new life flows just below the surface of the ground is, fortunately, much greater.)

All our wounds are sanctified, and all the time spent running away turns out to have been valuable, and nothing is ever lost which is given to God.

9

THE LORD'S PRAYER

The Holy Way is a Way of both prayer and action. Prayer is an opening to God's grace and to the presence of the Holy Spirit. Grace makes possible true human action in the service of God and neighbour.

Fallen man needs help to pray. It is not something that comes naturally to us any more. When the disciples ask Jesus to teach them to pray, his instructions are summarized in what we have come to call the Lord's Prayer, coupled with several important exhortations. In the Gospel of Matthew they are told to pray in their 'inner room' or 'treasury' with the door shut, 'and your Father who sees in secret will reward you' (6:6). They are also told to fast in secret (6:17-18), and their treasury is not to be used to store anything that moths or rust or thieves may take away from them, but only heavenly treasures, for 'where you treasure is, there will your heart be also' (6:21). The rest of Matthew chapters 6 and 7 is a continuation of these teachings on prayer—about the inner room of the heart and how to keep it empty of all but heavenly things. These instructions on prayer are situated in the larger context of the Sermon on the Mount, so that prayer and action are fully integrated in the teachings on Christian life.

The Lord's Prayer is offered at the beginning of each of the mysteries of the Rosary. As reported in the Gospels it consists of five or seven petitions. The five listed by Luke (11:1–4) expand into the seven listed by Matthew (6:9–13), which are the ones adopted by the liturgy of the Church and prayed in the Rosary. Here are the five in Luke:

Father,
1. *Hallowed be thy name.*
2. *Thy Kingdom come.*
3. *Give us each day our daily bread,*
4. *And forgive us our sins, for we ourselves forgive everyone who is indebted to us;*
5. *And lead us not into temptation.*

And here are the seven, from Matthew's Gospel (the extra two petitions are produced by expanding two of Luke's five):

Our Father, who art in heaven,
1. *Hallowed be thy name.*
{ 2. *Thy Kingdom come.*
  3. *Thy will be done, on earth as it is in heaven.*
4. *Give us this day our daily bread,*
5. *And forgive us our trespasses, as we forgive those who trespass against us.*
{ 6. *And lead us not into temptation*
  7. *But deliver us from evil.*

The structure of the prayer is interesting. In the case of the five, we might think of the human body in the form of a five-pointed star—the head and four limbs. The first petition, the hallowing of the Father's name, can be assigned to the head, the next two to the right and left hands, and the last to the feet.

In the case of the seven, we might associate them with the sacraments, or the days of creation, and also with the seven fundamental needs of the human person as described in the *Catechism of the Catholic Church* (2803–2854).

The petitions begin with God and end with deliverance from evil; so that if read in reverse order they represent an ascent to God from the depths of our worldly state. In both cases, the petition for daily bread is in the middle—number three of five, or number four of seven. This middle petition refers mystically to the Eucharist, which is the heart of the Church. (As Henri de Lubac put it, 'The Eucharist makes the Church.') For the Church comes from the heart of Jesus, from his love, demonstrated symbolically by the flow of blood and water from his side as he hung on the Cross. This is the river of the sacraments, in which we are baptized and from which we are born as children of God.

COMMENTARY ON THE SEVEN PETITIONS

1. *Our Father, who art in heaven, hallowed be thy name.*

The uniqueness of Christianity revolves around the unique relationship of Jesus to his Father, whom he called *Abba*, 'Daddy'. Through the Jewish prophets, man had been prepared to view God not simply as Creator of all things, but as Father, the head of our family, united to us in a Covenant to which he had bound himself for all time. In the blood of Jesus, a new Covenant is made and a new Name is given, a more intimate Name, one that only Jesus has a right to use. Into this right we enter not as individuals but as a community, in communion with each other, which is why we say *Our* Father, not simply *Father*.

The names of God are many—some say seventy-two, some say a hundred, some say an indefinite number. Each name represents God under some attribute, and God remains the Nameless One because in himself he transcends every attribute and every conception we have of him. But he knows himself, even if we do not know him.

The knowledge God has of himself is perfect, and God's conception of himself is the Father's begetting of the Son. 'No one knows the Son except the Father, and no one knows the Father except the Son and any one to whom the Son chooses to reveal him' (Matt. 11:27). Thus in the beginning, which means not just at the start but in the Archetype or Principle (the true 'beginning' of things, including time itself), the Word was with God, and Word was God (John 1:1). Since the *knowing* of the Father in the Son and the Son in the Father is also perfect, and identical with the divine nature, it is also a Person—the Holy Spirit. Thus God as he is in himself is Trinity. The Trinity is the knowledge of God in and by himself, transcending all knowing of him by creatures.

That is why the naming of God as Trinity, as Father, is the right not of creatures but of the Son; that is, of God himself, and why we can only name him 'as he is in heaven' in his transcendent glory when we are part of the Son, joined to him in baptism as members of the Church, as members of the corporate Person who is the Bride of God. This is the New Covenant in the Holy Spirit. We pray to the Father, with the Son, in the Spirit.

God's name is hallowed, kept holy or sacred, set definitively apart from all that is not God, by the fact that it can only be spoken from within the Trinity, the inner room to which God the Son has granted us access—since 'No one has ascended into heaven but he who descended from heaven, the Son of man' (John 3:13), who is also the Son of God.

The Name of God is the first sacrament. When God speaks, he reveals himself—just as when we speak, we reveal ourselves. Thus when he speaks in eternity the Word that is his Son, the Son is in fact the Name that reveals God. This Word is carried on the Breath of God which is the Holy Spirit. And because by his Word he causes the world to be, the world is a representation of the Word, and it is a 'Name' of God also. And when within the world he sends the Word into the womb of Mary, the Word becomes flesh. Thus the sacraments are born every time Jesus tells us that 'I am.'

2. *Thy Kingdom come.*

If the Name refers to the inner sanctum of God's own identity within the Trinity, the Kingdom is the radiation of that identity through creation. The Kingdom is to 'come,' which means it lies from our point of view in the future. It is the essence of all we pray for—union with God, the Coronation of the Virgin, the divinization of the creature by grace.

God's Kingdom comes by the radiation or sending of the Holy Spirit, as in the crowning of the Disciples with tongues of fire at Pentecost. In that sense the Church is the Kingdom; but the Church is only partially realized on earth until the times are fulfilled and all are safely gathered in. Many who appear to be part of the Church are spiritually cut off, and many who seem cut off from her are members of the Church invisibly, their numbers known only to God. 'But many that are first will be last, and the last first' (Mark 10:31).

In order to appreciate fully the import of this petition we should return to the Book of Revelation, where the Throne of God is unveiled. On the Throne of the Father is the Lamb who is the Son, and around it are the four Creatures, and the twenty-four Elders, and the Angels, bowed low and singing praise. The One who sits on the Throne makes all things new, and the Holy City descends from heaven like a bride.

The Kingdom is Sophia, God's Wisdom which is his majesty and beauty, into which the whole creation is taken up through the Incarnation of the Son, in the marriage of the divine and human natures.

3. *Thy will be done, on earth as it is in heaven.*

Almost breathlessly the Prayer moves from anticipation of the Kingdom to the grounding of that Kingdom in the earth by obedience to God. If the first Petition expresses Faith, the second Hope, then the third concerns Love. It is by love alone that the will of another can become my will, without force or compulsion but joyfully and perfectly. The distinction between heaven and earth remains, even in the Book of Revelation, but the same will is done in each, because the fulfilment of everything that pertains to the earth lies in the heavenly will alone.

The petition echoes the *fiat* of Mary at the Annunciation ('let it be to me according to your word') and of Christ in Gethsemane ('not my will, but thine, be done'). It is in these prayers that we see earth, or human nature, making it possible for God's will to be done as in heaven.

The will of heaven, which is love, is the Holy Spirit. Thus this petition is a prayer for the Spirit to descend from heaven to earth, and to fill the earth, as he began to do at Pentecost, and as he had already done in the soul of the Blessed Virgin.

4. *Give us this day our daily bread.*

It might seem pointless, foolish, to ask God for the most basic requirements of life, the ones that seem most under our control. Of course bread is for us to make, to fight for, to wrest from the soil, to buy from our neighbor. . . . Yet of course this petition makes the point that we are dependent on God for our very existence, and our survival from day to day. Bread may be the work of human hands, it may come to us from a bakery or supermarket, but it would not do so if God did not permit it, if his Providence did not arrange for us to receive it, and if he did not create every single ingredient out of his love.

When the disciples come to Jesus and ask him to eat, after he has been talking with the Samaritan woman, he replies, 'I have food to eat of which you do not know. . . . My food is to do the will of him who sent me, and to accomplish his work' (John 4:31–4). In the wilderness, tempted in his great hunger by Satan, he refuses to turn stones into bread, because 'Man shall not live by bread alone, but by every word that proceeds from the mouth of God' (Matt. 4:4). So for Jesus—who is in his own Person the 'word' that proceeds from the mouth of God—his nourishment, his daily bread, is to do the Father's will, and only secondarily to eat bread. The same should be true for us. The spirit in us is nourished by the right kind of obedience.

The spirituality of this obedience is described beautifully by Jean-Pierre de Caussade. In every moment God makes plain his will for us, by placing before us certain duties (be they as 'spiritual' as going to Mass or as mundane as household chores), or else by prompting us to do things that we could as easily have left undone. Whatever it is, however trivial or banal, God's 'bread' is in that thing and it is a sacrament for us, a source of nourishment for our soul.

The word 'daily' is a translation of the very unique word *epiousios*, which the Vulgate renders 'supersubstantial' or 'above' substance, referring to the higher substance of the Blessed Eucharist. Its plainer meaning is simply 'sufficient for the day', meaning bread that is enough to take us through the next twenty-four hours. In this sense it reminds us of the manna that fell in the desert to feed the tribes of Israel, but which could not be hoarded for the day after since it would quickly become corrupt.

5. *And forgive us our trespasses, as we forgive those who trespass against us.*

We ask to be forgiven what we owe to God. For to sin is to take something away from God, which means that we must now owe it back to him. Something is taken away from the glory of God by every sin. But no matter how small the sin, the debt is infinite by virtue of the infinity that is lost. That is why none can pay it back except the Son.

Here we confront the mystery of the Trinity once more, in the mystery of 'justification'. Without Christ, his Incarnation and Passion, men would have remained creatures of God; but they would have been nothing more than that. Their imperfect adherence to God and his natural law would have been compensated for in various ways. Every religion has ways of bringing or binding us back to God, in the form of symbols and rituals and sacrifices. But as Saint Paul wrote in his Letter to the Romans, none of this makes us truly righteous. The gap always remains infinite.

In that sense we can never be truly 'forgiven' without Christ. We can be tolerated by God, we can be blessed by him and comforted by him, as a creature is by its Creator, but there will always be a reconciliation still to accomplish, a penance to be made, a debt to be repaid; one that man who is not God cannot perform. But the man who is God can perform this sacrifice. He alone can pay this infinite debt, by giving his infinity, and he has done so.

This means that the forgiveness attained in Christ, through baptism (and regained after subsequent sin in the sacrament of penance and the Eucharist), is a whole other thing than any that might have been attained outside him. It overcomes the infinite chasm that the rejection of grace by our first parents had opened up. It pours into our hearts the living presence of the Holy Spirit, with the Father and Son. That is not the same as simply the presence that God has within us as the Creator in the hearts of his creatures. It is the Spirit of Sonship. It makes us no longer creatures, in a sense, but deifies us with the life of the Trinity.

6. *And lead us not into temptation*

Blessed is the man who endures trial, for when he has stood the test he will receive the crown of life which God has promised to those who love him. Let no one say when he is tempted, 'I am tempted by God'; for God cannot be tempted with evil and he himself tempts no one; but each person is tempted when he is lured and enticed by his own desire. Then desire when it has conceived gives birth to sin; and sin when it is full-grown brings forth death' (James 1:12–15).

God leads us into temptation the way the Holy Spirit led Jesus into the wilderness after his Baptism in the Jordan so that he might be tempted by Satan (Matt. 4:1). In other words, he permits us to be tempted, or creates opportunities for us to be tempted (not by himself but by the devil), and he always has a reason for doing so. But we *pray* not to be so led, unless it is God's will, because no one must presume that he is strong enough to resist the temptation. 'Watch and pray that you may not enter into temptation; the spirit indeed is willing, but the flesh is weak' (Matt. 26:41).

If we are tested, it is because we need to learn something. And though we may give way, God can give us the grace to resist. Certainly without his help the task would be hopeless. In defeating temptation we draw upon the victory of Christ against his three temptations; and we resist temptation only in Christ, in communion with him through the Holy Spirit.

7. But deliver us from evil

Now we reach the baseline of our plea. We need to be rescued from all the woes of the world and the enemies of the spirit. We have given into temptation, we have fallen into the gravity-well that leads to hell, we have come up against the one who seeks to obstruct God— the one who 'throws himself across' the Way of Jesus (*dia-bolos*).

The destruction of the Way in us is a fragmentation of the self, a shattering of the image of God, so that the 'I am' is lost. The light that comes from God and shines in the pure soul is darkened and fogged, refracted and misdirected. From this state of confusion, of being lost in the fog, we must seek to be rescued. We must allow our 'I' to be rebuilt. It is with this need that the Lord's Prayer confronts us at the end, so that we can begin again by appealing to 'Our Father' who shines above all the darkness, in communion with the Son whom darkness cannot overcome.

10

THE ROSE GARDEN

The Rosary of the Blessed Virgin Mary is the most widely disseminated and popular devotion among Catholics outside of the Mass. A circular string of beads resembling a necklace, each bead representing a prayer that is said whilst moving the fingers along the string, it can sometimes look like a mechanical substitute for 'real' prayer. But used correctly (that is, when prayed slowly and mindfully), it can lead to a much deeper, more active, interior participation in the Christian mysteries for those who find it congenial.

The Rosary is associated with Mary, but it is almost entirely focused on the life of her Son. Mary simply serves here as our initiator into the mysteries of Christ. In other words, the Rosary contains the Mother of God's own meditations on the Incarnation. *And he went down with them and came to Nazareth, and was obedient to them; and his mother kept all these things carefully in her heart* (Luke 2:51).

The Rosary is also a 'metaphysical' prayer. Mary is like the primordial waters lying open before the life-giving action of God at the beginning of the world. By praying we are trying to become like her, receptive to the will of God. Mary's *fiat* ('Let it be to me according to your word') echoes God's *fiat* ('Let there be light') in the very beginning of creation, and her Son's *fiat* ('Let not my will but thine be done') in the Garden of Gethsemane (Luke 22:42, etc.).

The Hail Mary
The main body of the Rosary is made up of five strings of ten beads, each of these 'decades' being separated by an extra bead marked off by a small space. The 150 beads each represent a short prayer called the 'Hail Mary', which is supposed to be recited while the bead is

passing through the fingers. At the beginning of each decade one prays the Lord's Prayer, and at the end a short prayer called a 'Glory Be' in praise of the Trinity.

The first words of the Hail Mary are those that were spoken by the Angel Gabriel when he appeared to her to announce the imminent conception of Christ. Every time we repeat the words of this prayer we are trying to approach Jesus through Mary.

> Hail Mary, full of grace, the Lord is with thee.
> Blessed art thou among women, and blessed is the fruit of thy womb Jesus.
> Holy Mary, Mother of God, pray for us sinners now and at the hour of our death.

There comes a time in the life of many Christians when the Hail Mary, brief as it is, suddenly expands until it encompasses the whole of life. It becomes possible to meditate upon it constantly. Each phrase contains a mystery that we never grow tired of gazing at.

Hail Mary—we address her from out of our darkness; or is it that we are called by the Angel's words into her presence?

Full of grace—Mary's title: she is what all of us should be, a creature brimful of her Creator.

The Lord is with thee—He is always with her, and in this 'with' are the secrets of what it is to be a person.

Blessed art thou among women—a blessedness that marks her out, yet brings all other women along with her.

Blessed is the fruit of thy womb Jesus—the hub of the mysteries, the Creator encompassed by the creature, the tree bearing fruit that contains the seed of all things.

Holy Mary, Mother of God—God has become a single cell, growing to be a child, and wakes in her arms.

Pray for us sinners now—for we are sinners now, lost in the woods, and we need her to find us.

And at the hour of our death—since death approaches all of us, and we will struggle to be born from the womb of the world.

The Structure of the Mysteries

The most obvious and important structural principle of the Rosary lies in the order of *mysteries* which according to tradition are assigned to be contemplated during each sequence of ten Hail Marys, and which are listed below. There are several sets of five mysteries, so each set each occupies a whole Rosary.

Of course, a 'mystery' here does not mean something that is deliberately being kept obscure. It is not something irrational or something secretive. It is, however, something that our human intelligence cannot fully understand, or get to the bottom of. It may consequently in a sense be 'hidden' (if not intentionally) from those who insist on grasping everything quickly and superficially.

The greatest practical difficulty that many people encounter in the devotion lies in the attempt to pray verbally at the same time as gazing interiorly upon the mysteries evoked through an image—a tableau or icon—in the imagination. To do so requires a mental discipline that brings the mind into closer alignment with the pattern of Mary's thoughts as she treasures these memories of her Son and 'ponders them in her heart'.

The five 'Joyful', five 'Sorrowful' and five 'Glorious' mysteries describe the life of human childhood, the adult life and the supernatural life. Taken as applying to the individual soul they describe, first, the life of the soul as it opens itself to grace, secondly the life of the soul as it struggles to follow Christ, and finally the soul's life as it experiences the transformation wrought by grace.

In his Apostolic Letter published in October 2002 (*Rosarium Virginis Mariae*), Pope John Paul II introduced a further set of five 'Luminous' mysteries to be prayed between the Joyful and the Sorrowful. These summarize Christ's public ministry between his Baptism and his Passion (his Baptism in the Jordan, the Miracle at the Wedding Feast in Cana, his Announcement of the Kingdom, his Transfiguration on the Mountain, and the Eucharist or Last Supper).

The New Mysteries

It may seem strange that a Pope so traditionally-minded as John Paul II, especially in matters of Marian devotion, should be willing to innovate in such a drastic manner by introducing a fourth set of Mysteries. The Trinitarian structure of the Rosary had been well established since at least the fifteenth century. The Rosary seems to have begun as a way of praying the 150 Psalms in three groups of 50—a kind of lay breviary. Partly for convenience, the Psalms were later replaced with Our Fathers, and later Hail Marys, in five sets of ten beads at a time, each set of 50 linked to one of the three cycles of Mysteries. But by adding another set of 50, with another cycle of Mysteries, John Paul II had effectively broken the tradition linking the Rosary to the Psalms. Although the link had become vestigial, I do not believe he would have done so without direct inspiration or authorization from heaven. So what meaning can we find in the change?

To begin with, the four sets of mysteries may be compared to the Cross, with its four arms. If we stand at the base of the Cross, we are present with Mary the Mother of God. Thus we begin our meditation by thinking of the Joyful Mysteries, recalling the Incarnation. Then we look up. Above the head of Jesus is the plaque affixed by the order of Pilate, bearing the message: 'Jesus Christ, the King of the Jews'. The two horizontal arms of the Cross linked by this proclamation therefore represent the Kingship of Jesus. One arm points towards the good thief who recognized him as King and the other to the unrepentant, who did not. The two arms also represent the Kingship as lived (the Sorrowful Mysteries, for on earth Our Lord lived his Kingship as the Passion) and as taught (the Luminous Mysteries). Finally, when we look up higher, to the top of the Cross, we are remembering the Glories of heaven to which the Cross conducts us.

The new fourfold structure of the Mysteries also recalls the four-fold structure of the Gospels, and each of the four sets of Mysteries seems to correspond to one of the Gospels in a special way. The Joyful Mysteries correspond to the Gospel of Matthew, whose symbol is a Man and who emphasizes the titles 'Son of Man', 'Son of Abraham', 'Son of David'. The Sorrowful correspond to Luke, whose symbol is the Ox and whose Gospel emphasizes the role of Jesus as sacrificial victim. The Luminous would then correspond with Mark, whose symbol is the Lion, and who proclaims the divine power of the Lord. Finally the Glorious Mysteries can be associated with John, whose symbol is the Eagle, and who teaches us about the intimate relationship between the Son and his heavenly Father.

Ancient and medieval thinkers found symbolic significance in numerical patterns. The Apostles' Creed through which one enters the Rosary has twelve sections, like the gates of the New Jerusalem. The Lord's Prayer which begins each sequence has seven, like the seven sacraments or the seven days of creation. The Glory Be with which each sequence ends is Trinitarian. Each sequence of beads is made up of ten Hail Marys, ten being the sum of seven and three, itself symbolic of the expansion of the totality of numbers contained in One. A Rosary contains five mysteries, five being the number of life and growth, found especially in flowers and leaves. Five is also closely related to the Golden Ratio and thus to many aspects of beauty in nature. By the addition of the five Luminous Mysteries, bringing the number of rosaries to four (the number of the walls of the New Jerusalem), Pope John Paul II brought the tradition to its completion.

Ways of Praying the Rosary

There are many forms of Rosary, both short and long (for example, Rosary Rings or Chaplets are very popular, which contain only ten marks or beads and a cross). The full Rosary is a circular string of five groups of ten beads interspersed by larger or slightly separate ones (marking the beginning or end of each decade). To go around the Rosary once with one's fingers is to pray one of the four sets of Mysteries (Joyful, Luminous, Sorrowful or Glorious).

The beginning of the Rosary normally consists of a short string consisting of a Crucifix, followed by a single bead at the beginning and end of a sequence of three. This leads to a holy image or medal, attached to which is the longer, circular part of the Rosary. The prayers assigned to the short string are the Apostles' Creed (for the Cross), an Our Father, three Hail Marys (for Faith, Hope, and Charity), and a Glory Be. In this way one enters the Rose Garden of Our Lady through the Cross, along the 'path' of the three theological virtues, and through the 'gate' represented by the medallion.

A complete circuit of the longer part of the Rosary includes five sets of ten Hail Marys, one set for each of five mysteries, each such 'decade' beginning with the Lord's Prayer and ending with a Glory Be. When one reaches the medallion again at the end of the circuit, one prays some closing prayers, including the *Salve Regina* or 'Hail, Holy Queen'. The idea is to close the gate of the Garden behind one and leave softly.

When praying the Rosary, it is customary also to 'offer' each decade for a particular 'intention' or for a particular person. Thus one might offer a decade for the healing or comfort of a friend or enemy, or for the ending of a war, or the establishment of justice in a certain situation, for example.

In Germany, a brief line referring to each Mystery is often inserted in between the two halves of the Hail Mary, after '...and blessed is the fruit of thy womb, Jesus'. This helps the praying soul to remember the Mysteries and to contemplate them in series. Thus one might pray as follows:

The Joyful Mysteries
And blessed is the fruit of thy womb, Jesus, whom you, O Virgin, conceived of the Holy Spirit
    . . . *Jesus,* whom you, O Virgin, took to Elizabeth
    . . . *Jesus,* to whom you, O Virgin, gave birth
    . . . *Jesus,* whom you, O Virgin, offered up in the Temple
    . . . *Jesus,* whom you, O Virgin, found again in the Temple

The Luminous Mysteries
    . . . *Jesus,* who was baptized in the Jordan
    . . . *Jesus,* who turned water into wine
    . . . *Jesus,* who proclaimed the Kingdom of God
    . . . *Jesus,* who was transfigured on the mountain
    . . . *Jesus,* who gave himself to us as Eucharist

The Sorrowful Mysteries
    . . . *Jesus,* who sweated blood for us

... *Jesus*, who was scourged for us

... *Jesus*, who was crowned with thorns for us

... *Jesus*, who bore the heavy Cross for us

... *Jesus*, who was crucified for us

The Glorious Mysteries

... *Jesus*, who rose from the dead

... *Jesus*, who ascended into Heaven

... *Jesus*, who sent us the Holy Spirit

... *Jesus*, who took you, O Virgin, up into Heaven

... *Jesus*, who crowned you, O Virgin, in Heaven

Many Catholics also insert a short 'Fatima Prayer' after each decade, after the Glory Be. It is a prayer for universal salvation (in the sense of 1 Timothy 2:4), and the words are as follows: '*O my Jesus, save us from the fires of hell. Lead all souls to heaven, especially those most in need of thy mercy.*'

The mysteries are often assigned to different days of the week. The *Joyful* used to be said on Mondays and Thursdays (and Sundays during Advent and Epiphany), the *Sorrowful* on Tuesdays and Fridays but daily in Lent, and the *Glorious* on Wednesdays and Saturdays (and Sundays from Easter to Advent). John Paul II suggested Thursday as the day for praying the *Mysteries of Light*, leaving Friday for the Sorrowful and moving the Joyful to Saturday. Thus one may still follow the traditional threefold sequence on Monday, Tuesday and Wednesday, before praying the whole set of four beginning on Thursday, finishing with the Glorious mysteries on Sunday. (In terms of number symbolism, this division of the week into two parts brings out the fact that seven, which is the number of the Covenant and of Creation, is made by the adding groups of three and four, just as twelve is produced by multiplying them.)

Opening and Closing Prayers

The Rosary may begin with this prayer:

Queen of the Holy Rosary, inspire in my heart a true love of this devotion, so that by meditating on the mysteries of our Redemption which are recalled in it, I may be enriched with its fruits and obtain peace for the world, the conversion of sinners, and the favor which I ask of you in this Rosary, which is to pray for me to the Lord our God, in the name of Christ our Savior, for [*insert your petition*]. I ask it for the greater glory of God, for your own honor, Mary, and for the good of souls, especially my own. *Amen.*

The Rosary normally ends with these prayers:

Hail Holy Queen, Mother of Mercy, our life, our sweetness, and our hope.

To thee do we cry, poor banished children of Eve. To thee do we send up our sighs, mourning and weeping in this valley of tears. Turn then, most gracious advocate, thine eyes of mercy towards us, and after this our exile, show unto us the blessed fruit of thy womb, Jesus. O clement, O loving, O sweet Virgin Mary! Pray for us, most holy Mother of God, that we may be made worthy of the promises of Christ.

O God, whose only begotten Son by his life, death, and Resurrection has purchased for us the rewards of eternal life, grant we beseech thee that, meditating upon these Mysteries of the Most Holy Rosary of the Blessed Virgin Mary, we may both imitate what they contain and obtain what they promise, through the same Christ our Lord. Amen.

[Optional:] May the divine assistance remain always with us. *Amen.* And may the souls of the faithful departed [*especially...*], through the mercy of God, rest in peace. *Amen.*

11

MYSTERIES OF THE ROSARY

As one prays each decade of the Rosary, it is helpful to focus one's attention (and thus feelings and prayer) around one particular mystery in the life of Jesus and Mary. The following commentary tries to bring out the way each of these mysteries relates to the other mysteries and to our own life—how each can lead us deeper into the life of faith.

After the name of each mystery I have put [in brackets like this] one of the things we might pray for during this meditation.

1. JOYFUL MYSTERIES: THE HIDDEN LIFE

*The soul prepares herself to welcome Christ, she manifests him
and eventually is forced to go deeper, through loss, into
the temple of the heart where he may be found again.*

The Annunciation
[to be humble]

The Angel greets Mary, who is little more than a child: 'Hail Mary'. In Latin, the word 'Hail' is *Ave*, the reversal of *Eva*, which is the name of our fallen Mother. This reminds us that the first mystery is to do with a reversal of the Fall. (*Ave* is also thought by some to be a shortened version of *absque vae*—meaning 'without woe'.)

'Full of Grace': the Angel pronounces this as though it was a name or title, and so it is: Mary is the one who is full of grace, for she is without sin; that is, without any space from which grace has been excluded.

Mary is 'immaculate' because she is sanctified for the sake of the Son who is to be born of her, who existed as God eternally before her own birth, and without whom no one born after Adam could

136

escape the presence of sin. God knows that her Son will pay the price of this perfect innocence upon the Cross. When she reaches the age when she might consent to his conception within her womb, her freedom to do so must not be impeded by any reluctance stemming from moral weakness.

Now nothing in her resists the will of God. She is free to oppose it, of course, but why should she? She knows or senses that it is in the will of the creator that the interests of the creature are best defended. Yet the future of the world hangs on her reply to the Angel, for the decision is not mechanical: it is an act she must make her own, a step she must take, which no one can dictate or do for her. Eve was just as free to reject the temptation of the Serpent, yet chose not to do so.

'The Lord is with thee.' In a sense the Angel is the Lord's presence to her, announcing in these words his arrival and what it means. In another sense she is the one with whom the Lord is *always* present. This second meaning is important, for if we lose the Lord, or a sense of his presence, we may find it again by going to Mary.

The Rosary is also the story of the Christian soul, and thus Mary's encounter with the Angel Gabriel may be taken to represent our own encounter with our angelic Guardian. We are thereby approaching that level of our being which Mary represents. We hear the voice of the Angel who is continually in the presence of God, we feel the touch of divine love, the necessary word of guidance.

In this meeting with the Angel the purpose of our life is revealed. Our mission is assigned to us, if we will accept it. How will we answer?

Each time we pray this Mystery we are trying to make it our own, to pour ourselves (as it were) into the mold of Mary, or to reach that place in ourselves where the Lord's will is to be done.

Mary replies, 'Let it be done (*fiat*) to me according to thy word.' Her *fiat* echoes God's *fiat lux* ('Let there be light') in the very beginning of creation, and her Son's *fiat* ('Not my will but thine be done') in the Garden of Gethsemane (Luke 22:42). She becomes in that moment of acceptance the Mother of the Son who is God.

The Visitation
[to love others]

The spiritual, inner encounter with God, and the conception of the divine life within the soul and body of Mary, immediately leads to a human encounter. It impels Mary to an act of charity, sending her across the hills to visit her elderly cousin Elizabeth, to share her joy and support her in a difficult pregnancy.

We imagine she would not have been allowed to go across country all alone, without companions, but it seems unlikely Joseph was with her, or that he yet knew of Mary's own pregnancy. The Bible tells us that she stayed for about three months. Since the Angel had come to her in Elizabeth's sixth month of pregnancy, this means she stayed with Elizabeth until the birth of the Baptist.

We, too, to the extent we are able to receive the grace God offers, find the motivation to turn away from ourselves towards another's need. This is part of the mission that is entrusted to us, just as it is part of Mary's mission to go to Elizabeth.

'Blessed art thou among women, and blessed is the fruit of thy womb.' Elizabeth's greeting becomes as much a part of the prayer we associate with Mary as that of the Angel. The two blend into each other, for behind both is the inspiration of the Holy Spirit which is the voice of prayer itself.

Once the soul has met God in the Angel, she can meet God everywhere, whether at home or at the end of a long journey, in the self or in others. Mary's encounter is now with the mother of a prophet, and with the prophet John himself, hidden but dancing in the womb before Mary, like King David before the tabernacle of the Lord. His motion, perhaps no more than a kick, is interpreted by Elizabeth with prophetic insight, and emphasizes the physicality of the Incarnation.

These are real babies, real wombs, real mothers. The events picked out by the Gospel writers are selected and stylized, almost hieratic or emblematic, to emphasize the meanings now known to be present in them.

We must place ourselves not only in the position of Mary, but in the position of Elizabeth, greeting Mary with joy, and praising the mystery accomplished in her. But it is a mystery in which Elizabeth has a part. The Holy Spirit who inspired her is also the Spirit of that love which unites her with her cousin and with us, so that in this Spirit we are all Mary, all Elizabeth, all Zechariah, all Joseph.

The Nativity
[to be poor in spirit]

Each set of five mysteries can be read from the center out. At the heart of the Joyful mysteries is this one, the mystery of the Nativity or Birth of Christ, or Christmas, while at the heart of the Luminous is the Prophecy of the Kingdom, at the heart of the Sorrowful is his Crowning with Thorns, and at the heart of the Glorious is the Descent of the Holy Spirit upon the Apostles (the Nativity of the Church). Each of these central mysteries in a sequence of five concerns kingship, for the Nativity is the birth of the true King albeit in obscurity, the Crowning with Thorns is a real coronation although it appears to be a form of humiliation, and at Pentecost the flames of fire come to rest on the heads of the Apostles. The entire series ends with the Coronation of the Virgin. After all, God is the King of Israel: the fulfilment of the Covenant is the coming of the Kingdom and the sharing of his royalty with the People of God ('You are a royal priesthood...').

But first and foremost, the Nativity is simply a birth, which is the bringing forth of the secret that Mary has cherished within her for nine months—the face that God has fashioned for himself in the womb of the world. This is nothing less than a re-making of the world, for the world as it existed before was perishing, falling into nothingness, whereas now it is united through this tiny child with the divine life of the Trinity.

Into relation with this child all people and things are being drawn, and in this relationship they will pass through death into a new existence. The seed of this life began to grow in the earth's soil at the Annunciation, but now it shows itself above ground, at Epiphany it will be acknowledged by the Wise, and on the Cross it will spread its branches over the earth.

In the image of Madonna and Child is represented the drama of the human personality, coming to birth in the meeting of two gazes and of two smiles, the mother's smile kindling the child's, the child's spontaneous smile evoking this sign of love from the enfolding cosmos.

The Mother here is the purely human, the Child is God. It is Joseph's mission to protect and raise this Child, which means first of all to shelter the Mother who is the Child's first home. Icons of the Nativity show him weary, perhaps doubting his fitness for the task, puzzling over God's plan. He is appointed to represent the heavenly Father and become an Icon of the Invisible.

The Presentation in the Temple
[to be pure and obedient]

The mysteries represented in the Rosary as 'Joyful' partly concern the continuity of the Old in the New Testament. The mystery of the Presentation shows the submission of Joseph and Mary to the Law and the Temple traditions, and it shows the recognition by Simeon and Anna of Israel's Messiah.

This is also a mystery about old age, when the hopes of our youth seem to been in vain and all the promises we made ourselves are left unfulfilled. We may easily be tempted to despair or bitterness. But God can transform everything, as every moment, if we remain faithful, or if (having despaired) we turn back to him.

An old man and an old woman, no doubt tolerated by the Temple authorities but hardly respected—perhaps on occasion mocked—faithful to the inspiration they have been given and empowered by the Spirit, see the significance of this one child among a thousand others.

Anna reads the destiny of the Mother in the face of the Child, for a sword is coming that will pierce her soul. It is the sword of Roman power, the power to kill the Son when he is betrayed by his friends. At a deeper level it is the burning sword of the Angel who guards the way back to the Garden in Eden—which is that place where all men are united in one Man. The return to unity, to inner peace, lies through the Cross of separation and desolation, in which every form of disunity and alienation is gathered together in one human existence.

These ten prayers also concern the mystery of purity, for the act of childbearing is sacred and the mother exists for a time outside the formalities of religion. Now she brings the fruit of her womb to become a part of the wider community, and in this case she brings to the Temple the source of all purity and all sanctification.

There is no stain of sin, no damage to the human will, either of Mother or of Son. They come to the Temple because we perform religious rituals primarily to give glory to God for his own sake—not to benefit ourselves.

Simeon and Anna would not have recognized Jesus unless they had maintained great purity in their heart, which is the organ of interior sight. If their imagination had been distracted by images of worldly pleasure or the passions of anger and jealousy, the light that shone from the Child would not have been evident to them. Like recognizes like, and the coming of the dawn to Israel brings peace to the watchman.

The Finding in the Temple
[*to search for God everywhere*]

This mystery looks forward to the public ministry of the Lord's teaching years, between his Baptism in the Jordan and his Passion. Here in his childhood (and even in adulthood he does not cease to be a child) he is already engaged in dialog with the teachers of Israel, and even his questions express a wisdom greater than that of Solomon.

The mystery also represents the twelve years up to that point, years in which he grew in the home of Joseph and Mary, and also in awareness of his mission to the People of Israel. It is the mystery of his obedience to Joseph and Mary, and therefore of his humility. It is the mystery of his hiddenness, even from the parents who know the secret of his conception, and therefore of the 'secret' teaching which, though manifest, is only revealed and understood to those who 'have ears to hear', at the right time and place.

Christ always stands in the Temple, in the Church, asking questions and answering them. His presence is always a challenge to the masters of the Law and Doctrine, for he stands among them as the truth embodied completely in a living person, not as a system of propositions or a book.

This is also the mystery of *conversation with the Word*: the Word of God speaking by means of words in a human language with his creatures. Here is an image of the Trinity reproduced in the second Person: his human mind forming an idea, the idea embodied in a word, and the word sent forth on his breath, uniting him in exchange with those who receive and understand.

It is the mystery of losing and finding, of losing perhaps *in order* to find, for when they found him it was to understand him better than before—and at the same time less than before, because they had been led deeper into the mystery of his mission.

We search for Jesus—that is, for God in findable form—and we search for him in the three days when he is absent from us (in the Tomb) or when we are absent from him (looking in the wrong place). We will find him, but he may be surprised that we did not find him earlier.

2. MYSTERIES OF LIGHT: REVEALING THE KINGDOM TO MERE CHILDREN

The soul is filled with light, the light of the world,
unrecognized by so many yet present everywhere
in truth, goodness, and beauty.

The Baptism in the Jordan
[*to be faithful to the promises of our baptism*]

'Hail Mary, full of grace, the Lord is with thee.' Up to now Jesus has lived with his mother, but now the Lord is beginning his ministry. He is leaving the obscurity of his hidden life with Mary to reveal the light of the kingdom. His baptism at John's hands marks the transition. When he steps into the waters of the river that runs through Israel, the earthly waters are mingled with the 'spring of water welling up to eternal life' (John 4:14), flowing from the heart of Jesus. Earthly waters become Living Waters: this is the mystical beginning of sacramental Baptism.

The descent of the Holy Spirit like a dove upon Jesus, as he stands in the waters and hears the voice of the Father, is the most extraordinary image of the Trinity in action, creating and re-creating the world. In the very first verses of Genesis the Spirit of God hovers over the waters as the world is created by the sound of God's voice.

God's first words are *Fiat lux* ('Let there be light'). That was the original 'luminous mystery'.

The Spirit is the breath of God, the Son is his Word. In the Son all things are made, in heaven and on earth and under the earth. The Son is the true Light that shines from the darkness of the Father. He is the Father's *Fiat*.

The solid earth is made between the upper and lower waters, after they are separated on the second day, and after the lower waters are gathered together on the third. Standing in the Jordan, Jesus stands in the midst of the lower waters, like a new-made continent, or like a new Ark in which good creatures may be kept safe from the Flood.

Like Moses walking into the Red Sea, like Joshua crossing the Jordan, Jesus leads his people through these waters into freedom and the Land of Promise. First, he must spend 40 days (as the Israelites spent 40 years) in the wilderness, tempted but not failing, as they were tempted and failed so many times.

The Spirit sends him into the desert places as God sent the fallen Adam out of the Garden into a wilderness, saying, 'In the sweat of your face you shall eat bread till you return to the ground, for out of it you were taken; you are dust, and to dust you shall return.' The Second Adam must have remembered these words as he yearned for bread, only too conscious of the mortality he had put on with his human nature. But he refuses to turn stones into bread for himself, for that is not his Father's will, and he will obey no one else.

The three temptations represent all possible temptations (physical, psychological, spiritual), and Jesus's victory over them creates in human nature the possibility of the three Vows (poverty, chastity, obedience). Thus he turns the wilderness of human nature back into a Garden, and the wild beasts and angels come and minister to him, as they did for Adam in his innocence.

The Wedding at Cana
[*to trust in Mary*]

His mission having begun with his return from the wilderness, now we begin to see signs that testify to Jesus's authority and manifest his nature. This one is the first of seven miracles recorded by the Evangelist John (corresponding perhaps to the seven days of creation and the seven 'I am' sayings), which include also three miracles of healing, one of the multiplication of bread, one of walking on water, and one of raising of the dead. In the Rosary, this one may be taken to stand in for all the other miracles recorded of Christ in Scripture.

This first miracle is precipitated by Mary, the Mother of Jesus. Noticing the lack of wine at the wedding, she prompts him to do something. Why should she do that, unless she knew he could perform miracles? Why would she persist in her confidence that he would act, even after he seemingly rebuffs her request, unless she knew him almost better than he knew himself, and was intimately aware of God's will for him? Mary was always filled with the Holy Spirit, almost an 'incarnation' of the Spirit, and just as the Spirit led Jesus from the Jordan into the wilderness, and then back to Galilee, so now Mary leads him into the performing of miracles.

Why this miracle? Just to make a wedding party go more smoothly? How banal! But we must remember the significance of marriage in the cosmic scheme of things, and in the parables of Jesus. A wedding is a symbol of the Kingdom, and of the final reconciliation of all things in Christ—the union of divine nature with human, of heaven with earth. On one level the miracle is simply a hidden act of kindness to the bride and groom, itself not without significance. On another, it is a manifestation (at least to the disciples) of the reality that is to be preached to the people: the coming of the Kingdom of God among them.

Jesus has recently transformed the natural waters of the earth into the waters of Baptism. Now he changes six jars of water into the finest wine to show his power over the elements themselves. He had refused to exercise that power to assuage his hunger by turning stones to bread, but now at the prompting of his mother he turns water into wine for someone's else's sake. It is a blessing on the wedding itself, indicating that when Jesus is present in a marriage it becomes a sacrament, partaking of the communion he offers to all men in the Church. It points forward to the Last Supper, the 'wedding feast of the Lamb', and to the Cross, which seals the new Covenant in his blood.

The Proclamation of the Kingdom
[for our hearts to be fully converted]

The Greek word *kerygma* means the preaching or proclamation of the 'good news', and this mystery refers to the moment when Jesus read aloud in the synagogue the scroll of Isaiah, proclaiming it fulfilled:

> 'The Spirit of the Lord is upon me, because he has anointed me to preach good news to the poor. He has sent me to proclaim release to the captives, and recovering of sight to the blind, to set at liberty those who are oppressed, to proclaim the acceptable year of the Lord' (Luke 4:16-21; cf. Is. 61:1-2).

The immediate reaction of the people is admiration, but it quickly turns to anger, for he tells them he can perform no miracles there. They try to throw him off a hilltop, but he walks through the crowd and disappears. He does not run and hide, or dodge and weave, but 'passes through the midst of them'. How is that possible, through a crowd that wants to kill him? Perhaps it is thanks to a miracle (invisibility, or intangibility), but however it happens we are reminded that nothing and no one can harm us unless God permits it.

This Mystery also recalls the Sermon on the Mount (e.g. Matt. 5:1–20), where he teaches the spirituality of the Kingdom—his equivalent of the Ten Commandments. The Beatitudes are a composite portrait of his true followers: the poor in spirit, those who mourn, the meek, those who hunger and thirst for righteousness, the merciful, the pure in heart, the peacemakers, those who are persecuted. In Luke 9 it is linked to the sending of the Twelve, the feeding of the Five Thousand, and Peter's inspired recognition of him as the anointed Christ of God.

The Transfiguration
[to love meditation and prayer]

Before the week of his Passion, which involved his final confrontation with the powers of evil, Jesus takes his three closest disciples up into the mountain to pray. Luke tells us this was about eight days (Mark says it was six) after his prophecy of the Kingdom: 'But I tell you truly, there are some standing here who will not taste death before they see the kingdom of God' (9:27–8). Thus in one way, the Transfiguration is a glimpse of that Kingdom, which the disciple John was to see more fully when he was an old man, in the visions narrated in the Book of Revelation.

Jesus takes his disciples with him to pray. He is teaching them to pray, leading them in prayer, showing them what prayer means. His face is altered and his clothing becomes dazzling white as he talks to Moses and Elijah about his coming 'exodus' (Luke 9:31). In Jerusalem he will lead the people of the Covenant out of the Egypt of sin, across the desert of death, and into the Promised Land. Prayer means talking on familiar terms with the greatest prophets, who are still alive with God. And though it involves going higher up in the spiritual dimension—up the mountain not down in the valley—it does not mean leaving the body behind, for the body is transfigured.

No one saw where Moses was buried, and Elijah was taken up bodily to heaven in a chariot of fire. The human body is an essential part of the highest prayer, for the body belongs to the whole person who is transfigured in God. The disciples are heavy with sleep but remain awake. They are not fully conscious, for their bodies still hold them back. They themselves are not yet transfigured; they are merely witnesses.

Peter's suggestion that they make booths for Jesus, Moses, and Elijah is connected with the Jewish Feast of Booths or Tabernacles (*Sukkot*), when the people would journey on pilgrimage to Jerusalem, and for six days whole families would eat meals together, entertain guests, and sleep in their booths. Here the Kingdom proclaimed by Jesus is being identified as the goal of the Jewish pilgrimage. And just as the Glory or *shekinah* of the Lord was present with the Jews in the Tabernacle built by Moses to house the Ark, and just as the Lord spoke to Moses face-to-face in his tent (Ex. 33:7–11; 34:29–35; 35:1–19), so the Lord God is present with the disciples in the body of Jesus, and just as the voice of God was heard on Sinai speaking from the cloud, so the disciples hear the Father's voice telling them to listen to the Son.

The face of Moses shone with light after he had spoken with God. Jesus also speaks with God face-to-face in prayer, and his face and clothes shine even more brightly, for he is greater than Moses. He both speaks to God and is God, in the mystery of the Trinity, for the Son is the face God turns towards himself, and the face he turns to us.

The Eucharist
[to be devoted to Jesus in the Blessed Sacrament]

Immediately before Christ entered into his Passion there was the Last Supper, at which he instituted the Eucharist along with the Episcopate. Thus the last of the first ten Mysteries, referring to the Eucharist, immediately precedes the first of the last ten Mysteries, which is the Agony in the Garden leading to the arrest and trial of the Son of God.

All the Luminous Mysteries are enfolded in the gift of the Eucharist. Baptism begins our initiation into the royal priesthood of Christ; the Eucharist is its completion.

'Eucharist' means thanksgiving. The essence of divine and eternal life is a receiving of existence or identity and a giving of thanks to God, which is a giving of glory and praise to the maker and source of everything we have received and that can be received. This eternal life is a participation in the love of the Holy Trinity which is the archetype of all sacrifice and of every marriage. The Eucharist is the wedding feast of the Lamb.

It is a Mystery of Light because it is the full communication of truth, the Truth who is a Person, the Word of the Father, 'the true light that enlightens every man' (John 1:9), the light that the darkness has not overcome.

In the Eucharist is the real presence of our Lord, the presence that nourishes prayer, the presence that makes the Church. Through the consecration and offering by the priest, the appearances of bread and wine become expressive of a new divine intention. Christ no longer intends to give us a mere symbol of himself—which bread and wine always are—but his very self in reality. By making this intention apply to a specific piece of bread, a specific cup of wine, he changes the reality while leaving the atoms and molecules unaltered.

The Eucharist is the Holy Grail, the cup of mercy and healing and immortality, containing the essence of all sweetness, the 'one great thing to love on earth', the source of romance, glory, honor, and fidelity (Tolkien, Letter 43), the fruit of the Tree of Life.

3. SORROWFUL MYSTERIES:
THE PASSION OF THE DIVINE BRIDEGROOM

*The soul suffers with Christ the purgation of all
that opposes the light, a darkness that must be
conquered from within.*

The Agony in the Garden
[*to repent of our sins*]

The saving Passion of our Lord begins in the garden of Gethsemane, to reverse the effect of a Fall that took place in the garden of Eden (and it will bear fruit in a third garden—see the first of the Glorious Mysteries). The Lord waters the ground with his sweat and blood, so that the seed he plants in the earth, in the sleeping disciples, will grow in the Church.

He prays to his Father that the 'cup' will pass him by, but submits to his Father's will. Does he pray this as the second Person of the Trinity or as a human being? As God, his will is the same as that of his Father. As man, he has a human will too, for this pertains to his nature as man. The two are not in conflict, for although he has to make the act of submission, the resistance comes not from his human side but from the natural abhorrence that his human will has to master. The unity of the two wills, human and divine, is not a unity of identity—the human nature is not the divine nature—but a unity brought about by love.

The suffering which his body and soul fear, this cup which he dreads, is the result of the Fall—of the separation that has opened up between God and creation. Man's will has opened the wound; the will of Jesus must close it.

The cup is once more the Grail, the vessel which contains the 'blood' or life of Christ separated from his body. That blood is the bearer of the Holy Spirit. It is the sacramental substance that communicates divine grace to every part of the extended body of Christ which is the Church.

The three Apostles Peter, James, and John, who barely kept awake on the Mount of Transfiguration, now cannot stay awake and pray, as he asks. He prays the same prayer three times: once for each of them, for it is on their behalf, as representing all his followers, that he struggles. They sleep the sleep of the flesh (as Lancelot slept in the presence of the Grail). They cannot concentrate, cannot attend.

'Pray that you may be spared the test.' But they did not, and so the test will come. They have not understood the essence of what is now to transpire on the Cross. They were not awake to see the Lord accept the cup on their behalf, or be strengthened by the Angel.

The Scourging at the Pillar
[*to mortify our senses*]

The cords of the Roman soldiers strip away the skin and drown him in agony. The beauty that God made for him, the beauty of his body, is marred and torn. Every stroke corresponds to some just punishment for something we have done, of which he is innocent. He resents nothing but feels everything.

The pillar to which he is tied represents the center of the universe, the axis around which it turns, the Tree of the Knowledge of Good and Evil, the sacred mountain, Mount Zion. For everywhere the Son of Man is, that is the center of the universe.

The soldiers may be doing their duty, following orders, or they may be enjoying the job a little too much. Hardened by their work, they are hardened against human feeling, and their consciences do not feel the blows from each stroke of the lash, which falls on them though they do not realize it.

The Crowning with Thorns
[*to love humiliation*]

The middle Mystery of this series of five is the one that corresponds to the Nativity, the Proclamation of the Kingdom, and Pentecost in the other series.

Jesus, the one who sees all, is blindfolded by men and made into a joke for their amusement, but this is only the reverse side of the mystery of his glorification. It is what glory looks like when it is seen in the distorting mirror of sin.

He is challenged by the soldiers to prophecy—*who hit you then?* He knows but does not say, for he is ready to bury their wickedness in his forgiveness, and they will know that forgiveness, burning with shame when the knowledge comes.

The crowning is a real coronation, for in the acceptance of this mockery for love of us he makes it golden, just as his wounds will shine after the Resurrection.

He needs nothing to be king of the universe, only to be doing his Father's will.

The Carrying of the Cross
[to be patient under trials]

He tells us we must each carry our Cross, but that the burden will be light. For him it is not light at all, since he feels the weight of it in order that we might be comforted by his presence with us when we carry our own.

If it seems heavy to us, then we are not letting him bear it in us, as he has done already. We think perhaps that we will spare him further pain, but really we are refusing to walk with him, refusing his companionship. Such is his love for us that the best way for us to console and assist him is to let him comfort us.

All this is easy to say, and less easy to do. When the burden comes, it seems impossible to bear, and so Jesus himself fell three times under it. In the end Jesus had to be helped by another. No one is really alone.

What makes it worse is that the burden is something that will be our instrument of torture. But for Jesus it is his throne and the instrument of salvation. It is the doorway to heaven and the veil of the Father. It is his Mother and his Brothers.

The Crucifixion
[to be forgiven our sins]

Nailed to the Cross are our sins. All that we have done wrong, all that we might do wrong, is stabbed into the wood and fixed there. The interior of sin is revealed for those who can bear to look. Jesus has made himself a mirror. This is what we are doing to ourselves by choosing what seems pleasant over the order of the universe that we know in our heart.

There are two thieves crucified on either side, one repenting and one rejecting. It is the scene of the Last Judgement, when men will welcome or reject the presence of God in their own hearts. Below are standing Mary and John, each entrusted to the other by the Word of God. John represents all the disciples, even those temporarily absent through fear and confusion. Mary is giving birth to the Church.

The stream of blood and water that flows out from the dead Christ is akin to the blood mingled with water that flows out from under the altar of the Temple when the sacrifices are made. The body of Jesus is the new Temple, his Sacred Heart the new altar. The water and blood, become Eucharist for us, are the spring that gives eternal life, a river of grace that flows through the seven sacraments.

That river of grace is caught, in the visionary world, by an angel, in a golden cup, the Holy Grail. This sacred Vessel is the Church, the Blessed Virgin standing beneath the Cross, the Ark. The cup signifies that nothing is lost. The river of the sacraments flows between heaven and earth, between the soul and the body of Christ separated from each other by death, a separation that makes room for us to become the extended body of Christ, in whom his Spirit lives.

4. GLORIOUS MYSTERIES: THE RETURN TO GOD

*The soul's illumination now spills over into the body
to transform it into a spiritual body over which
death has no power.*

The Resurrection
[for Faith in Christ]

If all human beings are in Adam, and Adam is in Christ, then all of us have died and all been resurrected by the power of God. But the lives of human beings are spread out in time and space, so that when we look at Christ's life on earth we are looking both into the past and into the future. Our resurrection has happened in Christ, but not yet in us.

Faith is the beginning of our resurrection. It is the first fruit of the Tree of Life, which God gives us so that we might live forever. It is an act of will, a decision to trust in the Word of God, but we could not make it without the help of God's grace in us. That is why theologians call faith an 'infused' theological virtue. This means that it is a divine-human act, an act of cooperation with God, and as such it is founded on the union of divine and human natures in Christ.

The disciples do not at first recognize Jesus, because the resurrected body is (in a sense) not the same as the one that died. For
'there are celestial bodies and there are terrestrial bodies; but the
glory of the celestial is one, and the glory of the terrestrial is
another. . . . It is sown a physical body, it is raised a spiritual body' (1
Cor. 15:40, 44). It is still a body, not a spirit, and it is still the body of
Christ, and bears his wounds, but it is changed, and its appearance
is no longer at the mercy of our earthly sight but—like all that is
spiritual—invisible unless deliberately revealed.

The Ascension
[for Hope, and the desire for heaven]

Hope measures the distance between what we grasp obscurely in
faith and what we possess securely, when in the beatific vision love
becomes our eternal life. Paul expresses this hope when he says that
God has 'raised us up with him, and made us sit with him in the
heavenly places in Christ Jesus' (Eph. 2:6), as though we had
already ascended simply by receiving him in the sacraments.

He ascends by his own power, not by a chariot as Elijah ascended,
and he goes to 'where he was before' (John 6:63). For as Jesus told
Nicodemus, 'no one has ascended into heaven but he who
descended from heaven, the Son of man' (John 3:13). He is the way,
and he is also the destination. Where he was before is with God in
the mystery of the Trinity.

In his divine nature he had never left the Father's side, but he
ascends now in his human body. Through that body, which is connected to all human life and its cosmic environment, the whole
world is drawn into resurrection. 'Then I saw a new heaven and a
new earth; for the first heaven and the first earth had passed away,
and the sea was no more' (Rev. 21:1). So 'God himself will be with
them; he will wipe away every tear from their eyes, and death shall
be no more, neither shall there be mourning nor crying nor pain
any more, for the former things have passed away' (Rev. 21:3–4).

Pentecost
[for Love, and the Gifts of the Holy Spirit]

The opposite of Babel—tongues divided, but tongues like fire, uniting the new community in a single witness, and speaking to all who would listen, in every language. Peter leads the apostles in speaking of Jesus, and the signs to come, and the possibility of salvation for those who call on the Lord's name. His words are like fire, and about 3000 are baptized that day.

Each set of mysteries represents a turn of the spiral, so that just as the first and second Glorious Mysteries correspond to the first and second Sorrowful (the rising from death to the acceptance of death in Gethsemane, and the flagellation of the flesh to its glorification in the Ascension), and the others may be read in this way too, so the third Mystery, the crowning of the Church with tongues of flame, corresponds to the Crowning with Thorns, and the eloquence of the disciples at Pentecost to the silence of Jesus before his accusers.

The Holy Spirit descends on the Apostles from heaven, seven weeks after Easter Sunday and ten days after Ascension Thursday. This Christian festival corresponds to the Jewish festival of Shavuot, fifty days after the Exodus, when God gave Moses the Ten Command-ments. Now the law that is given to man is the Holy Spirit of love.

The Spirit is from the Father and from the Son. Jesus has breathed it forth and returned it to the Father on the Cross (John 19:30), and received it back in the Resurrection, only to breathe it upon them when he conveys the power to forgive sins (John 20:22). Now it comes from heaven, where he is with the Father. As in the Nativity, what was hidden in Mary has now come to the view of the whole world, and the many nations bear witness to the new light (the wise men, the crowds).

The Assumption
[for devotion to Mary and the grace of a good death]

Mary follows Jesus, who takes her up to be with him in heaven, above all the angels, when the time comes for her to die. Her destiny is that of the archetypal Christian soul, and her escape from the lim-itations of time and death represents the final victory of Christ, who made the Cross a bridge to heaven and the tomb a portal to life.

For us who must die, there is a period of waiting in the separation of body and soul, until the general resurrection when all matter will be transformed. But for Mary there can be no period when her body is touched by corruption, for all possibility of stain has been removed by the grace that flows down from the Cross into time and space. By the power of the Father, she is the entire source of the human nature of the Son, and so her body cannot be separated from his. The human nature he assumes and redeems in his Person is present first in her.

Our love for Mary is one with our love for beauty and goodness, of interior peace and measured wisdom, of flowers and mountains and green valleys and the deep ocean, of stars and the happiest moments of human life, the kindness of friends and the love of family and the bliss of lovers. Nothing of our earthly life will be lost, because Mary treasures all things in her immaculate heart.

The Coronation
[for the triumph of the Immaculate Heart of Mary]

God became man so that man could become God, according to the Church Fathers. 'Beloved, we are God's children now; it does not yet appear what we shall be, but we know that when he appears we shall be like him, for we shall see him as he is' (1 John 3:2). The goal of our earthly existence is to become 'like him', by becoming full of grace, full of the Holy Spirit. When we look at Mary, we see the dignity in which our soul and body, our own person, is called to share.

The world is saved by Jesus Christ in Mary. Once raised to heaven she is crowned Queen, because in heaven 'to serve is to reign' (John Paul II). In her our human nature is revealed as the highest work of God's art. A human person has become the face that creation turns towards the Face of God. Being illuminated by his light she is clothed with the sun, and the angels themselves form the diamonds in her crown. The moon on which she stands is the old earth, the memories that constitute her past.

Balthasar says (in *The Threefold Garland*), that God himself 'is the crown that descends upon all that she is'. He is the eternal circuit of love into which we are drawn. Then each 'will finally know who he is in reality, and consequently each will at this time be able to make of himself a fully authentic and unique gift. And this self-giving will be common to all, so that we will not only plunge eternally into God's ever newer depths, but also into the inexhaustible depths of our fellow creatures, both angels and men.'

12

THE WAY OF THE CROSS

The fourth Sorrowful Mystery of the Rosary together with the Fifth may be expanded into a series of fourteen meditations, traditionally known as the Stations or Way of the Cross. These are meditations on the Way of Jesus Christ in his Passion—his self-offering and acceptance of death for the sake of redeeming sinners, from the moment when he was condemned to death by worldly authority, until the moment when he is laid in the tomb.

Images representing these fourteen Stations are almost always placed around the walls of a Catholic church, starting near the altar on the left-hand side (if you are facing the altar), along the left-hand wall to the back or entrance of the church, then continuing along the opposite wall, to finish near the altar on the right-hand side.

During Lent, and at other times, the faithful may individually or in groups process from one Station to another, kneeling and praying for a few moments at each image: it is a kind of pilgrimage of the heart. The list of Stations is arranged in the following order to show the way they would appear in the building, and the order in which they would be followed by a pilgrim moving around the church. The reflections that follow, like those on the Rosary, are entirely personal but may help to stimulate your own thoughts and prayers.

1. Jesus condemned to death	14. Jesus is laid in the tomb
2. Jesus receives his Cross	13. Jesus is taken down from Cross
3. Jesus falls for the first time	12. Jesus dies on the Cross
4. Jesus meets his mother	11. Jesus nailed to the Cross
5. Simon helps Jesus carry Cross	10. Jesus stripped of his garments
6. Veronica wipes the face of Jesus	9. Jesus falls for the third time
7. Jesus falls for the second time	8. Jesus speaks to women of Jerusalem

1. Jesus is condemned to death

We are all condemned to death.

We are all condemned, handed over to the forces that will destroy our body. We are handed over by Adam when he accepts the fruit from Eve and rejects the word of God.

Adam and Pilate both try to put the blame on others, to 'wash their hands'. They have lost that sense of 'justice' which consists in *obedience to truth* (Pilate: 'What is truth?'). For as Adam is quick to point out, it is Eve, the Bride that has been given to him by God, who causes the divine 'word' to be disobeyed, contradicted, sacrificed. (Yet he was probably standing alongside her all the time.) Eve in her turn blames the Serpent. But together, Adam and Eve have effectively crucified the Obedience and Love that would have given them eternal life.

Pilate and the Jews are replaying the parts of Adam and Eve in the Fall, but now a new factor has entered into the story—one that will transform the outcome. The one who takes the punishment for their disobedience is God.

So we see why the Way of the Cross necessarily echoes the events in Eden's Garden. God had placed a Tree in the center—or is it two trees, the tree of the knowledge of good and evil, and the tree of life, both in the same central place? Now in the barren garden of Golgotha, the Cross is the tree of knowledge, and the One who carries it, in order to be carried by it, is himself the tree of life.

Pilate seems to recognize Jesus as the King of the Jews, the embodiment of truth. He 'finds no crime in him'. Yet Pilate, with one part of himself suspecting who Jesus is (he will write *The King of the Jews* upon the Cross), hands him over to be crucified nevertheless.

The People ask for the release of Bar-abbas: literally, the 'Son of the Father'. It is because they think Jesus is falsely claiming to be the Son of the heavenly King that they demand he be put to death and a criminal released in his stead.

Later Jesus will ask his Father to forgive the People, for they do not know what they are doing. He suggests to Pilate that he has little freedom in the matter, for his responsibility is to maintain order, and the crowd has turned nasty. (Yet even so, could not Pilate have risen above his situation and defended to the death a man whom he knew to be falsely accused? It may be part of the gentleness of Jesus that he does not demand or expect it of him.) The one who hands Jesus over to Pilate, namely Judas, 'has the greater sin'. But the responsibility goes back further than Judas: it goes back to Adam. It is Adam's guilt that must be expiated here—and *mine*, for I also hand him over when I sin, on some level of my being knowing that he is a King.

2. Jesus receives his Cross

Jesus took our deaths upon himself.

The Carpenter must take this dead wood, and fashion from death an image of the love that overcomes death.

Jesus embraces his Cross as Saint Francis embraced Lady Poverty. We see here the intimate relationship of the two trees in Eden. The tree of life (which is Jesus) embraces the tree of the knowledge of good and evil, which is the tree of death.

The two beams of the Cross may have been carried separately, until they were brought together at the end of the journey. For in dying we are judged: meaning that then all our acts are brought to, connected with, the vertical line of heaven.

Jesus accepts the Cross, in the sense that he remains free even in the compulsion of his 'punishment'. By *taking possession* of the Cross that is forced upon him (the Cup that he is given to drink), he does not lose his freedom but gives it a particular (universal) form. He crystallizes it.

The Cross therefore is the form of his death. The Cross is the shadow of man. It is what all men fear. It is whatever human nature fears and shrinks from. It is the darkness, the humiliation, the ignominy, the ugliness, the powerlessness, the rejection, the immobility.... He embraces this, and he does it for us. In each of us, he can do the same. When we face the shadow, he is able to embrace it and transform it. Deep within, he is there praying in us, through his Spirit: *Not my will but thine be done.*

Jesus makes the solid Cross no longer an impenetrable obstacle to us, but a gateway, a way back into Eden. In a sense, he willingly impales himself on the Angelic Fiery Sword that guards the way of return. For the way back to Paradise leads through death, through the baptism of fire that separates soul from body.

The tree of the knowledge of good and evil is the tree we know too well: the one that has brought us death, which is its only fruit. But that fruit could only be plucked through disobedience to the will of God. What if one should pluck the same fruit in *obedience*? Then the tree would be transformed into the tree of life. There would only be one tree, no longer two. But Adam could not do this. It could only be done in the middle-point of history, a history of the unfolding of disobedience, 'in the fullness of time'—and by One who was capable of obedience.

By embracing the Cross, Jesus unites himself with it, and makes the two trees into one. He gives to the tree of life, which is his own body, the form of the tree of death. He gives to the world, on which he is to be crucified, the *form of the Church*.

3. Jesus falls for the first time

The man who falls has been tempted,
but never fell. Now the Fall begins in him.
The Tempter failed to make him turn stones
into bread; now he seeks his revenge.

He falls to his knees. Symbolically, I suppose, there are three falls because of the three parts of human nature—legs, torso, and head (body, soul, and spirit). The first fall represents the acceptance of the Cross by Christ in his animal or mobile nature. Or each fall represents the effects of sins against goodness, beauty, or truth.

But Jesus does not fall in order to be *symbolic*. He falls because his legs give way. He can no longer walk under the weight. Yet because he is God, everything he does and everything that happens to him is a revelation.

As Caryll Houselander says, he is 'living through the experience of *ordinary* men', and this first fall is the fall of shame, of disillusionment, of frustration, that we all suffer at the beginning of adulthood. Those who set out in confidence are soon enough humbled. The first effect of sin is to deprive us of the power to carry on, to deprive us of the freedom to move, to bring us down into the dust from which we came.

Mark the Ascetic writes that 'It is impossible to forgive someone else's offences whole-heartedly without true knowledge; for this knowledge shows to every man that what befalls him belongs to himself.' In our case, the things that befall us, which make us suffer, *belong to ourselves* because we have deserved all this and more. Or we can consider that what befalls us is a gift because it enables us to share in the life and work of our Lord. In the case of Jesus, these things belong to him simply because he has been given them by his Father, and he has accepted them for the sake of the mission his Father gives, which is one of mercy to us.

As the body of Jesus begins to accept the weight of the Cross, as sin begins to do its work in him, we begin to realize that our own weakness and pain is the way we can glimpse—and perhaps share—the experience of Jesus. Whatever we suffer is only a fragment, an aspect, a drop, of the full human experience of the effects of sin.

Only Jesus can experience those effects in their fullness. Our very sins prevent us from being fully conscious of anything. How often, when faced by natural beauty, have we felt that we are not capable of even taking it in? The same applies to evil. Jesus is pure enough to see and feel the reality that we cannot face, that we have no place in ourselves to receive. He is the one who is personally offended in every sin, every compromise with the truth, every betrayal of a friend, every act of adultery, every theft, every lack of attention. *Now he begins to feel the weight of this reality.*

The Cross he has started to carry is a kind of 'sacrament' of sin. In the Cross all sin, all that blocks grace, all that is counter to the Holy Spirit, all that kills love in us, is mysteriously present. He falls three times because he has defeated the Devil three times in the wilderness. Now he permits the Evil One to take his revenge.

Why is it necessary for him to suffer all this personally, consciously? It is necessary because he is the incarnation of the fullness of God and the fullness of man. The Father does not hold back anything of the divine nature that he can give to his Son; the fullness of human nature must be united with that. Not that his human experience becomes infinite: that would not be human. Rather, the human in him achieves its *maximum capacity*. 'No cry of torment can be greater than the cry of one man. Or again, *no* torment can be greater than what a single human being may suffer' (Wittgenstein).

There is no human experience that does not find an echo or a place in him. His outline encompasses all others. In his experience we find our own completed. He brings our own lives to their conclusion.

4. Jesus meets his Mother

Silence speaks louder than words,
and the Word speaks in silence.

Perhaps, too, one may view the First 'Fall' of Christ as the descent of the Word into the world—a Fall that would reverse Adam's Fall into sin. The mystery of the Incarnation consists in the fact that God became man. And after he descended into the womb, and was born, the *first thing he saw was his Mother's face*.

Time is always a kind of cycle, in which some things change but the universal laws unfold in constancy—and around Christ all those laws are tightly wrapped, for he is the *center of time*. His track to Calvary recapitulates the stages of his life and of ours. His whole mission to save, which is the meaning of his name (Jesus = God saves), implicit even in the way he is born, is summed up in the actions of his Passion, by which he actually accomplishes that salvation.

Mary sees her Son paying the *price of the miracles* she asked him to perform, and especially the Sign he gave at Cana. 'They have no more wine.' Fallen humanity has no wine left, only water. Human couples want to marry, but they have no sacrament to bind them together as one, no grace to help them. *So Jesus must produce the wine*. His own blood will be the bond that unites them.

Her Son is about his Father's business. By accepting that fact a sword pierces her soul, for she is walking for us, with him, the road back to Eden through the Way guarded by the cherubim. Between the two of them, Mother and Son, is a great gulf—the gulf of the sins of man that neither of them have committed, but which she understands for the first time by seeing them, each and every one, displayed in him.

He gives a form to the great space of evil and sin in the world by the manner of his death, like a man forming a kind of *portrait of the darkness*. He will turn it inside-out, turn darkness to light, water into wine.

The mystery of *co-redemption*. The Mother and the Son, the Woman and the Man: each suffers for the other, the suffering of each magnifies that of the other. Her suffering as Mother fills out to the limit what had been 'lacking' in his. He wanted most of all to spare her this.

At the same time, perhaps, would there be a kind of *consolation—* if he allowed himself to feel it? She, at least, knows his dual nature and the mystery of his birth, the fact that he is the Truth and the Son of God. So her presence is a reminder of his mission, if he needed one, and a secret companionship on his chosen path. He does not need to say to her, 'My hour has come.'

What is the expression on her face? How does she greet Jesus? Does she try to encourage him to be strong, to be brave? Does she try to smile through her tears, to show that she understands? Or will she actually understand only later, when he rises from the dead?

Maybe she prays that someone will help her Son to carry the Cross.

5. Simon of Cyrene helps to carry the Cross

*After the encounter with the Mother
comes the encounter with the Stranger.*

The rest of mankind is seemingly not involved in this drama which takes place in Jerusalem on one particular morning. We go on about our lives and our business. The Roman Empire bustles about. One man's journey is interrupted, however. Simon is just a passer-by, roped in to help. He becomes a disciple.

Suddenly we realize that we are all involved, whether we know it or not. Every one of us will be asked to suffer some part of Christ's Passion. It is up to us how we react to that; with what grace (or lack of it) we shoulder the burden. Are we resentful, annoyed, at being compelled by circumstance to interrupt our plans, or change them altogether? Are we moved with compassion? Do we see the man's need and respond with generosity of spirit? Do we let the experience change our lives for ever? Do we let it *save* us?

Names in Holy Scripture are hardly coincidental. Simon's name recalls that of Simon Peter, the man to whom Christ gives a new name, 'Rock', and on whom he builds his Church. *That* Simon was inspired by the Spirit to acknowledge Jesus as the Son of God. Is this Simon similarly open to the promptings of the Spirit? Why does Scripture note the name? Is this Simon another kind of Rock?

This Simon is the Stranger, the passer-by: the very opposite of a Disciple, let alone an Apostle. Yet now he follows Christ, or perhaps he goes ahead of him, takes his place for a moment. Only Christ can go the whole way.

Simon Peter should have been there, at Christ's side, available to help. 'Let me carry the Cross for you, Lord. You should not have to do that, at least.' But Peter had fled, had ceded his place to a stranger—one with the same name, because *he is given part of the mission of Peter.*

The mission we are each given will be completed, if not by ourselves then by another. (So much the worse for us.) And it is Christ who completes all our missions, and gives us the strength to do whatever the Father asks us to do. It is *as part of Christ* that we suffer, that we strive and love and die and are reborn to eternal life. There is no person, no place, no thing that needs be closed to his life. Least of all the life of this stranger, who one day will embrace Simon Peter in heaven.

6. Veronica wipes the face of Jesus

The mystery of the Holy Face

Why did not *Mary* wipe her Son's face? Instead, another Stranger steps forward and takes the Mother's place in the drama. But whereas Simon took Peter's place because Peter was not there, Veronica takes on the maternal role of Mary who *is* there—and, as it were, with her permission, in answer to her prayers.

Simon of Cyrene and now Veronica: first the man, then the woman. The man helps Jesus to shoulder the Cross. The woman wipes the blood and sweat from his face. But the man acts because he is compelled; the woman because she has pity.

The face of God. In the old days, one might not look on it and live.

Now one looks *in order to* live. Jesus came to imprint his face upon the world. It is a woman who gives him the material: the cloth, the womb.

It is an act of compassion and love. When we act in such a way, to comfort the afflicted, we receive imprinted on our souls the image of Christ, the features of Christ. The veil of Veronica is not merely a relic, but represents her soul. It may have been the cloth she used to cover her own head, now become an Icon.

This is the beginning of sacred art, the first image not made by human hands, a pure grace received by the artist, who must nonetheless be there to receive it, holding out the cloth against all resistance, offering the substance to God, despite the jostling crowd and the hostility of the soldiers.

The first Icon is a mask of blood and sweat and spittle that reveals the mission and love of Christ. More beautiful Icons will be made later, Icons made from paint and from gold; but always their foundation will be the same: the moisture and the minerals of the earth, the dust and 'slime' of the ground from which Adam was made, now bearing the imprint of the Incarnation.

A veil without features is like the opposite of an actor's mask, the *persona* (from which we get our word 'personality'). For Christ to give it his own features is as if to say, your mission is mine, you will find yourself in me.

God reveals himself not just as God, but as Person. We were made in the image and likeness of God, and we lost that likeness through sin. Now by taking on the ugliness of sin, Jesus restores the divine likeness in us.

7. Jesus falls the second time

The weakness of God is stronger than men (1 Cor. 25).

If the first fall was the acceptance of the weight of the Cross in his animal or mobile nature, the second is its acceptance in his psychic nature, his human soul, his imagination—and the third will be its acceptance in the deepest part of his soul—his spirit or intellect. To accept the Cross in the soul is to bear it upon the heart.

The weakness of God is a function of his power, which is always the power of love. In the essence of love is to give and to receive, not to take. To *give the self* is to place oneself into the hands of another, while giving up power over him. And yet, to *give the self* requires the ultimate power over oneself, amounting to total self-mastery. For we cannot give what is not our own.

The weakness, the powerlessness of God is expressed in the weakness of Jesus, as he fails to carry the Cross for a second time (even the part that has been left to him, now that Simon is helping). That weight, that Cross, is a 'sacrament' of all sin. It is being carried by him because of sin; it weighs on him as sin. To be crushed by it is only possible because of the strength of divine love, which enables the innocent to go into the place of sinners. As if a bubble of light were to force itself to the bottom of a dark ocean.

This weakness is a greater power than sin, because it is a deliberate act which takes possession of sin, in order to set the sinner free. The 'strong man' has broken into the house of the Devil.

All sin, though it begins with an act of freedom, is a renunciation of freedom. The only act which magnifies freedom is an act of virtue.

Freedom is the capacity to act for oneself, or to *be* oneself in acting, to take responsibility for one's behavior. I cannot fully be myself if I am merely a part of myself. A free act summons all that I am. Sin, on the other hand, divides me. In sin I do not adhere to the truth of my own being, or that of the world. I am not myself, in fact I lose myself. I identify with some point on the periphery, on the circumference, not with the center of the circle, which is in God.

Every time Jesus falls, he descends further from the vertical, from the axis of heaven, to embrace the horizontal, the plane of the earth. Then when he rises again, it is to take the earth with him on to the vertical axis of the Cross. But he will have to be placed there in the end by the hands of others, having been reduced to the passivity of earth.

8. Jesus speaks to the women of Jerusalem

Weep not for me. Weep for yourselves and your children. (Luke 23:28)

Is this admonition a refusal of their compassion? Is it a warning of what will befall, now that the world has rejected the Messiah? Or is it rather a revelation by him of the inner significance of the Way of the Cross? 'Do not think of me as separate from yourselves and your children. I am within you. I am showing you what you have done to yourselves.'

Are we not like the women of Jerusalem, when we follow the Stations of the Cross in our churches, trying to weep, feel pity for this great man so wrongly used? Does Jesus rebuke us here?

Pope Leo the Great said: 'Anyone who has a true devotion to the passion of our Lord must so contemplate Jesus on the Cross with the eyes of his heart that Jesus' flesh is his own.'

To weep for ourselves and our children is to see ourselves walking the Way of the Cross. It is to lose ourselves in him; to find ourselves in him. We must unite ourselves with him if his sacrifice is to be effective.

This is the turning point in our own journey, the moment between two falls. If we are following the Way of the Cross in images along the walls of a church, we start to move back towards the sanctuary. Jesus has come to the porch; he has come to the people; he has gathered the women, the mothers and their children, to himself. Those who have understood this can take, with him, the final journey.

9. Jesus falls for the third time

Like the serpent in Eden, he goes on his belly in the dust.

Now Jesus begins to resemble the serpent that was raised on the staff by Moses for the healing of Israel, the serpent made of brass, which was first melted and forged into the likeness of the thing that brought them death in the wilderness.

The sin of Adam made him resemble the serpent. The New Adam returns to Paradise in the serpent's form. He must eat the dust, he must taste the punishment of the tempter and the one who yields to temptation.

Smitten to the ground by the weight, this time the weight of all the people, of the mothers and the children, he descends lower than he has ever gone. He is flat on his face. Now it is the earth herself, not Veronica, that rises to press his face.

He is flat, horizontal. From here he must be lifted, and lifted again, until he is stretched vertically above the world.

He falls three times because we fall three times. He resisted the Devil three times in the desert, but now is the Devil's time. A strange echo of the temptations: to cast himself down from the roof of the temple, to rule the world from a great height, to eat the stones as though they were bread. . . .

Now he is on the threshold. He has fallen for the third and last time: body, soul, and spirit. Poverty, chastity, and obedience. He is ready for the wedding feast.

10. Jesus is stripped of his garments

We must be stripped of everything.

He will enter his Passion naked, as Adam and Eve left the Garden clothed. He will restore the Original Innocence, nakedness without shame. But he must do so through humiliation.

We must stand naked, not before men, but before God. We must repent. The sins we have clothed ourselves in must be taken from us by force.

The things that distract us, that separate us from the light and from God, the things that we have made and put between him and us, we must allow to be removed.

To enter the nuptial bed, a man must take off his clothes. This is the man who is the Spouse of all mankind. *They know not what they do.* Everything will look different from the other side, from eternity. What is happening is the opposite of what appears to be happening. (It often is.)

In the ancient world, athletes competed naked. Here is the supreme Athlete, and the ultimate Race.

In Eden, God clothed us before forcing us to leave. On Calvary, man strips God before forcing him to leave.

His Mother had seen him naked before—as a child. (Also John the Baptist, when Jesus came out of the Jordan.) Now all see him, as though the secrets of God were laid bare, pearls before swine. His nakedness represents the *esoteric*, the truths that all think they know but which only those truly know whose hearts are pure, for only they can 'see God'.

The soldiers had already stripped him and mocked him, covering him with purple and giving him a crown of thorns, before driving him on his way. They were showing in unconscious prophecy what is to about to be done: the God-Man is about to be given his robes of state, his crown and throne.

They strip him of his single garment before nailing to him a garment of wood. What was once a living tree planted by God is now a tree of dead wood, bringing only death. This is the garment he must assume. He must cause the life to flow within it and from it again.

11. Jesus is nailed to the Cross

They do not know it, but they are returning the fruit to the Tree.

It is said that each of our sins penetrated his body like a nail. Each suffering in the Passion was the result of particular sins committed against him.

In his divine nature, Jesus foresaw every sin we will commit. He watches us commit them, and each causes him grief in his human nature. He foresees also the prayers of the saints, and our own acts of repentance, which are not the end of our sins. He offers each of his sufferings for those sins.

Those who drove the nails into his *hands* did not know that they were placing there all the sins we commit with our hands, by grasping and holding and letting go, the sins of greed and selfishness, of aggression and violence, of making and unmaking... sins against poverty.

The nails in the *feet* are the sins of movement, of going and coming, of running away and running towards, of avoiding and hiding, of choosing the wrong path... Sins against obedience.

The *crown of thorns* is placed there by the sins of the mind and the spirit, sins of pride, sins against chastity, against purity in the imagination, against truth and wisdom, against hope.

By these nails and sufferings we penetrate him, we are attached to him. We are his Cross. The Church is his Cross. The Cross is his Bride. The Cross is those he has redeemed, to whom he is united. The Cross becomes Holy, for it is the instrument he chooses to bring about the salvation of the world and his own death; it is sanc-tified by his blood.

Love is wounded and pierced by being *attached*, as the Buddha said. Love does not come down from the Cross. We hang there, stretched between Heaven and Earth and East and West, until drained of life.

12. Jesus dies on the Cross

My God, my God, why have you forsaken me? (Mark 15:34)

Stretched in four directions, now he breathes out his Spirit in the fifth direction, and is pierced from a sixth. The 'six directions' of space can no longer separate us from the love of God. Stretched on the Cross with his Mother and Disciple below he forms a tableau, almost like a flat picture with height and breadth but no depth. Now death supplies the depth-dimension, the front and back.

It is we who are missing in this tableau, unless we dare to place ourselves with Mary and John. We stand at a distance, gazing. The Spirit breathed out from the body reaches out to us, brings us into the picture, makes us a part of it—makes us 'Church'—adds the third dimension. The Centurion's lance penetrates the body in the opposite direction to the Spirit's trajectory, but in the same dimen-sion, releasing the blood and water that make the Spirit flesh in us.

Or are we present here as the thieves crucified on his right and left? The three crosses on Calvary are three moments in time: past, present, and future. The thief who mocks is the Past: he is ourselves before the advent of Christ and devoid of grace. The thief who repents is the Future. He is ourselves touched by the grace of the Savior and freed of his sins. The Lord is the Present, the Actuality, in relation to whom all else is simply before or after, seed or fruit.

The three crosses form a kind of 'electrical circuit'. The man at the center of time takes the energies of sin from the first thief into himself. He transforms them, and transmits them to the man on the other side, taking him to Paradise.

The seven sayings or 'words' from the Cross correspond to the seven petitions of the 'Our Father', and each is carried on a single breath, bearing with it the meaning of one of the seven sacraments of the Church that is being formed out of the Passion. The cry of dereliction, which he takes from the Psalm, refers to the heart of his mission as High Priest and mediator of the new Covenant. With it he institutes the new priesthood, the priesthood of the Shepherd who will go into the uttermost darkness to retrieve his lost sheep from the Evil One. The sacrament of Holy Orders is to do with this bridge thrown down between heaven and hell, across the gulf that (in the parable of Lazarus and Dives) separates the rich man from the Bosom of Abraham.

The Son is forsaken because he is joined to those who are forsaken, separated from the Father by their sins. He fills that void with the spirit of obedience. He is like Isaac, who submits to Abraham's knife. (And in a way he suffers as Abraham suffered; being obedient, as Abraham was obedient, to the necessity laid upon him by the divine will.) The sacrifice is an act not of killing but of obedience; it is the priesthood of one who offers himself. Thus it throws open a window on the Trinity. We see the otherness of the Son from the Father, as well as the love that unites them.

13. Jesus is taken down from the Cross

He walks the Paths of the Dead.

The image we have of the Pieta, of the dead Son in his Mother's arms, or her lap, represents a sorrow we shy away from imagining. The Son's suffering is over: now the Co-redeemer is left to receive it into herself. Her soul is split in two by the Word which acts like a sword in her. She is divided in order to receive.

As at the Annunciation, she receives the Body of the Lord, but now the Soul of the Lord has been taken away from it, just as then it was given. She cannot follow. She is the ocean into which he sinks now, the peace of death his body longed for as he hung on the Cross, even as his Soul continues its journey to the land of the lost.

The gift of tears. Now the bridegroom has been taken away, and his disciples can mourn. But in one way he has left them only to consummate the marriage. The path of love takes him away from his friends, in order to enter a new domain of intimacy, the secret places where new life will be conceived.

The Paths of the Dead. In this whole world there is no death, except for those who are left behind. There is only the journey into darkness or light. Into the darkness where sin forces its reward from a reluctant God, he follows them. The reward of sin is its punishment: it is to know itself fully for what it is, a living death and torment of separation. This is the punishment that the Son has taken on himself and which he now brings to the dead. He has become their reward, their punishment. He is their flame of fire, their undying worm. He is also their teacher, perhaps their rescuer.

On the surface of death, the Mother dreams. She can do as little as one who is dead, but her weakness is the strength of God. She is the Annunciation. She assents even as her heart shrieks against death. That is the division, the cleaving of her soul. These are the labor pains of the Church.

To us, what does this man's death represent? Frustration, perhaps. The crushing of our hopes for ourselves and those we love, the bitterness of that failure, the resentment of that bitterness, the anger from that resentment, the hatred that wells up in us, the hatred of ourselves that is aimed at others. We are those to whom Christ is coming, to rescue us. That is the path of death that he now walks, following us as deep as we can go to hide from him, in order to lead us to an unthinkable, unimaginable end.

Faith may be dead. Hope may be dead. Love lives on.

14. Jesus is laid in the tomb

Out of the depths I cry to you, O Lord. (Psalm 130)

Like an arrow in its target, the Lord sinks deeper into the earth, carrying within him secretly and in disguise the poison that will destroy death.

Until now, perhaps, *passivity* (of which being dead is the extreme case) has been an imperfection, a sheer lack—of activity, of goodness, of being. But Christ has assumed that corpse-like passivity into the Trinity, where death now becomes an expression of the divine Act, a part of the Incarnation. No longer passivity, it has been transformed into disponibility, or *receptivity*: the state of being able to be used by the divine will. In Baptism we join our natures to that of Christ, our death to that of Christ, our powerlessness to his all-accomplishing will.

This darkness, the acceptance of the will of another even to the separation of body and soul, is the beginning of a great flood of graces from the Passion. The first thing it makes possible is the Blessed Virgin's *fiat*, years earlier, when she accepts to become the Mother of God. For that was no mere passive obedience, as in the acceptance of an action forced upon her by a greater power: it was a deed consciously undertaken and motivated by love; being active it could not have been passive. To make the will of another one's own is not merely to submit one's own will to that of another, but it is to become one with the other. That is how we are joined to him. Thus God is received into man.

Jesus is laid in the tomb by the man Joseph, who represents the human 'father' of Jesus. The two men shared the same name, because their missions were so similar, the one being a symbolic extension of the other. Joseph of Arimathea, according to tradition, is also the keeper of the Grail that served the Last Supper and caught the Precious Blood (there in the Upper Room, if not also on Calvary). The Cup, the Womb, the Tomb: all receptacles for the Body of Christ—in life, in death, and in his sacramental existence which is both life and death, or transcends them equally.

What goes into the tomb with Christ is everything we have lost, or which is taken away from us by time, illness, and death. Old people are more conscious than others of the things that slip away: chances that will not come again, smiles and voices that will not be heard, beautiful places now paved over. All of these things pour like an endless stream into the grave, and all of them are kept safe by Jesus, and all of them will rise with him in the morning.

> My soul waits for the Lord,
> More than watchmen for the dawn;
> Yes, more than watchmen
> long for the morning.
> Psalm 129:6

13

THE FINAL MYSTERY

The last mystery of the Rosary is the Coronation of the Blessed Virgin. The ceremony of coronation is an image derived from an aristocratic society which may be unfamiliar to us. She is not being elected President. And yet we instinctively understand it. Every little girl wants to be a Princess; every father of a little girl wants to make her one.

The yearning of human nature to be the brightest star in the firmament, to be the Beloved, the Queen of Hearts or the King of the World, measures the scope of our humanity. Deep down, our desires are for the infinite, and can be satisfied by nothing less. Deep down, we know that we are really *that* special, or that we might become so. It is this desire, this passion, that is our downfall when its energies are diverted towards the thousand goals that are not worthy of us. We are always falling short of the end we were made for. But Mary does not fall short, and her elevation from handmaid to Queen, echoing the tale of Cinderella, is a vindication of our human passions and a demonstration of that destiny. It is a destiny that we can only inherit in humility, for to become everything we must first become nothing.

Any child who discovers 'I am loved' is experiencing a coronation. Love makes us princes and princesses, kings and queens. It surrounds us with symbols of our state, anoints us with the oil of gladness, places us on high. And we know we are not worthy of it, for all of this is a sheer gift. It is not something to which we can feel we have a right, or something which we already possess potentially within ourselves. If we look within, we know we are nothing, we have nothing. Only in the eyes of others can we see ourselves as beloved.

Humility is realism. It is seeing ourselves as we are, not as worse than we are. We do not have to *pretend* to be pathetic.

All glory belongs to God. There is nowhere else for it to come from. Yet all of creation is glorious, because creation is God's act of sharing that glory with others, and making them capable of participating in it. Once again, the final mystery of the Rosary is paralleled in the Book of Revelation by the closing vision of the City of God descending like the Bride of God.

The Obstacle

There is one thing that stands in the way of all this glory, and it is sin. Charles Williams once defined sin as 'the preference of an immediately satisfying experience of things to the believed pattern of the universe'. It is a decision to do my own will in this moment, even though I know it differs from God's will (or not caring whether it does or not).

Only God can see God. It follows that we can only see God if we become God. *Blessed are the pure in heart, for they shall see God.* To have a pure heart is to have the possibility of becoming God, that is, of receiving God and being received by him. The heart is where we connect with God. Any impurity there will break the circuit, and infinity will no longer be transmitted: grace will not flow. *The unclean shall not pass over it.* We will be living only on the grace we have already received, cut off from the life of God that makes us ever-more.

Impurity in the heart is an attachment to the self. It takes many different forms, and we do not always recognize it as such. The self is not something we should be attached to, for it is God's job to love me, not mine. I can only love myself in God. In fact, I can only love *anyone* if I love them in God. To put it another way, when I love someone, I am seeing them in God, or glimpsing the way God sees them.

Once I choose the limited good, rather than the unlimited good which is God's will, even in one tiny matter, it becomes easier to commit the same sin later. From being an apparently harmless experiment, a little adventure, it becomes a habit, and then an addiction and finally a prison with no way out. I find I no longer have the power to do otherwise, for the decisions I have taken have divided me against myself and I am no longer whole. Only a person who is whole and in command of himself can make a free decision on his own behalf. Divided, we cannot even whole-heartedly *want* to become holy, or to know God.

Thank heavens, then, that God has died of our sins on the Cross, and given us a way to become who we were meant to be. In the sacrament of Confession and through the Eucharist we are given once more the gift of freedom.

These brief reflections on the final mystery of the Rosary (which is also the final mystery of the Book of Revelation) may serve to bring this book, too, to its conclusion. Between the Rosary and the Apocalypse there is a profound correspondence. Our Lady and Saint John stand together at the foot of the Cross, in the hour of glory. From John flows the Book of Revelation, from Mary the Rosary, both leading us ever deeper by a spiral path into the mysteries of the world in Christ.

Holy Queen

We return to the prayer with which the Rosary finishes. If possible it should be sung in Latin with the traditional melody. But here is the English translation.

*Hail Holy Queen, Mother of Mercy, our life, our sweetness
    and our hope.*
To you do we cry, poor banished children of Eve.
*To you do we send up our sighs, mourning and weeping in
    this valley of tears.*
*Turn then, most gracious advocate, thine eyes of mercy towards
    us, and after this our exile, show unto us the blessed fruit of
    thy womb, Jesus.*
O clement, O loving, O sweet Virgin Mary!
*Pray for us, most holy Mother of God, that we may be made
    worthy of the promises of Christ.*

Each of these sentences is worth pondering. She is our Queen, because she is the Mother and virginal spouse of our King, who is Mercy incarnate. She is our life, because without her we perish in the darkness and the cold. She is our sweetness because she makes everything taste wonderful. She is our hope because we know we can rely on her.

We cry to her because we are banished from her. Separated from our Mother by sin, we are reunited thanks to her holiness.

We send up our sighs, but these are really the sighs of the Holy Spirit: 'it is the Spirit himself bearing witness with our spirit that we are children of God, and if children, then heirs, heirs of God and fellow heirs with Christ' (Rom. 8: 16–17). We are in a valley of tears because we cannot see over the hills to the light in the sky above. We are trapped in sorrow, unless someone should lift us up.

Turn then, most gracious advocate, thine eyes of mercy towards us, and after this our exile, show unto us the blessed fruit of thy womb, Jesus.

She is our 'advocate', one who speaks on our behalf. The word is used by Jesus to refer to the Holy Spirit, who is so closely united with Mary that she is his fullest expression in the world (Saint Maximilian Kolbe calls her his 'quasi-incarnation'). Her eyes of mercy— this refers to the gaze of a true mother, in whose light the child awakens to know himself loved in the world of being.

Make us know we are loved, O Mary. Open the gates of our exile, and show us the fruitful kingdom, *O clement, O loving, O sweet Virgin Mary! Pray for us, most holy Mother of God, that we may be made worthy of the promises of Christ.*

APPENDICES

1: REVELATION AS LITURGICAL COMMENTARY

What follows is a more detailed guide than could be given earlier to the incredibly complex series of visions that make up the bulk of John's narrative.

Recent scholarship suggests that Revelation was intended to be read aloud in the Christian assembly as a commentary on the liturgy, which in its essentials has remained the same since the earliest days of the era.[1] As Austin Farrer already indicated in the middle of the last century, the pattern of the book is not one of earthly history,

> but of celestial liturgy performed by Christ and the angels: the taking and unsealing of a book, the offering of incense, the blowing of trumpets; the opening of a heavenly temple, revealing the Ark of the Covenant and a series of other portents on high; the pouring of libations from angelic bowls.[2]

These heavenly actions, he continues, 'spill over in earthly effects, and end with the total conquest of earth by heavenly grace', but the purpose is not to present a chronological history. It is rather to present a liturgy that fulfils the purpose of the Temple and brings it

---

1. Although we do not know the exact form the liturgy took in John's day, we can be sure that it began like ours with prayers and readings, went on to the Gospel and sermon, and culminated in the Eucharistic offering and Communion. Justin Martyr describes the Eucharist as preceded by extensive readings from apostles and prophets in his *First Apology* (c. 155). The *Didache* (c. 100) spoke of Christians to confessing their sins to be reconciled with their brothers before taking part in the Eucharist. (See the survey of early Christian sources in Cheslyn Jones et al, *The Study of Liturgy*, especially 170–72, 182–8.) Scott Hahn gives a detailed liturgical reading to Revelation in *The Lamb's Supper*, and more succinctly in the final chapter of his book on the history of the Covenant, *A Father Who Keeps His Promises*.

2. Austin Farrer, *The Revelation of St John the Divine*, 23.

to an end, so that 'in the world to come there is no sanctuary other than the presence of God and of the Lamb.'[3]

Farrer's book is invaluable, but to bring out this theme we may equally follow an outline given by Ian Boxall:[4]

Chap. 1:1–8. Prologue and opening. (Christ the Alpha and Omega.)

Part I. Preparation of the Church and the opening of the Lamb's scroll.

Chap. 1:9–3:22. Inaugural vision and the seven messages to the churches.
Chap. 4:1–8:1. Throne vision and the seven seals of the Lamb's scroll.
Chap. 8:2–11:19. Seven trumpets.

Part II. Unveiling of the Lamb's scroll and visions of the Church

Chap. 12:1–15:4. Seven visions.
Chap. 15:5–19:10. Seven bowl-plagues.

---

3. Ibid., 44.

4. In his book *The Revelation of St John*. Other commentaries I have found helpful include Richard Bauckham, *The Theology of the Book of Revelation* (together with his more detailed literary study, *The Climax of Prophecy*); Ian Boxall, *Revelation: Vision and Insight*; John Sweet, *Revelation*; as well as Farrer's *The Revelation of John the Divine*. I discovered Farrer's earlier *A Rebirth of Images* rather late in my own study, which would have probably been derailed by a detailed consideration of Farrer's commentary with its great wealth of insight (although it should be noted that he had revised many of his ideas by the time of the later book). As noted there are several ways of ordering the text of the Apocalypse. John Wick Bowman in *The First Christian Drama* divides it into seven main 'Acts' rather than Ian Boxall's six, by breaking after the seven bowl-plagues at 17:1 and defining the overthrow of Babylon as a separate Act, with the seventh beginning at 20:4. John Sweet has a simpler outline, breaking the text into four sets of seven: the letters to the churches, the seals of the scroll, the trumpets, and the bowls. Farrer sets out the underlying structure of the book in the form of a square set on its corner, the four sides of which refer not only to the four elements and the seasons of the year, with the astrological signs, tribes and precious stones set in order around the figure, but also the seven great calendar-feasts and, of course, the seven days of creation.

Chap. 19:11–22:11. Seven final visions of the Church.

Chap. 22:12–21. Epilogue. (Christ the Alpha and Omega.)

Part I. Preparation of the Church and the opening of the Lamb's scroll

Inaugural vision and seven messages

John is told to write to the churches about what he sees: 'what is and what is to take place hereafter' (1:19). In other words, he is to reveal to the young Christian communities the meaning and goal of history. The whole Book of Revelation is this letter to the churches, but first John presents a series of condensed messages, describing the tests and temptations that each of the seven churches undergo as they struggle to remain faithful to the sacramental life of the Church (chapters 2 and 3 of Revelation). In these messages are contained glimpses of the imagery and prophecies that will be expanded upon in the rest of the book. The function of the messages is to console the Christian community under persecution, but also to call it to repentance.

The fact that there are seven churches is, of course, no accident. The number seven represents completeness, and these communities are being taken as representative of the full spectrum of Christian experience in the world. Each of the seven churches, John tells us, is a 'golden lampstand' (one branch of the *menorah*) and each has an angel (a star) which is held in the hand of God. The seven stars are also, as Austin Farrer argued, the seven planets, which gave their name to the days of the week, representing the plenitude of time held in the hand of Christ.

Throne vision and the seven seals of the Lamb's scroll

In chapter 4 John sees a door in heaven, and through it the throne of God surrounded by thrones for twenty-four Elders (one for each hour of the day), seven torches representing the sevenfold Spirit of God, a sea of glass, and four living creatures full of eyes in the forms of lion, calf or bullock, man, and eagle, each with six wings, each praising the Trinity (cf. Ezek. 1:10; Isa. 6:2–3). As they sing their praises of God, the Elders cast down their crowns and join in the praise.

The vision is of a heavenly liturgy, an eternal act of praise and worship. John seems to be saying that liturgy, after all, is what heaven *is*. John's visions all take place in the divine Presence and within the heavenly Temple—the Temple that is the Body of Christ—and the Christian reader is invited to see this heavenly worship going on all around him in the earthly assembly.

In chapter 5, John is shown a scroll sealed with seven seals, which only 'the Lamb that had been slain', with its seven horns and seven eyes representing the seven spirits, is worthy to open. To us, a lamb with seven horns and eyes might seem a rather grotesque image, if we can visualize it at all. John is using a symbolic language in which horns represent power and eyes spiritual knowledge. (The Hebrew word for 'horn', *qrn*, is the same as that for 'shine'; so we may wish to visualize the horns of the Lamb as rays of light. You may recall the famous statue of Moses by Michaelangelo, in which the prophet is bizarrely shown with two horns because the Bible describes his face as 'shining' so brightly after talking with God that he had to wear a veil.)

Having first called the assembly to repentance, the liturgy of heaven continues with a reading of the Holy Scriptures, for as every creature in heaven and earth, under the earth and in the sea, along with the millions of angels, joins in the praise of God, the scroll is opened by the Lamb, just as the readings are interpreted for the Christian assembly by a priest representing Christ, who personally opened the Scriptures for his disciples on the road to Emmaus and in Jerusalem (Luke 24:27, 45).

In chapter 6 we see the result of the opening of the seals in a new series of visions. A white horse carries a crowned rider representing the false messiah (the true one will appear later, in chapter 19), a red horse brings War, a black horse brings Judgment, a pale green horse brings Death. After the four horsemen are released from the first four seals, the fifth seal reveals the souls of the martyrs crying out for justice from under the altar, and the sixth the ending of the cosmic order in earthquake and star-fall. (These are the *unavoidable disasters* of which Jesus speaks in the Gospels: Matthew 24, Mark 13, Luke 21.)

The opening of the seventh seal is preceded by an interlude in chapter 7, beginning with the four angels at the corners of the earth restraining the winds from the earth, sea, and trees, and with the Dawn Angel coming to seal 12,000 of the saved from each of the twelve tribes.[5] Then a multitude *beyond count* of the saved (those outside Israel?), washed white in the blood of the Lamb who has died for all, are seen to be involved in the heavenly liturgy. But when the seal is finally opened there is silence in heaven 'for about half an hour' following which trumpets are given to the 'seven angels who stand before God' (8:1–2)—the archangels or planets governing the dance of time.

According to Margaret Barker, what John's visions have been describing up to this point is largely based on the elaborate Jewish Temple rituals, transposed on to the cosmic level.[6] The half-hour silence corresponds to the vesting or ceremonial clothing of the High Priest (cf. Zech. 2:13–3:5), whose 'coming to the earth'—his emergence, in the ancient ritual, into the great hall of the Temple, surrounded in clouds of incense and surrounded by the rainbow light of the first day of creation, inaugurating the reign of God—is about to be announced by seven trumpets. This vesting ceremony also corresponds to the Catholic priest's preparation for the Eucharistic Prayer. As for entering the silence, this is like entering the eye of the whirlwind, the still center around which everything turns. There is an echo here of the seventh day of creation, the day of rest and contemplation. One series of visions has reached its climax. Something new is about to begin.

5. This Angel 'with the seal of the loving God' is identified by Saint Bonaventure, in his revision of the prophecies of Joachim of Fiore, with Saint Francis, who both possessed the seal of the stigmata and 'sealed' his followers with the *tau*-sign 'T.' According to Bonaventure, this signified a final seraphic Order of Johannine contemplation in which the meanings of Scripture (the 'fullness of truth' promised by the Holy Spirit) will be revealed. On all this see J. Ratzinger, *The Theology of History in St Bonaventure*, 33–55.

6. According to Margaret Barker in *The Hidden Tradition of the Kingdom*, 18, and her earlier book, *The Great High Priest*, the Temple rituals reflected the seven days of creation: each day, and each part of the Temple, represented a stage, with the holy of holies standing beyond both matter and time.

Seven trumpets

Each of the seven trumpets that are now sounded, beginning at Rev. 8:7 after the great silence announces a disaster that will befall the world outside the community of the saved, until the seventh, which is delayed. If we are reading this sequence as a commentary on the Christian liturgy, the seven liturgical trumpet blasts which presage the joining of heaven to earth must represent stages or aspects of the Eucharistic offering, and the 'little scroll' that John is given to eat before the sounding of the seventh his reception of Communion.

The first four trumpets mark the destruction of one third of the cosmos, grouped according to the third, fifth, and fourth days of creation respectively: earth and foliage (8:7), oceans (8:8–9), rivers and waters (8:10-11), sun, moon, and stars (8:12–13). The next two trumpets afflict those men 'who have not the seal of God' with torment and with death, but fail to arouse repentance (9:20). These six trumpets together show us the shadow side of the Offertory or Epiclesis, the fate of that part of the world which is excluded (by its refusal to repent) from the sacrifice of the Mass and the community of the Church. The plagues unleashed by the trumpets, like those released by the bowls later, echo the ten plagues described in the Book of Exodus.

An angel 'wrapped in a cloud, with a rainbow over his head', prophesying 'no more delay' (10:1–7), now gives John the little scroll to eat, sweet to taste and bitter in the stomach, recalling the scroll eaten by the prophet Ezekiel (Ez. 2:8–3:3). This contains the next set of prophecies he must deliver to the churches. If 'we are what we eat', John must now *become the book*: he must assimilate, and become identified with, God's word. If the scroll represents the Eucharist, the 'bitterness' he feels is related to the nature of the prophecies he must now divulge.

Since Jesus is the Word of God in person, the representation of the Eucharist by an edible scroll is of course quite appropriate. The possible Eucharistic symbolism here is strengthened by the fact that the angel 'with a rainbow over his head' who holds the little scroll (Rev. 10:1) is speaking with seven thunders words that John is told to seal up and *not write down*—for the holiest things should be exposed only to those fully prepared and initiated.[7] This mighty angel linking sea, land, and heaven recalls the mysterious figure evoked in the most ancient of our Eucharistic prayers: *Almighty God, we pray that your angel may take this sacrifice to your altar in heaven. Then, as we receive from this altar the sacred body and blood of your Son, let us be filled with every grace and blessing. . . .*[8]

According to Bauckham, this cosmic angel is distinguished from all the other angels in the book as the mediator of revelation to John, since the scroll contains the heart of this prophecy that the Seer is to communicate.[9] In any case, the immediate result of John's eating the little scroll is another visionary experience, in which he glimpses what will be unfolded in more detailed visions later concerning the war with the Beast. He is given a measuring rod like a scepter (Rev 11:1) and told, again like Ezekiel, to measure the Temple and those who worship there.[10]

The city will be trampled by the nations for 42 months, and the witnesses, who are also called 'olive trees' and 'lampstands' (here probably representing the prophets, in the spirit of Moses and Elijah)[11] will prophesy for 1260 days, before the Beast kills them. They will revive 3½ days later to ascend to heaven.

The eating of the little scroll and the conclusion of the trumpet section marks the mid-point of the book. From this section we have a view that enfolds both what came before and what will follow. It culminates with the blowing of the trumpet (the so-called 'last

---

7. Farrer makes the point that according to the logic of the book so far, John's reader or hearer might have expected the author to give us a series of prophecies in the seven thunderpeals akin to those of the seven seals and seven trumpets, but is relieved to find the sequence cut short by the voice from heaven swearing 'no more delay.' The divine purpose will be fulfilled in the days of the seventh trumpet, with the eating of the scroll and what follows it.

8. Or, in the words of a more literal translation: *In humble prayer we ask you, almighty God, that these gifts be borne by the hands of your holy Angel to your altar on high in the sight of your divine majesty, that all of us who receive the most holy Body and Blood of your Son through this sharing at the altar may be filled with every grace and blessing from above...*

9. R. Bauckham, *The Climax of Prophecy*, 253–7.

10. 'Measuring' in the prophetic tradition usually represents divine protection, for what is known by God will never perish.

trump'), and the announcement that 'The kingdom of the world has become the kingdom of our Lord and of his Christ, and he shall reign for ever and ever' (Rev. 11:15). This recalls the effect of the seven trumpets sounded by the people of God under Joshua at the angel's command, which flattened the walls of Jericho (Joshua 5:13–6:27). The twenty-four Elders fall on their faces before God, the heavenly Temple is opened, and the Ark of the Covenant revealed within it (all this echoes the beginning of the 'Liturgy of the Word' in Chapter 5, with the vision of the throne and the presentation of the seven-sealed scroll, although at that point the Ark was not revealed).

Part II. Unveiling of the Lamb's scroll and visions of the Church

What then follows this significant mid-point is another three-fold sequence of seven visions that echoes and elucidates the preceding three, as though to make with them the kind of symmetrical pattern known as 'concentrism', a common rhetorical device in the Hebrew Scriptures.

> 1. *Inaugural vision and seven messages*
> 2. *Throne vision and the seven seals*
> 3. *Seven trumpets*
> [—The little scroll—]
> 3. *Seven visions*
> 2. *Seven bowl-plagues*
> 1. *Seven final visions of the Church*

Read in this way, the first group of seven visions after the mid-point would refer to the immediately preceding vision-sequence of trumpets (corresponding to the preparation of the Eucharist), the seven bowls would refer to the opening of the seals (corresponding

---

11. These two witnesses recall Moses and Elijah standing on either side of Jesus at the moment of his Transfiguration in the synoptic Gospels. The 'two witnesses' go back to Zechariah (chap. 4), where the prophet is shown two olive trees on either side of a sevenfold lampstand and is told that these are 'two anointed who stand by the Lord of the whole earth.' Christians will also remember the icon of the Crucifixion, with Mary and John standing on either side as witnesses of Christ's passion. The great Roman martyrs Peter and Paul form another familiar pair.

to the preaching of the Gospel that opens the minds of the faithful), and the final seven visions would refer back even further to the messages to the churches (these corresponding to the calling and preparation of the faithful to hear the Gospel at the beginning of the Christian liturgy). But let us look at them in more detail.

Seven visions

The seven visions concern, first, a woman clothed with the sun, giving birth, threatened by the Dragon, and escaping on eagle's wings (cf. Ex. 19:4). In Chapter 13, the second vision concerns how the Dragon gives his authority to a Beast who rises from the sea, and (in the third vision) another from the earth. These latter two visions portray the mysteries of human iniquity that are assimilated and overcome in the Eucharistic sacrifice. They are the revelation of an 'Anti-Trinity': the Dragon (the anti-Father), the Beast from the sea (the Anti-Son or Antichrist whose female form is Babylon), and the Beast from the earth (the Anti-Spirit).

The fourth or central vision (in the series of seven) at the beginning of Chapter 14 shows us the Lamb and his 144,000 followers on Mount Zion, followed by three angels who proclaim the fall of the Beast and his followers. Being the central vision, it reflects the book as a whole (14:1–13). The fifth vision shows us 'one like a son of man, with a golden crown on his head, and a sharp sickle in his hand' (14:14), who reaps the harvest of the earth. The harvesting of the grapes follows in the sixth vision, and the seventh gives us the Song of Moses and of the Lamb, marking the new Exodus, sung by those who had conquered the Beast, standing beside the sea of glass (15:2–4).[12]

In all this, especially the mention of 'harvest', the Eucharistic references are plain enough.

Seven bowl-plagues

Now we come to the section that I have said refers back to the Liturgy of the Word. As it begins, 'the temple of the tent of witness

12. Thus the series of seven visions ends as it begins, with a reference to the Exodus.

in heaven was opened, and out of the temple came the seven angels with the seven plagues, robed in pure bright linen, and with golden sashes across their chests' (15:5–6). The impression of a liturgical celebration is unavoidable. The pouring of the seven bowls result in plagues and disasters that repeat those associated with the seven scrolls in the parallel passages in chapters 4 to 7, and with the first six trumpets in chapters 8 and 9: these undoubtedly represent the 'judgment' of God on sinful humanity (16:5, 7). We can connect this very easily with the Liturgy of the Word or the reading of the Scriptures, since it is in the light of these that the human soul is judged and purified.

The seventh bowl involves a triple catastrophe for the cities of men: 'The great city was split into three parts, and the cities of the nations fell, and God remembered great Babylon, to make her drain the cup of the fury of his wrath' (16:19). Thus the seventh bowl thus introduces the extended vision in chapters 17, 18, and the first part of 19 of the fate of the 'Great Whore', who is Babylon, the City of Sin, and the Beast on which she is seated. These are thrown down, in a catastrophic judgment lamented by the kings of the earth and celebrated in heaven. The culminating scene of rejoicing (19:1–10) clearly echoes the opening of the 'seven seals' section in Chapter 7, as we might by now expect.

It is worth noting that the seven bowl-plagues complete a series of three divine judgments issuing from the throne-room of God: the seals, the trumpets, and the bowls. As Richard Bauckham has pointed out,[13] in each case the seventh member of the series portrays the arrival of God's kingdom, but the three series overlap: 'the seventh seal-opening includes the seven trumpets and the seventh trumpet includes the seven bowls.' Thus each series reaches the same goal, but 'from a starting point progressively closer to the end.' This helps to explain why the three series are also of increasing severity: the seal-openings affect a quarter of the earth, the trumpets a third, while the bowls affect absolutely everything.

---

13. R. Bauckham, *The Theology of the Book of Revelation*, 40.

Seven final visions of the Church

Finally, John sees heaven opened and the Word of God riding to war to defeat the Beast and its armies. The Dragon is bound for a thousand years before being cast into the fire, the dead are judged and book of life opened, and a new heaven and a new earth revealed. The 'holy city, new Jerusalem' comes down out of heaven from God, 'prepared as a bride adorned for her husband' (Rev. 21:2), contrasting vividly with the whore Babylon described earlier. Here the poetry of John's book is at its most moving, and most consoling. 'God himself will be with them; he will wipe away every tear from their eyes, and death shall be no more, neither shall there be mourning nor crying nor pain any more, for the former things have passed away' (21:3–4).

The streets of the city are paved with gold, but it is gold that is 'transparent as glass.' In the center of the City is the 'throne of God and of the Lamb', from which flows the river of the water of life 'through the middle of the street.' At the center also, on both sides of the river, is the 'tree of life' with its twelve fruitings and its leaves for the healing of the nations (cf. Ezekiel 47:12).

References to the book of life, the City-Bride, even the sharp sword coming from the mouth of the Alpha and Omega, along with many other phrases in this section, echo directly the statements and promises of the seven messages to the churches in the first three chapters of Revelation. As mentioned, these messages in turn represent that moment in the liturgy when the congregation opens itself to recognize those faults and failings that the Spirit identifies so accurately, and prepares to hear the Gospel.

So the rhetorical symmetry of the book does seem to reflect the likely structure of the early Christian liturgy. The pattern is threefold: beginning with a rite of preparation and repentance that opens the faithful to the Word, moving on to an exposition of the Scriptures, and ending with a Communion in the Body and Blood of the Lamb, by which the Christian is finally converted into a prophet and agent of his Lord. Then the threefold pattern reverses, and we are taken back to the beginning. Read in this way, the Book of Revelation is intended to have a spiral structure that leads us up to the

Eucharist, then back at a higher level to the beginning of the liturgy. Thus an endless cycle of meditation is created, penetrating ever more profoundly into the Word of God and leading us closer to the liturgy of heaven.

Revelation as Mystagogy

The three distinct sets of visions leading up to John's eating of the small scroll may be seen as corresponding to three main parts of the Mass or Divine Liturgy leading up to the reception of the Eucharist. The same pattern is then echoed in reverse order. By putting together the appropriate passages from the first and second half of the Book we might find the basis for a spiritual commentary on the three main parts of the Mass.

Penitential Rites

From the first half of Revelation. Chap. 2:1–3.22: the seven messages to the churches. Calls to repentance, promises of salvation.

From the second half of Revelation. Chap. 19:11–22:11: the seven final visions of the Church. Enacting the final judgment of God, binding the Devil, vision of the new Jerusalem.

Liturgy of the Word

First half. Chap. 4:1–8:1: the throne vision and the first six seals of the Lamb's scroll. A call to witness, a reading from the Scroll, the sealing of the tribes.

Second half. Chap. 15:5–19.10: the seven bowl-plagues. Learning what is to come. Babylon exposed and cast down in prophecy.

Offertory, Consecration, Communion

First half. Chap. 8:2–9:21: the seventh seal, oblation at the heavenly altar, and the sounding of the first six trumpets. Destruction of 1/3 of the cosmos.

Mid-point. Chap. 10:1–11:19: the eating of the small scroll and sounding of the seventh trumpet. 'The kingdom of the world has become the kingdom of our Lord and of his Christ' (11:15).

Second half. Chap. 12:1–15:4: the woman clothed with the sun, war with the Dragon, reaping of the earth. A recapitulation of John's prophecies seen from within the Eucharist.

2: ON READING THE BIBLE

Only if we read the Bible 'with the help of the Holy Spirit, by means of whom it was written',[1] does Scripture truly come alive for us. Then it is more than just marks on a page. The diversity and variety of Scripture is accounted for by its multiplicity of human authors, many of them at odds with each other, and the weaving together of the text over many generations in different historical circumstances. But the unity of Scripture remains. It derives from its origin in 'one historical subject, the people of God, which, despite all the changes of its history, always retained its inner self-identity.'[2] If we don't believe in this historical subject—in the Chosen People or the Church—we will be unable to notice this overarching unity. This means, too, that we have to accept that the Church has a certain authority to interpret Scripture. For it is the same Spirit who unites into one beautiful whole the words of Scripture, and who unites the diverse members of a worldwide society into a Church, an organic community (indeed, a corporate person) breathing with one life.

Ultimately, God utters only one Word in his eternity. That one Word, which is the inner meaning and content of the entire Bible, is Jesus Christ. We cannot be said to have understood any passage of Scripture unless we have perceived it in relation to him, in the Holy Spirit. What we need, and must pray for, is an ability to see through the human words on the page in the light of faith. We need new eyes to penetrate the familiar (perhaps sometimes over-familiar) surface of the text and unveil the features of Christ. This is precisely what Pope Benedict XVI has tried to do in his book *Jesus of Nazareth*. The brief Foreword of the first volume of that work probably contains the most succinct summary of this approach to reading Scripture currently available, and the same

1. *Dei Verbum*, para 12.
2. H.U. von Balthasar and J. Ratzinger, *Mary—The Church at the Source*, 39.

Pope's *Verbum Domini* (2010) is the most authoritative and detailed study of the question.

Biblical scholars, even Catholic ones, have not always been as faithful to the Spirit of Scripture as they might have been. As a result, there is some justification for the low regard in which they have come to be held by many of the faithful. Since the nineteenth century there has been so much talk of 'demythologizing' the text of Scripture, or of dismantling it 'critically' in order to distinguish the most 'authentic' fragments from the rest, that non-academic readers have almost given up trying to hear the text with their own ears. The Reformers' great experiment of opening up the Bible to everyone begins to look like a failure. For on the one hand we have a community of scholars who can never agree on anything. (Following the model of the secular sciences they claim nevertheless always to be moving in the right direction, even if they do not expect to discover the final truth any time soon.) On the other we have a plethora of sects created by individuals who interpret the Bible for themselves, on the assumption that they can hear the Holy Spirit speaking within them whilst being cut off from the community of others in whom the Spirit also dwells.

The achievements and adventure of modern Biblical scholarship was helpfully summarized by the Pontifical Biblical Commission in a book published in 1993 called *The Interpretation of the Bible in the Church*. One of the first things the document does is examine the principles operating within each of the types or styles of Biblical interpretation. It begins with the 'historical-critical' method. Careful study of internal and external evidence leads to a range of conclusions: that the so-called 'Books of Moses' were not all written by a single man, that the Psalms were not composed by King David, that the Gospel of John was the product of a Johannine community rather than the Apostle, and that the Book of Revelation was not written by the same author as the Letters of Saint John. The document does not denounce this method, or such conclusions, as incompatible with Catholic faith. On the contrary, it deems the method 'indispensable' for the scientific study of Scripture. The questioning of original sources and authorship does not affect belief in divine inspiration working through and guiding the human authors, whoever they may have been. (The Church teaches that Holy Scripture is written *both* by God *and* by human beings. There is as little conflict here as there is between the human and divine nature of Christ, or between Christian faith and reason.)

The document of the Biblical Commission then goes on to examine the way literary criticism gives way to form-criticism and then redaction-criticism, which tries to study the editorial process by which texts evolved over time. (The Holy Spirit can be an editor too.) It then continues with rhetorical, narrative, and semiotic or structuralist methods, the 'canonical' approach that pays attention to the texts in their overall context, and the use of human sciences such as psychology and sociology. It looks at liberationist, feminist, and fundamentalist interpretations, and finally the hermeneutical approach which draws attention to the philosophical assumptions operating in every attempt to interpret the text, no matter how seemingly neutral or objective. All of these methods have value, it says, and each of them has contributed and will continue to contribute very valuable insights. Then the document steps back and draws its own conclusions.

Ancient exegesis, which obviously could not take into account modern scientific requirements, attributed to every text of Scripture several levels of meaning. The most prevalent distinction was between the *literal* sense and the *spiritual* sense. Medieval exegesis distinguished within the spiritual sense three different aspects, each relating, respectively, to the truth revealed [allegorical], to the way of life commended [moral] and to the final goal to be achieved [anagogical]. . . .

In reaction to this multiplicity of senses, historical-critical exegesis adopted, more or less overtly, the thesis of the one single meaning: a text cannot have at the same time more than one meaning. All the effort of historical-critical exegesis goes into defining 'the' precise sense of this or that biblical text seen within the circumstances in which it was produced.

But this thesis has now run aground on the conclusions of theories of language and of philosophical hermeneutics, both of which affirm that written texts are open to a plurality of mean-ing.[3]

We have therefore moved beyond the era of historical-critical interpretation. All four senses must again be taken seriously. The *literal* sense is still regarded as primary, but it is not the same as the 'literalist' sense beloved by fundamentalists. It means simply what the original authors intended to communicate. A phrase such as 'Let your loins be girt' (Luke 12:35) does not mean 'Put on a loin cloth', but simply 'Be ready for action.' The Bible contains pieces of mythology, poetry, imaginative fiction, and liturgical invocation as well as versions of historical narrative. The reader of Scripture must be alert as to which genre is intended. Nor is there always only one literal meaning, since even in secular poetry 'a human author can intend to refer at one and the same time to more than one level of reality.'[4] The literal sense is also open to development, since a text is written down and preserved precisely in order to free it from its original circumstances and allow it to illuminate other times, other circumstances for later generations.

> It does not follow from this that we can attribute to a biblical text whatever meaning we like, interpreting it in a wholly sub-jective way. On the contrary, we must reject as unauthentic every interpretation alien to the meaning expressed by the human authors in their written text. To admit the possibility of such alien meanings would be equivalent to cutting off the biblical message from its root, which is the Word of God in its historical communication; it would also mean opening the door to interpretations of a wildly subjective nature.[5]

The question is, how strictly do we take the word 'alien' here? This will depend on our assumptions, and the whole mind-set with which we approach the text. What the document calls the 'spiritual

3. Pontifical Biblical Commission, *The Interpretation of the Bible in the Church*, 81 (my italics). See J. Granados *et al.* (eds), *Opening Up the Scriptures* for an up-to-date discussion.

4. Ibid., 83.

5. Ibid., 84.

sense' of the text is an interpretation that goes further than the literal *without* being alien to it. For example, when God in the Old Testament promises to establish David's throne 'for ever' he is speaking rhetorically (since David's kingdom has long since come to an end).[6] But the promise can also be read spiritually in a completely literal sense as applying to Jesus Christ, who 'dies no more' (Rom. 6:9). The spiritual sense of Scripture is what we find in Scripture when we read in tune with the Holy Spirit, under the guidance of the Church, and in the light shed upon it by the Incarnation. Reading the Bible in this way is like viewing a stained glass window from within the Church when sunlight is shining through it, compared to seeing it from outside where the image is not properly visible.

There is also what is called the *sensus plenior* or 'fuller sense', which refers to a new and deeper literal sense or meaning, not intended by the human author but made known to us by the authority either of another Biblical author or of the Church herself—for example, when texts referring to Jesus, his Father and the Spirit are explained with reference to the doctrine of the Holy Trinity, which is not explicitly taught in the Bible. (The same might apply to the doctrines of purgatory, Original Sin, the Assumption, and the Immaculate Conception.) The point is that if God is the co-author and editor of Scripture, he can guide human authors to the choice of expressions that contain deeper meanings known at the time only to himself.

---

6. 'And your house and your kingdom shall be made sure for ever before me; your throne shall be established for ever' (2 Samuel 7:16).

3: GEMATRIA —
THE REAL BIBLE CODE

In ancient Hebrew and Greek, before the advent of what we now call Arabic numerals, there were various ways of representing numbers and quantities. Each letter of the alphabet, for example, was the equivalent of a number.[1] This meant that a literary text could also be read as a numerical code, and it seems that many of the authors of Scripture used this technique to embed several layers of meaning within the same piece of writing. The name for this technique is *isopsephy* or *gematria* (related to the word geometry, which in turn refers to the 'measure of the earth'). The Pope refers to it in the first volume of his book *Jesus of Nazareth* when he explains the structure of Matthew's genealogy of Jesus in three groups of fourteen generations by the fact that 14 was the numerical value of the name of David.[2]

Gematria is one example of a much wider use of numerical symbols in Scripture. I have noted in this book the presence of number symbolism not just in the Apocalypse but in the Gospels: the 153

---

1. Hebrew has 22 letters. Each could be used to represent a number from 1 to 22 ('ordinal value'), or else after the tenth letter each could refer to successive tens and hundreds: 20, 30, 40 ... 90, 100, 200, 300, 400 ('normative value'). Furthermore the *letter names* themselves might be spelled out in either 22 or 400 gematria, making a total of four main ways of relating letters to numbers. Duane L. Christensen argues that these four systems are symbolized in the Hebrew Bible itself by the four rivers that flow out of Eden's single river (Gen. 4:10). See 'Four Rivers, Two Trees, and the Garden of Eden', filed under 'Master Table' at www.bibal.net. To make matters more complicated, there are also two ways of counting with 'reduced' values, in which the letter or word is reduced to a single digit from 1 to 9 (thus 2, 20 and 200 would all be equivalent to 2, and 240 to 6, for example).

2. Joseph Ratzinger/ Pope Benedict XVI, *Jesus of Nazareth*, 9. A bold attempt to reconstruct early Christian gematria was made in the 1920s by Simcox Lea and Bligh Bond in their two-volume work, *The Apostolic Gnosis*.

fishes is an obvious giveaway, and sophisticated symbolic number games may well underlie the accounts of other incidents in the life of Christ, including the feeding of the 5,000 with 5 loaves and 2 fish leaving 12 baskets (Mark 6:34–44), and of the 4,000 men with 7 loaves and a few fish leaving 7 baskets (Mark 8:1–9).[3]

Gematria as such comes into play only when the number is 'disguised', as it were, by a name. A good example would be the occasion when Jesus gives to Simon the name 'Peter', or Cephas. The numerical value of the Greek 'Cephas' is 729, a number important to the Pythagoreans, being the cube of 9 and twice the number of days in the solar year. Peter is thus associated with the 'foundation stone' on which the Church will be built, and with the sun (also with the hierarchies of heaven, if one jumps ahead rather anachronistically to the teaching of the monk Dionysius). The value of the Greek *petra*, meaning 'stone', is 486, which is the surface area of a cube made up of 729 smaller cubes.

Numerologists have explored in great detail the properties and correspondences of many important names, titles, and phrases in the Hebrew and Greek Bible. The first words of God, *Let there be light*, have the numerical equivalent of 232, which is the same as the phrase *The word of the Lord*, defining the essence of revelation itself. One of the richest in mathematical possibilities is the very first verse of Genesis: *In the beginning God created the heavens and the earth.*[4] The numerical value of this sentence is 2701, which is the product of two prime numbers, 37 and 73. It also happens to be the sum of all numbers from 1 to 73, which itself is a significant number, being the numerical value of the Hebrew word for Wisdom.[5] (It is worth noting in passing that the Greek word 'Logos' has the value of 373.)

---

3. The reader who wishes to go further into this may like to visit www.jesus 8880.com. For an exemplary discussion of another symbolic number that occurs widely in Scripture and Tradition, see Timothy Scott, 'Remarks on the Universal Symbolism of the Number 72', *Eye of the Heart*, Issue 1 (May 2008), 119-40, available online at *www.latrobe.edu.au/eyeoftheheart.*

4. Cf. http://freespace.virgin.net/vernon.jenkins.

5. In Timothy Scott's article cited above on the number 72, he explains the close symbolic relationship of this number with both 71 and 73, all three being symbolic extensions of 70, the tenfold multiplication of the perfect number 7.

Geometrically the two prime factors of 2701 are related to the Platonic solids and various symmetrical structures in two and three dimensions, though the details need not concern us here. The numbers 37 and 73 mirror each other, and the digits of each add up to 10, the sacred number of the Pythagoreans, as do the digits of 2701. (We will encounter 37 again below, in another connection.)

The number of the beast who arises from the earth in Rev. 13:11, the beast who speaks like a dragon and makes fire come down to earth, marking everyone on the hand or forehead so they can buy and sell, is said to be 666, and the reader is explicitly invited to ponder the meaning of the number. John tells us it is a *human* number, the 'number of a man'. It is often pointed out that it is the sum of the characters in the name of Nero plus those in the title Caesar,[6] and that Nero's persecution is likely to have been taking place during the period when the Apocalypse was written. But the number may also have a broader reference—not just to one Emperor, but all of them, indeed to every ruler of the earth (representatives of the 'prince of this world').

It is possible to arrange the first 36 (3x12) numbers in a 'magic square' of six lines, every line of which adds up to the number of the Sun, which is 111, whether read vertically, horizontally, or diagonally, thus:

6   32   3   34   35   1
7   11   27   28   8   30

6. For example, in Simcox Lea and Bligh Bond, *The Apostolic Gnosis*, 44. Austin Farrer thinks that St John tends to base his gematria on Greek, whereas this depends on the Hebrew form of the name (*A Rebirth of Images*, 292). In a so far unpublished book ('Unveiling the Apocalypse'), Emmett O'Regan points out that 666 is the numerical equivalent of the Greek word for 'beast' when translated into Hebrew, suggesting that the author was familiar with both languages. He also finds an equivalence between our English 'w' and the Hebrew letter *waw*. Since this letter represents the number 6, he argues, we might even see the 'mark of the beast' in the ubiquitous code for the internet, 'www'. Jean Hani cites yet another interpretation: 666 is apparently the numerical equivalent of 'like God' (*k-elohim*), as the Tempter promised Adam that he would become in Genesis (*The Symbolism of the Christian Temple*, 30). Please also see the detailed exposition of gematria in connection with the 'number of the beast' by Richard Bauckham in *the Climax of Prophecy*, 384-407.

19	14	16	15	23	24
18	20	22	21	17	13
25	29	10	9	26	12
36	5	33	4	2	31

This six-sided magic square of the sun, adding up to 666, is associated in early gematria with the 'earthly Sun' or Demiurge. In Jewish Kabbalah it is the numerical equivalent of 'Spirit of the Sun' (*Sorath*). By making it the name of the beast, John may be contrasting the 'earthly divinity' of the rulers of this world with that of Jesus, whose own number (the value of the Greek letters of his name) is 888. Whereas 6 is a number associated with incompletion (the six days of creation without the Sabbath), and 7 with perfection, the number 8 lies a step beyond natural perfection, in the realm of grace.[7]

Lea and Bligh Bond detect the presence of the 12th prime number, 37, in many or most of the various titles given to Jesus, and 888 is no exception, being 37 multiplied by 24. 888 is also regarded as a 'solar' number, but concerned with the 'spiritual Sun', and with the triumph over death. Thus the tripled 8 both transcends and integrates the created world. It is interesting that the first Christian Emperor Constantine adopted the title *Sol Invictus*. Solar imagery is a uniting factor between Christianity and Paganism, for the sun is a natural symbol of grace, power, life, and divinity.

The name Jesus can be represented by the first non-trivial magic square of prime numbers, which sums to 111 in each of 8 directions (including the diagonals), making 888 in total, with 37 in the central square:[8]

67	1	43
13	37	61
31	73	7

7. The numbers 6 and 8 are reconciled in the figure of the cube, which has six sides and eight corners. One of the corners would be the 'cornerstone', identified with Jesus.

Jesus Christ has the numerical value of 2368, made up of 888 for IESOUS and 1480 for CHRISTOS. (The difference between this and the numerical sum of the first verse of Genesis in Hebrew is 333.) Interestingly, these three numbers are in a close natural approximation to the Golden Ratio—3:5:8—making Christ the Golden Mean.

This can be nothing more than an introductory note concerning a huge subject, surely one that is unjustly neglected by Biblical scholars. Currently the playground of eccentrics (it is easy to see how it could become obsessive), gematria deserves further investigation as a tool almost certainly employed by the biblical authors themselves.

.

8. The intervals being 6, 6, 3 x 6, 6, 6, 3 x 6, 6, 6. I am grateful to Robert Bolton for noticing this pattern.

4: MARGARET BARKER'S TEMPLE THEOLOGY

In this book I have made some use of the ideas of the Biblical scholar Dr Margaret Barker, whose books concerning apocalyptic literature in the Bible are immensely interesting, but sometimes rather disturbing. The implications of her work are radical, if not revolutionary, and I felt I needed to examine them a bit more closely here. In the body of the book, I have cited her in support of my own argument at times, but she also has a strong argument of her own which may lead in a rather different direction, and the roots of this divergence need to be explained.

Dr Barker's 'Temple theology' traces the roots of Christian theology back into the first Jewish Temple, the Temple of Solomon, destroyed by a cultural revolution in the time of King Josiah around 600 BC. (Refugees from these purges settled in Egypt and Arabia, taking with them, she believes, elements of this tradition that later resurface in Islam and among the Gnostics.) The Temple was rebuilt by Zerubbabel around 520 and lasted another 600 years until the Romans destroyed it in AD 70. But Dr Barker believes the First Temple tradition continued 'underground' in tension with the Second. The legend of the Flood was intended as a coded description of the Exile. For representatives of the First Temple—perhaps including Ezekiel, Isaiah, and the excluded Enoch through to the Qumran community contemporary with Jesus—the Second Temple was apostate; it was, in fact, impure, a 'harlot'. First Temple writers were responsible for the book of Exodus, Second Temple for Deuteronomy. The theology of the two traditions was quite different: the First was a mystical doctrine of secret initiations, with visionary experiences of the kingdom and throne of God, the Second was more prosaic, concerned with the Law, with practical rules for everyday life, and with words rather than visions.

201

She reads the Christian Book of Revelation not as a late addition to the scriptural canon but as belonging to the very earliest stratum of New Testament writings. In fact she makes the startling claim that *'The visions of the Book of Revelation underlie the Gospel narratives and explain the choice of biblical texts that accompany events.'*[1] It represents the resurgence of the First Temple tradition, a synthesis of the visionary, apocalyptic esotericism that the Second had tried unsuccessfully to suppress. It was therefore closely linked to the Dead Sea Scrolls. John—the Evangelist and author of the Book of Revelation—may have been the High Priest of the early Christian community, and his hostile references to the 'Jews', which have been misused by anti-semites throughout history, are in fact references to the followers of the corrupted Temple tradition, who are blind to the signs of the Kingdom. She quotes the Roman author Josephus: 'Jews is the name they are called by *from the day they came up from Babylon.'*[2]

Barker also suggests that the Hebrew Christian John was at odds with Paul, the 'Apostle to the Gentiles', and that his seven messages to the churches in Asia were intended to turn them against Paul (successfully, according to 2 Tim. 1:15), who is described at Rev. 2:14 as that 'Balaam' who 'taught them to eat food sacrificed to idols'.[3] Traces of this conflict (eventually resolved through the leadership of James Peter and the passage of time) appear in chapter 15 of the Book of Acts.

For John, in Barker's view, the whore Babylon represented the Second Temple, the New Jerusalem the return of the First. And as the author of the Letter to the Hebrews knew well, Jesus was the long-expected 'great high priest' of the First Temple, known as Melchizedek, the Resurrected One, returned to perform the atonement sacrifice of the last days—prophecies treasured by the sectarians of the hidden tradition (Heb. 5:10). Her interpretation places

---

1. M. Barker, *The Hidden Tradition of the Kingdom of God*, 94.
2. Ibid., 116. My emphasis.
3. M. Barker, *The Revelation of Jesus Christ*, 70. An alternative account of Revelation's reference to Balaam as a coded reference to the Iranian dualists or magi can be found in Jean Daniélou's *Primitive Christian Symbols* under 'The Star of Jacob'.

the visionary ascent—enabling first-hand knowledge of the things of heaven—at the very center of the early Christian experience.

The Old Testament texts, in Dr Barker's reading, are not as monotheistic as they appear. On the basis of the earliest documents available, including the scrolls at Qumran, she distinguishes several 'Gods' in the Old Testament: *God Most High* (El Elyon), worshiped by Melchizedek according to Genesis 14:18–20, is distinct from the *Son of the Most High*, a second God or aspect of God known as Yahweh, the LORD or Almighty, who is also the 'Logos' of Philo and the Angel Metatron the 'throne sharer', the guardian angel of Israel. Since the 'High Priest' of El Elyon is also his 'Son', Melchizedek himself can be identified with this second God in person, the God served by the Aaronic priesthood of Abraham's line.[4] She recalls that when Gabriel appears to the Virgin Mary he refers to Jesus as the 'Son of the Most High' (Luke 1:32).

So far, none of this is particularly problematic for the Christian believer, and in fact it sheds some light on the Letter to the Hebrews (and on the Gospels). Father John Redford's painstaking and orthodox examination of the historical basis of the Fourth Gospel cites Dr Barker with approval: she cautions us 'against assuming that, at the time of Christ and immediately before it, Judaism was so rigidly monotheistic that Jesus claiming divinity was totally contrary to Jewish ideas.'[5] It is certainly possible that there were varied concepts of God as of the priesthood among the ancient Hebrews and Essenes, some of which leave their traces in the Christian scriptures. We know, also, that prophets were common in the early church, and that tensions ran high between the Hebrew Christians and the Hellenizers. None of this calls into question the Christology taught by the Church a thousand years later. The presence of two 'Gods' in the Old Testament might simply indicate the intuition of a distinction that the doctrine of the Trinity would later explain more fully.

There remains, however, an ambiguity in Dr Barker's presentation that may pose a more serious problem. The royal high priesthood of Melchizedek, she says, comes about not through natural

4. M. Barker, *The Hidden Tradition of the Kingdom of God*, 63, 69–70.
5. J. Redford, *Mad, Bad, or God?* 223.

birth, but by death and resurrection into a state 'without father or mother or genealogy', that 'has neither beginning of days nor end of life' (Heb. 7:3, 24). *Resurrection* therefore means nothing more than an initiation that enables the Priest to enter the Holy of Holies. It is this 'resurrection', it seems to be implied, that makes Jesus into the Christ, the new High Priest. This takes place not after his bodily death but before, at the moment of his baptism in the Jordan (presumably at the hands of the Essene community or some such group). Interpreted in this way Dr Barker would be placed among those who believe that Jesus *became the Christ* only when he was baptized at the age of thirty, and that the story of his bodily Resurrection after the Crucifixion was merely symbolic.[6]

Such conclusions had earlier been drawn by Henry Corbin, the orientalist who succeeded Louis Massignon at the Sorbonne and became entranced by mystical Islamic theosophy. In his comparative studies of Middle Eastern visionary traditions Corbin found the basis for a reconstruction of Templar chivalry, a spiritual doctrine that he thought derived from the primitive Judeo-Christian community of which the Apostle James was the bishop. After the death of James and the destruction of Jerusalem by the Romans in AD 70, the Hebrew Christian remnant became separated from the mainstream and was eventually labelled heretical (Ebionites). According to Corbin, it was these heretics who preserved the true teaching of Christianity, which is in continuity with that of the Essenes at Qumran and was passed on through various mystical brotherhoods into the Middle Ages.[7]

Corbin believed that 'the Christ' was not a man but a *theophany*, a manifestation of the celestial Son of Man, the *Christos Angelos*. For Corbin, the man Jesus only became identified with this immortal 'Christ' after his baptism in the Jordan. The orthodox Christian belief that God assumed a human nature in the womb of Mary in

---

6. Father Redford interprets her differently, saying: 'the idea that Jesus had a significant experience at his baptism which revealed to him his own vocation and mission is not alien to biblical scholarship' (ibid., 149). In fact, we know from the Gospels that Jesus grew in wisdom (Luke 2:52), even if on some level he always knew that his Father was in heaven (Luke 2:49).

7. H. Corbin, *Temple and Contemplation*, chapter 5 on the *Imago Templi*.

order to save us from our sins is regarded by Corbin as the beginning of the collapse of the distinction between God and the world, a desecration that was the basis of modern secularism and materialism.[8]

This discussion is of fundamental importance. It makes a big difference whether Jesus came back from the dead or not, and whether he was divine from the moment of his conception or became so later. Christianity affirms the union of two natures, divine and human, in the womb of Mary. It does so on the basis of the Trinity, which allows us to distinguish one equally divine Person from another, as well as God from world, within a union that is all the deeper for being founded on difference. The paradox is fundamental, and one has to choose whether to accept it, or not. Corbin does not, and it would be good to know whether Margaret Barker is following in his footsteps. The fact that she ignores the infancy narratives (which were dropped by the Ebionites) may be suggestive.

The realm for which Corbin coined the word 'imaginal' is a region of the soul that needs to be clearly distinguished both from the intuitive or metaphysical intellect and from the discursive rational faculty. It is a region in which the invisible realities that the intellect apprehends in abstraction appear clothed in images drawn from the world of the senses. Depending on whether the visionary is oriented towards or away from the source of spiritual light— upwards or downwards, so to speak—the vision may however conduce towards a good or an evil end. In the case of the biblical apocalyptic literature (Ezekiel, Daniel, Revelation), the Church has accepted that the visions recorded there form an essential part of the canon—something that does not apply to the apocryphal literature. This does not mean that such writings contain nothing of value, and nothing that can illuminate the beliefs of the early Christians or even the nature of the invisible. It does mean that from the Church's viewpoint what is true and valid in them will tend to be fragmentary, or mixed with error.

The canon of Scripture has been chosen so that, out of the balance of one fragment with another, the whole figure of truth may emerge. To give equal weight to texts that were excluded from the

---

8. See Tom Cheetham, *Green Man, Earth Angel.*

canon may be legitimate scholarly procedure, but a Christian might well argue that it tends to distort the revelation entrusted to the Church. For 'to interpret Scripture theologically means not only to listen to the historical authors whom it juxtaposes, even opposes, but to seek the one voice of the whole, to seek the inner identity that sustains the whole and binds it together.'[9]

It seems from Margaret Barker's work that the Resurrection was indeed anticipated in the myth and ritual of the Temple tradition. But a Catholic might want to add that Christ was not a High Priest of the Old Covenant; he was the High Priest to which the Old Covenant looked forward, and of which Melchizedek himself was but an obscure image. Jesus lacked a beginning and an end not because he had been initiated into eternal life (that would apply more to ourselves, with reference to Baptism), but because he was already *eternally existent* as the Son of God, and being born in time had raised his flesh into an everlasting kingdom. These are the lines along which, I believe, Catholic exegetes will have to argue if they want to preserve the Church's faith whilst integrating many valuable insights from Margaret Barker's ongoing researches.

9. Von Balthasar and Ratzinger, *Mary—The Church at the Source*, 39.

5: THE SEVEN SACRAMENTS

It is appropriate here to include summaries of some of the material in my book The Seven Sacraments. *In that book I suggest that by virtue of the internal coherence of tradition and the influence of the Holy Spirit, each of the seven sacraments of the Church corresponds to one of the seven petitions that make up the Our Father, one of the seven miraculous Signs listed by John in his Gospel, one of the metaphysical Days of creation, and one of the Last Words from the Cross.*

Baptism: Giving the Name

'Our Father, who art in heaven, hallowed be thy name'
Second sign: healing the official's son (John 4:46–54)
'I am the way, and the truth, and the life; no one comes to the
　Father, except through me' (John 14:6)
Sixth day: Adam and Eve
'It is accomplished' (John 19:30)

Marriage: Kingdom Come

'Thy kingdom come'
First sign: changing water into wine (John 2:1–11)
'I am the true vine' (John 15:1)
Seventh day: the Sabbath
'Woman, behold your Son' (John 19:25–7)

Ordination: Between Heaven and Earth

'Thy will be done on earth as it is in heaven'
Fifth sign: walking on the water (John 6:19)
'I am the good shepherd' (John 10:11)
Third day: land in the midst of the waters
'My God, why have you forsaken me?' (Mark 15:34)

Eucharist: Bread of Heaven

'Give us this day our daily bread'
Fourth sign: feeding the Five Thousand (John 6:1–15)
'I am the bread of life' (John 6:35–71)
Fourth day: creating the sun and stars.
'I thirst' (John 19:28)

Reconciliation: Unveiling Sin

'Forgive us our trespasses, as we forgive those who trespass
    against us'
Third sign: healing the paralyzed man (John 5:1–14)
'I am the door' (John 10:9)
Fifth day: life stirring the waters
'Father, forgive them, for they know not what they do' (Luke
    23:34)

Confirmation: Witness to the Light

'Lead us not into temptation'
Sixth sign: healing the man born blind (John 9:1–40)
'I am the light of the world' (John 9:5)
Second day: creating the sky
'Father, into your hands I commend my Spirit…' (Luke 23:46)

Anointing: Healing Power of the Cross

'But deliver us from evil'
Seventh sign: raising Lazarus (John 11:1–44)
'I am the resurrection and the life' (John 11:25)
First day: creating light
'Today you will be with me in paradise' (Luke 23:43)

*The Sacraments Reflected in the Mass. I also take the opportunity
here to re-present what actually happens in the Mass, dividing the
action into seven main sections, and correcting some mistakes that
crept into the earlier version of this account: (1) the Introductory Rite,
(2) the Penitential Rite, (3) the Liturgy of the Word (which runs from*

the Gloria to the Gospel), (4) the *Offertory*, (5) the *Consecration*, (6) *Holy Communion* and (7) the *Rite of Dismissal*. Each of these parts echoes one of the sacraments, in the following order: (1) *Baptism*, (2) *Reconciliation*, (3) *Confirmation*, (4) *Ordination*, (5) *Eucharist*, (6) *Marriage*, and (7) *Anointing*. Each part of the Mass is examined in turn, bearing this association with the sacraments in mind.

1. Introductory Rite (*Baptism*). This sacred rite always begins with the sign of the Cross, which is also the symbol of the holy Trinity, in whose name every Christian is baptized. The gesture serves as a symbolic gateway into sacred space and sacred time. I always feel a strange reluctance to look at my watch during the Mass, once the ritual has begun. To enter into the spirit of the celebration is to be partially removed from secular time and implanted within the world of the angels.[1]

1. Penitential Rite (*Reconciliation*). This rite constitutes a kind of 'clearing of the decks', spiritually speaking. It is not a substitute for sacramental confession, which it presupposes, but a communal act of repentance for the minor sins committed since sacramental absolution was last received in private. This is no encouragement to wallow in guilt, but a realistic and formal way of reorienting ourselves toward God in order to be able to receive what he wishes to give us. The invocation, 'Lord have mercy, Christ have mercy, Lord have mercy,' is directed to God as Trinity.

2. Liturgy of the Word (*Confirmation*). Here God gives us his Word. The readings from Scripture, both Old and New Testament, are to be *heard liturgically*; that is, they are not merely Bible stories that may be either quite familiar or quite obscure, either as literature or as history, rather they are the proclamation of God's revelation to us in the present moment. Perhaps they will sound to us as

---

1. The Church's liturgy is described in the Letter to the Hebrews: 'But what you have come to is Mount Zion and the city of the living God, the heavenly Jerusalem where the millions of angels have gathered for the festival, with the whole Church in which everyone is a "first-born son" and a citizen of heaven' (Heb. 12:22–3, J.B. translation). 'The Mass is, actually, a sacramental participation in the liturgy of heaven, the cult officially rendered to the Trinity by the full host of the spiritual creation. The presence of the angels introduces the Eucharist into heaven itself,' says Jean Daniélou, S.J. in *The Angels and Their Mission* (62).

though we had never heard them before, since the moment in which we hear them is new. There is a sacramental virtue in the words that corresponds to Pentecost and thus to the sacrament of Confirmation. Provided that we manage to open our ears and hearts to them, such words can become like seeds falling onto fertile ground, bearing the Holy Spirit's life-force within them. It is part of the priest's work to reflect on the readings in his homily (sermon) in order to help them have this effect. He is, thus, planting seeds in the souls of his congregation. This part of the Mass is concluded with a recitation of the Creed, which sums up the whole of Revelation in an inspired form, uniting the fragments of the Bible just read with the great ocean of truth.

3. Offertory (*Ordination*). Now we move from the Liturgy of the Word to the heart of the Mass. The congregation offers bread and wine prepared on their behalf for the priest to consecrate. A collection plate may be passed around. These tokens represent human work and lives, as well as the whole created world that has entered into the making of these substances – through the soil, the plants, the farm animals who played their part, indeed even the lowly earthworm that tilled the soil, the wind and rain and sunshine. The priest takes these gifts and offers them to God. He invokes the Holy Spirit. This is what the office of priest exists for: the priest is a living *epiclesis* (invocation). The whole world – and not just the human world – is involved in the liturgy, and all that has been offered here will be raised up on the last day as part of a resurrection earth.

4. Consecration (*Eucharist*). The Last Supper was the anticipation of the Passion or death of our Lord on the Cross, which in turn was the earthly image and incarnation of the eternal sacrifice in heaven. The priest raises up all our earthly giving, every aspect of our lives that has not been deliberately held back or turned away from God's face, to become a part of the self-giving of the Son to the Father, in heaven as it is on earth. The consecration, bound up as it is with the invocation, takes place in the view of most Catholic theologians when the priest utters the words of Christ, 'This is my body...' At that moment Christ is speaking directly through the priest. Sacramental priesthood gives way to the real thing, as Christ takes up all that we have offered and includes it in the gift of his own body and blood, the living bread which came down from heaven for the life of the world.

5. Holy Communion (*Marriage*). We do not have to receive the consecrated body and blood of our Lord at every Mass, but the priest does, and most people also want to. Why, since the great sacrifice has already been accomplished at the altar of God? You might as well ask why a couple having made their vows of Marriage should want to postpone the honeymoon. United with Christ in the sacrifice that has made us one flesh, that interior union is consummated with the mingling of our bodies, a symbolic giving and receiving that enables a new spiritual grace to come into our lives, making them more spiritually fruitful.

6. Rite of Dismissal (*Anointing*). Though brief, the dismissal (*Ite missa est*) brings the whole liturgy together in a single act of blessing and sending (*missio*). We are sent out into the world to complete the action of the Mass in our own lives: at home, at work, at school. If we have participated effectively in the Mass, we will have been healed of our sins and prepared even for death, as we are in the sacrament of Anointing. We go out from the sacred precinct marked, finally, with the sign of the Trinity.

BIBLIOGRAPHY

(Please see the author's blog for further discussion:
http://thechristianmysteries.blogspot.com)

Arthur J. Arberry, *The Koran Interpreted* (Oxford University Press, 1964)

R. W. J. Austin (tr.), *Ibn Al'Arabi: The Bezels of Wisdom*, Classics of Western Spirituality (New York: Paulist Press, 1980)

Hans Urs von Balthasar, *The Glory of the Lord*, Vol. VII, 'Theology: The New Covenant' (San Francisco: Ignatius Press, 1989)

————. *Theo-Drama*, Vol. III, 'Dramatis Personae: Persons in Christ' (San Francisco: Ignatius Press, 1992)

————. *Theo-Drama*, Vol. IV, 'The Action' (San Francisco: Ignatius Press, 1994)

————. *Theo-Drama*, Vol. V, 'The Last Act' (San Francisco: Ignatius Press, 1998)

————. *Theo-Logic*, Vol. II, 'Truth of God' (San Francisco: Ignatius Press, 2004)

————. *First Glance at Adrienne von Speyr* (San Francisco: Ignatius Press, 1981)

————. *Prayer* (San Francisco: Ignatius Press, 1986)

————. *The Threefold Garland: The World's Salvation in Mary's Prayer* (San Francisco: Ignatius Press, 1982)

Christopher Bamford (ed.), *Rediscovering Sacred Science* (Edinburgh: Floris Books, 1994)

Margaret Barker, *The Great High Priest: The Temple Roots of Christian Liturgy* (London: T&T Clark, 2003)

————. *The Hidden Tradition of the Kingdom of God* (London: SPCK, 2007)

————. *The Revelation of Jesus Christ* (Edinburgh: T&T Clark, 2000)

John D. Barrow, *The Constants of Nature: From Alpha to Omega* (London: Vintage, 2003)

Stephen C. Barton (ed.), *Where Shall Wisdom be Found?* (Edinburgh: T&T Clark, 1999)

Richard Bauckham, *The Climax of Prophecy: Studies on the Book of Revelation* (Edinburgh: T&T Clark, 1993)

_____. *The Theology of the Book of Revelation* (Cambridge University Press, 1993)

Robert Bolton, *The Order of the Ages: World History in the Light of a Universal Cosmogony* (Ghent, NY: Sophia Perennis, 2001)

Bonaventure, Saint, *Bonaventure: The Soul's Journey Into God, The Tree of Life, The Life of St Francis*, Ewert Cousins (tr.), Classics of Western Spirituality (New York: Paulist Press, 1978)

_____. *Collations on the Six Days*, The Works of Bonaventure, Vol. 5, tr. José de Vinck (Patterson, NJ: St Anthony Guild Press, 1970)

Jean Borella, *Guénonian Esoterism and Christian Mystery* (Hillsdale, NY: Sophia Perennis, 2004)

Louis Bouyer, *Cosmos: The Word and the Glory of God* (Petersham, MA: St Bede's, 1988)

Ian Boxall, *The Revelation of St John*, Black's New Testament Commentary (Peabody, MA and London: Hendrickson and Continuum, 2006)

_____. *Revelation: Vision and Insight* (London: SPCK, 2002)

Sergius Bulgakov, *The Bride of the Lamb*, trans. Boris Jakim (Grand Rapids, MI: Eerdmans, 2002)

_____. *Sophia: The Wisdom of God - An Outline of Sophiology* (Hudson, NY: Lindisfarne Press, 1993)

Titus Burckhardt, *An Introduction to Sufi Doctrine* (Wellingborough: Aquarian Press, 1976)

Walter Burkert, *Lore and Science in Ancient Pythagoreanism* (Cambridge, MA: Harvard University Press, 1972)

Richard A. Burridge, *Four Gospels, One Jesus? A Symbolic Reading* (London: SPCK, 1994)

Stratford Caldecott, *The Seven Sacraments: Entering the Mysteries of God* (New York: Crossroad, 2006). Additional material not included in the book is freely available from the author's web-site on the pages concerned with the book at www.secondspring.co.uk.

_____. *A Companion to the Book of Revelation* (London: CTS, 2008)

_____. *The Fruits of the Spirit* (London: CTS, 2010)

_____. *Beauty for Truth's Sake: On the Re-enchantment of Education* (Grand Rapids: Brazos, 2009)

Tom Cheetham, *Green Man, Earth Angel: The Prophetic Tradition and the Battle for the Soul of the World* (State University of New York Press, 2005)

Yves M.-J. Congar OP, *The Mystery of the Temple: or The Manner of God's Presence to His Creatures from Genesis to the Apocalypse* (London: Burns & Oates, 1962)

Henri Corbin, *Temple and Contemplation* (London: KPI in association with Islamic Publications, 1986)

Hieromonk Damascene, *Christ the Eternal Tao* (Platina, CA: Saint Herman of Alaska Brotherhood, 1999)

Jean Daniélou SJ, *The Angels and Their Mission* (Westminster, MD: Newman Press, 1957)

———. *The Angels and Their Mission* (Westminster, MD: Newman Press, 1957)

———. *Primitive Christian Symbols* (London: Burns & Oates, 1964)

Celia Deane-Drummond, *Creation Through Wisdom: Theology and the New Biology* (Edinburgh: T&T Clark, 2000)

Jeane-Pierre de Caussade, *The Joy of Full Surrender* (Brewster, MA: Paraclete Press, 2008)

Henri de Lubac SJ, *The Christian Faith: An Essay on the Structure of the Apostles' Creed* (San Francisco: Ignatius Press, 1986)

———. *Catholicism: Christ and the Common Destiny of Man* (San Francisco: Ignatius Press, 1998)

Meister Eckhart, *Meister Eckhart: Sermons and Treatises*, Vol. I, tr. M.O'C. Walshe (Boston: Element Books, 1991)

Evdokimov, Paul, *Woman and the Salvation of the World* (Crestwood, NY: St Vladimir's Seminary Press, 1994)

Austin Farrer, *A Rebirth of Images: The Making of St John's Apocalypse* (Westminster: Dacre Press, 1949)

———. *The Revelation of John the Divine* (Oxford University Press, 1964)

Gia-Fu Feng and Jane English, *Chuang-Tsu: Inner Chapters* (London: Wildwood House, 1974)

Pavel Florensky, *The Pillar and Ground of the Truth: An Essay in Orthodox Theodicy in Twelve Letters*, trans. Boris Jakim (Princeton University Press, 1997)

Paul Friedländer, *Plato: An Introduction*, Bollingen Series LIX (Princeton University Press, 1969)

Etienne Gilson, *Being and Some Philosophers* (Toronto: Pontifical Institute of Medieval Studies, 1949)

José Granados, Carlos Granados, Luis Sánchez-Navarro (eds), *Opening Up the Scriptures: Joseph Ratzinger and the Foundations of Biblical Interpretation* (Grand Rapids, MI: Eerdmans, 2008)

Romano Guardini, *The Lord* (Chicago: Regnery Gateway, 1954)

———. *The End of the Modern World* (Wilmington: ISI Books, 1998)

Scott Hahn, *A Father Who Keeps His Promises: God's Covenant Love in Scripture* (Ann Arbor: Servant Publications, 1998)

————. *The Lamb's Supper: The Mass as Heaven on Earth* (New York: Doubleday, 1999)

————. *Letter and Spirit: From Written Text to Living Word in the Liturgy* (London: Darton, Longman & Todd, 2006)

Jean Hani, *The Symbolism of the Christian Temple* (San Rafael, CA: Sophia Perennis, 2007)

David Bentley Hart, *The Beauty of the Infinite: The Aesthetics of Christian Truth* (Grand Rapids: Eerdmans, 2003)

Vincent Foster Hopper, *Medieval Number Symbolism: Its Sources, Meaning, and Influence on Thought and Expression* (Mineola, NY: Dover, 2000)

Laura DeWitt James, *William Blake and the Tree of Life* (Berkeley: Shambala, 1971)

John Paul II, *Man and Woman He Created Them: A Theology of the Body*, tr. Michael Waldstein (Boston: Pauline, 2006)

————. *Memory and Identity: Conversations at the Dawn of a Millennium* (New York: Rizzoli, 2005)

Cheslyn Jones, Geoffrey Wainwright, and Edward Yarnold SJ (eds), *The Study of Liturgy* (London: SPCK, 1978)

Charles H. Kahn, *Pythagoras and the Pythagoreans: A Brief History* (Indianapolis, IN: Hackett Publishing, 2001)

C.F. Kelley, *Meister Eckhart on Divine Knowledge* (New Haven: Yale University Press, 1977)

Peter Kreeft, *You Can Understand the Bible: A Practical Guide to Each Book in the Bible* (San Francisco: Ignatius Press, 2005)

Simcox Lea and Bligh Bond, *Materials for the Study of the Apostolic Gnosis*, Parts I and II (Wellingborough: Thorsons, 1979 and 1985)

Ernest G. MacClain, *The Myth of Invariance: The Origin of the Gods, Mathematics and Music from the Rig Veda to Plato* (York Beach, ME: Nicolas-Hays, 1976)

Gerhard May, *Creatio Ex Nihilo: The Doctrine of 'Creation Out of Nothing' in Early Christian Thought* (Edinburgh: T&T Clark, 1994)

John Michell, *How the World is Made: The Story of Creation According to Sacred Geometry* (London: Thames & Hudson, 2009)

John D. Miller, *Beads and Prayers: The Rosary in History and Devotion* (London: Burns & Oates, 2002)

Francesca Aran Murphy, *The Comedy of Revelation: Paradise Lost and Regained in Biblical Narrative* (Edinburgh: T&T Clark, 2000)

Robert Murray SJ, *The Cosmic Covenant: Biblical Themes of Justice, Peace, and the Integrity of Creation* (London: Sheed & Ward, 1992)

Seyyed Hossein Nasr, *Religion and the Order of Nature* (Oxford University Press, 1996)

The Philokalia: The Complete Text, compiled by St Nikodimos of the Holy Mountain and St Makarios of Corinth, Vol. 2, trans. G.E.H. Palmer, Philip Sherrard, and Kallistos Ware (London: Faber & Faber, 1981)

Clifford A. Pickover, *A Passion for Mathematics: Numbers, Puzzles, Madness, Religion, and the Quest for Reality* (Hoboken, NJ: John Wiley, 2005)

Josef Pieper, *The End of Time: A Meditation on the Philosophy of History* (London: Faber & Faber, 1954)

_____. *The Four Cardinal Virtues* (University of Notre Dame Press, 1966)

Servais Pinckaers OP, *The Sources of Christian Ethics* (Catholic University of America Press, 1995)

Plato, *Timaeus and Critias*, tr. Desmond Lee (London: Penguin Classics, 1977)

Harry Lee Poe, 'The Problem of Time in Biblical Perspective', in Harry Lee Poe and J. Stanley Mattson (eds), *What God Knows: Time and the Question of God's Knowledge* (Baylor University Press, 2005)

Pontifical Biblical Commission, *The Interpretation of the Bible in the Church* (Vatican City: 1994, available online)

Joseph Ratzinger/ Pope Benedict XVI, *Jesus of Nazareth: From the Baptism in the Jordan to the Transfiguration* (London: Bloomsbury, 2007)

_____. *The Theology of History in St Bonaventure* (Chicago: Franciscan Herald Press, 1971)

_____. *The Spirit of the Liturgy* (San Francisco: Ignatius Press, 2000)

_____. *Introduction to Christianity* (San Francisco: Ignatius Press, 2004)

_____. *'In the Beginning...': A Catholic Understanding of the Story of the Creation and the Fall* (Grand Rapids, MI: Eerdmans, 1995)

G. Reale, *Towards a New Interpretation of Plato* (Washington, DC: Catholic University of America Press, 1997)

John Redford, *Bad, Mad or God? Proving the Divinity of Christ from St John's Gospel* (London: St Paul's, 2004)

Ruth Rees, *The Rosary in Space and Time* (Chicago: Liturgical Training Publications, 2004)

Marko Ivan Rupnik, *In the Fire of the Burning Bush: An Initiation to the Spiritual Life* (Grand Rapids, MI: Eerdmans, 2004)

John H. Sailhammer, *The Pentateuch as Narrative*: A Biblical-Theological Commentary (Grand Rapids, MI: Zondervan, 1992)

Francis de Sales, *Treatise on the Love of God* (London: Burns & Oates, 1884)

John Saward, *The Beauty of Holiness and the Holiness of Beauty: Art, Sanctity and the Truth of Catholicism* (San Francisco: Ignatius Press, 1997).

Leo Schaya, *The Universal Meaning of the Kabbalah* (London: George Allen & Unwin, 1971)

Leo Scheffczyk, *Creation and Providence* (London: Burns & Oates, 1970)

D.C. Schindler, *Hans Urs von Balthasar and the Dramatic Structure of Truth: A Philosophical Investigation* (New York: Fordham University Press, 2004)

Steven J. Schloeder, *Architecture in Communion: Implementing the Second Vatican Council through Liturgy and Architecture* (San Francisco: Ignatius Press, 1998)

Kenneth L. Schmitz, *The Recovery of Wonder: The New Freedom and the Asceticism of Power* (Montreal and Kingston: McGill-Queen's University Press, 2005)

Michael S. Schneider, *A Beginner's Guide to Constructing the Universe: The Mathematical Archetypes of Nature, Art, and Science* (New York: HarperCollins, 1994)

————. *Constructing the Cosmological Circle: Symbol and Instrument for Universal Harmony* (2006), available from www.constructingtheuniverse.com

Wolfgang Smith, *The Quantum Enigma: Finding the Hidden Key* (Hillsdale, NY: Sophia Perennis, 2005)

Adrian Snodgrass, *Architecture, Time and Eternity: Studies in the Stellar and Temporal Symbolism of Traditional Buildings*, Vol. 1 (New Delhi: Sata-Pitaka Series, 1990)

Adrienne von Speyr, *The Word becomes Flesh: Meditations on John 1–5* (San Francisco: Ignatius Press, 1994)

John Sweet, *Revelation* (London: SCM Press, 1979)

Robert Temple, *He Who Saw Everything: A Verse Translation of the Epic of Gilgamesh* (London: Rider, 1991)

Paul Vallière, *Modern Russian Theology: Bukharev, Soloviev, Bulgakov - Orthodox Theology in a New Key* (Grand Rapids and Edinburgh: Eerdmans and T&T Clark, 2000)

Arthur Versluis, *TheoSophia: Hidden Dimensions of Christianity* (Hudson, NY: Lindisfarne Press, 1994)

Adrian Walker, 'The Poverty of Liberal Economics', in Doug Bandow and David L. Schindler (eds), *Wealth, Poverty, and Human Destiny* (Wilmington: ISI Books, 2003) 19-50

Michael Ward, *Planet Narnia: the Seven Heavens in the Imagination of C.S. Lewis* (Oxford University Press, 2008)

Celia Wolf-Devine, *The Heart Transformed: Prayer of Desire* (New York: St Pauls, 2009)

John D. Zizioulas, *Being as Communion: Studies in Personhood and the Church* (London: DLT, 1985)

――――. *Communion and Otherness: Further Studies in Personhood and the Church* (London: Continuum, 2006)

```
        J
I     H  S
      V
      H
```

Lightning Source UK Ltd.
Milton Keynes UK
UKOW051820021111

181364UK00001B/7/P